TOO WET TO PLOW

Too Wet To Plow

Americana and Homespun Philosophy in Beautiful Prose, Poetry, and Art

FRANK FUIS, JR.

Illustrated by the Author

FIFTH PRINTING

Exposition Phoenix Press

Exposition-Phoenix Press

Pompano Beach, Florida

All material in this book that appeared in other publications is reprinted with permission.

First Printing, 1977
Second Printing, 1981
Third Printing, 1983
Fourth Printing, 1985
Fifth Printing, 1989

Enlarged reproductions of certain illustrative art in this volume can be made available at reasonable cost. Write to Norris World Enterprises, Box 333, Norris, Tennessee 37828 for further information.

ISBN 0-682-48844-5

Printed in the United States of America by Exposition-Phoenix Press
Pompano Beach, FL 33062.
Distributed also by Norris World Enterprises, Norris, TN 37828

To the memory of my wife Hazel (née Stephens) and son Dennis Charles; also to the memory of my mother Anna (née Zimmermann) who encouraged my literary efforts, and to my father Frank who had personal reservations about them

ACKNOWLEDGMENT

For the cheerful and helpful assistance rendered me in the selection, compilation, preparation, and completion of this work, I wish gratefully to acknowledge the following: My wife Ethel, son Brian, sister Anna and brother-in-law Arvy, James Simms, Robert L. Vickery, Wayne Schrader, Jewell Hayes, Calvin Lunsford, Betty Ann Jolly, Burnett Ball, and the late William Hirth.

Many of the fine persons who figured in the inspiration of subject matter herein are named with no disparagement intended. In writings, if any, which may be taken as having derogatory implications, names used are purely fictitious.

ABOUT THE AUTHOR

The author, artist, and poet, Frank Fuis, Jr., whose work is published herein, was born in St. Louis, Missouri, on March 7, 1911, of Austrian and Swiss parentage, the father and mother having in their early years, and soon after turn of the century, adopted America as their permanent home. Because his father, the senior Frank Fuis, preferred a greater degree of independence than city employment offered, he moved his family—wife Anna Zimmermann Fuis, daughter Anna, and son Frank—to a small farm deep in the Missouri Ozarks when the latter was three years of age. The rustic beauty of the Ozark Hills, coupled with later rigors of outgambling the odds connected with wresting a living from a hill country farm, served to make young Fuis sensitive to the values of life in the great God-given heritage we have.

Frank's work, habits and life in general were biased by an innate sense of perfection which proved both a virtue and a frustration. The love for art, music, and literature at times seemed incompatible with clearing new ground, cleaning out the barns, or following a plow day after day. But each person is the sum total of the many factors which influence his development, and Frank was no exception. One event which chagrined young Fuis was that the demand of work on the farm delayed had worldwide significance, in the design of equipment in which our astronauts brought back the first rock samples from the moon, and in items of equipment which were used in the NASA Lunar Laboratory in Houston, Texas. Frank is a life member of the Tau Beta Pi and the Phi Eta Sigma honorary scholastic societies, and the International Platform Association. In addition his professional, humanitarian and literary accomplishments have earned him recognition for listings in *Who's Who in Tennessee, Who's Who in the South, Who's Who in the South and Southwest, Personalities of the South, Two Thousand Men of Achievement, Who's Who in Finance and Industry, Community Leaders of America, Who's Who in the United States,* and the *Dictionary of International Biographies,* Cambridge, England.

T.E.W.

CONTENTS

About the Author v
Foreword xii
Frontispiece xiv
Too Wet to Plow (Title Poem) xv
O Pen of Mine xvi

PART I BAREFOOT BABBLINGS 1
My Broom Is a Horsey 2
Pockets 4
The Foot Race 6
Pathways 9
Springtime in the Hills 10
The Anemone 12
Ingratitude 14
The Old Rail Fence 16
Warts 19
Swinging on the Gate 20
The Barnyard League 22
Mulberry Mouth 25
The Churning Chore 26
Blanche 28
The Scarecrow 30
Nature's Melody 32
The Dinner Bell 34
Wading in the Pond 36
Baby Cottontail 39
Threshing Time 40
Bib Overalls 43
Washday Blues 44
Smokin' 46
Romping in the Hayloft 49
The Way to School 50
Schoolday Autograph Verses 53
Autumn in the Ozarks 54
The Rabbit Trap 57
Throwin' Rocks 58
Cider Time 60
Buster's Comeuppance 62
Molasses-Making Time 66
Halloween 68
November Rains 70
The Washtub Bath 72
Christmas 74
The Ciphering Match 76

PART II ADOLESCENT ADO 79
Pitchin' Horseshoes 80
Just Who Am I 82
The Stream of Life 84
Smile Awhile 87
The Love of Mother's 88
May Baskets 90
The Treacherous Road 93
Lonely Days 94
A Trip to the Sawmill 96
Plowin' Newground 99
Runnin' Ol' Blue 100
Caves 103
A Faithful Horse 104
Bringing Home the Cows 106
Ozarks Rendezvous 108
The Old Country Store 110
The Toiler's Tribute 113
Town Picnic on the Fourth 114
Picking Blackberries 116
Our Party Line 118
The Sunset 120
The Play Party 122
The Quiltin' Bee 124
O Robin Fair 127
The Gift of Wealth 128
Summer Afternoon 130
Workin' Out the Poll Tax 133
Revival Meetin' Time 134
Big Britches 137
Twilight Shadows 138
The Drought 140
Oaken Shakes 142
Newfangled Changes 145
Country Singing 146
Autumn Wanderlust 148

The Pie Supper 150
Egotism 153
The Shivaree 154
The Ol' Fireplace 156
Self Gratification 159
The Possum Hunt 160
The Tie Hacker 163
O Wintry Wind 164
Sliding on the Ice 167
To a Dying Year 168

PART III ADULT AGENDA 171
The Square Dance 172
Scratchin' Out a Livin' 175
The Farmers' Co-op 176
The Tin Lizzy 178
Education 182
The Class of '34 184
My Church 189
When the School Year Is O'er 190
Empty Little Shoes 192
I'm Just a Bill 194
The Chestnut Grove 198
Influenza Blues 200
The Sunshine Everywhere 202
Jesus Is My Friend 204
C-H-R-I-S-T-M-A-S 206
Barefoot Trails 208
The Engineer (Essay) 210
Waltzing Shadows 214
H-A-Z-E-L 216
T-E-N-N-E-S-S-E-E 218
America, O Land So Fair 220
Across the Blue Pacific 222
The Old Grist Mill 224
Mornings 227
Building a Church 228
Tomorrow 231
Pitter, Patter, Little Feet 232
Rewards of Suffering 234
Have I Played Fair Today 236
On Parting 238
Hazel, or Heaven's Bouquet 240
The Weight of Tears 242
Back to Shore 244
In Memoriam 246
We Blaze a Trail 248
Headlights into the Snowstorm 250
My Redhead 252
I'm Glad I'm Me 255
I Trust the Lord 256
Fleeting Magnanimity 258
Life's Unknown Gifts 260
It Wouldn't Be a Boy 262
The Disciples 264
A Toast to Gertie 266
Joe and Schmoe 268
Fortunes of Poverty 273
Are You Kiddin' 274
How Many Tears 276
Fluffy 278
Lionism 280
Grandparenthood 282
The Nonagenarian 284
Circumstance Hero 287
The Atomic City 288

PART IV RAMBLINGS AND REMINISCENCES 291
Beside the Still Waters 292
A Boy Again 294
Destiny 296
Birthdays 299
The Public Sale 300
Grandstand Harry 303
The One-Room Country School 304
Lilacs 'Round My Door 306
The White Oak Tree 308
The Lullabye of Mother's 311
Smoke Nostalgia 312
The Ancient Road 314
Point of View 317
And the Creeks Rose 318

How Tall 320
House of Yesterday 322
The Engineer 325
School Days 326
The Old Woodyard 328
The Witness Tree 330
Home Remedies 332
The Old Courthouse 336
O Country Road 339
Tricks that Memory Plays 340
Won't You Sing Me to Sleep 343
The Battlefield 344
Keys to Happiness 348
The Blessings of Rural Childhood 350
Parens Cum Laude 357
The Master Engineer 358
Christmas in the Hills 377

FOREWORD

In this unique presentation of all original poetry, prose and art, the author has recorded with warmth and sensitivity the topics, events and observations which deal with customs, lore and traditions going back a century or more in American history—particularly that of the Missouri Ozarks, and to a degree that of rural Appalachia—but all of it descriptive, applicable and appealing to everyone regardless of his place in the far-flung reaches of America. The subject matter deals with many of those everyday activities, homespun philosophy, and human values which make up the sum total of our great heritage. Written for and about people at the crossroads of grass-roots America and for those on the streets of our national scene—people like himself who live, work and play, laugh and cry, in the environs of daily down-to-earth events—the author intentionally presents his work in a style that circumvents any pretense at sophistication. With the philosophy that there is beauty in simplicity, the material in *Too Wet to Plow* touches at the unaffected ways known to the author and the fine people with whom he lived and worked for over half a century.

The writer believes that much of America's past threatens to become lost in the turmoil of modern industrialization and space-age technology. Himself an engineer by profession, he was personally caught up in the mainstream of unprecedented advances in twentieth century progress, but through it all he has remained sensitive to the "little things" in our proud traditions, and has always sought to capture them in his writings.

Too Wet to Plow is a compilation of writings, some of which began before the author was in his teens, and much of which has been published through the years. It will be noted, however, that composition of the work herein is unique in the publishing field. Unlike conventional books of poetry in which there is no continuity, and in which the reader often must guess the motives, significance, historical time, values and other background facts related to the poems, *Too Wet to Plow* has an innovative format of presentation—a style all its own!

In general this uniqueness of presentation is accomplished by prefacing each poem with a *commentary* that gives the reader background information portraying the source of its inspiration. Through the entire work the material has been "engineered" to this open-book format with the commentary always appearing on the left-hand page facing the poem on the right, both bearing a common title, and both always beginning at the *top* of their respective pages. Thus the commentary both introduces the subject of the poem, and sets the stage for the reader with the effect of making the poem virtually come alive with meaning and purpose.

For the work as a whole, the author has arranged the material in a somewhat chronological order, much as one encounters them in the successive stages of life itself—themes on childhood, adolescence, adulthood, and lastly, a proud reflection over the highlights of nearly a lifetime of interesting and exciting happenings. So, unlike most books of poetry, there is here a definite continuity, a near autobiographical progression, as it were, which ties the whole into a related entity. In this way the reader of the poems and the complementary essay material virtually "grows up" with the author in Part I, lives the school days with him and works in the fields in Part II, takes on adult responsibilities, marries, sees the advent of children and later, grandchildren in Part III, and even drifts back through memory lane to relive some of the fondly remembered scenes of America's rural past in Part IV.

In conclusion, the reader will relate again and again to the many topics included in this comprehensive book, even as the author, ever sensitive and responsive to the vital world about him, captured in terms, beautiful, simple and expressive the ways and traditions of persons, places, and things of the outdoor world—all of which have enriched his life and activities in many wonderful ways, and which in a total sense have made up the heritage of the greatest nation on earth!

THE PUBLISHER

TOO WET TO PLOW

Father's reached a weighty verdict
  Which affects the day for all—
Walking yesterday's last furrow,
  Compacts in hand an earthy ball;
Kicking at the soil's new profile,
  Knits a deep assessing brow,
Casts about with firm decision:
  "Son, it's plumb too wet to plow!"

'Twould be only fair to say so,
  Straining to suppress a shout,
That there's always some rejoicing
  As we turn the horses out.
They with lofted heads and tailfare
  Frisk to graze with sheep and cow—
Makes you wonder who's most grateful
  When come days too wet to plow!

While we know work must continue
  Lest we end up mighty sad;
Yet, there's none can change the weather
  And there's nothing that's all bad.
Man, besides, needs unplanned changes—
  Breaks the routine up somehow.
So it's best we not feel guilty
  When it's just too wet to plow!

O PEN OF MINE

O pen of mine, pray write a line,
  A line of great abiding worth
Whose depth and scope bear joy and hope
  To cheerless mortals 'round the earth.

O pen in hand, I would command
  That you unleash but words sincere,
In years ahead to still be read
  And still be true and good to hear.

O pen of might, I'd have you write
  Of things where honest values win;
Of age and youth, of love and truth,
  To ease the burdened ways of men.

O pen of mine, pray write a line
  To reach a hapless kindred soul,
That, though his heart be rent apart,
  Would tend to make him once more whole!

Part I

Barefoot Babblings

MY BROOM IS A HORSEY

The accompanying poem is one in which the virtues of an active imagination are much in evidence. Imagination is every child's magic carpet—that exciting medium which transports him to the never-never lands beyond the horizons of present realism. Equipped with this capability, he can bring color to a drab existence, surmount grave adversities, and crown his days with purpose and meaning.

In our formative years there are developed many of the traits and interests which serve us all the days of our lives—and imagination is by no means the least of these. At this stage there are no particular demands for exotic or extravagant playthings, for with the gift of a vivid imagination a stick becomes a horse no less real than the steed of a knight or the pony of a cowboy; an empty spool takes on the importance of a busy mill wheel; and a dilapidated old building may even turn for a moment into the Taj Mahal!

For children in homes where fantasy is discouraged, a dull and blighted existence may result in later years. The child who is not privileged to ponder the mysteries of jolly old Saint Nicholas, the Easter bunny, the tooth fairy, or the wily goblins of Halloween, may grow up very matter-of-fact, to be sure, but he will miss many of the most exciting and memorable events of childhood. As for me, I am glad I have those memories. I feel strongly, therefore, that a child's occasional retreat to the lands of make-believe makes for a valued broadening of perception which helps develop a keen ability to envision new achievements in his adult years. Certainly a dreamer must precede a doer, and here imagination is the foundation and forerunner of creativity. No one can deny that the road of progress is paved with stones of achievement which once were mere figments in the imagination of some dreamer along the way.

In my own childhood I could hardly have known that my life's work would be in the fields of engineering, designing and invention. In these kinds of endeavor, imagination must play a major role, and thus proves itself an indispensable professional asset.

For their days ahead, and for the joys of living them, there is every reason for cultivating imagination in the minds of our youngsters.

Silhouette is that of son Brian.

MY BROOM IS A HORSEY

My broom is a horsey, oh so frisky, you know;
I jump in my saddle and a-riding I go!

Away through the orchard like a cowboy so free,
Around the cow pasture to the butternut tree.

Then out to the meadow and the hay ricks so fair
To startle the plover and the cottontail hare.

I fear not the forest where the animals run—
The bears all go hiding when a-riding I come.

It's fun as I gallop in the open and free—
Adventure is calling my good horsey and me.

I ride like a warrior and as brave as they grow;
But nighttime is coming so away home I go!

POCKETS

Value, we are told, is a relative thing; and the chattels in a boy's pockets are valuables in a very real sense. Amazing it is how much worth can be attached to paraphernalia a boy carries about with him! Then, too, it is no wonder that pockets in a youngster's jeans wear through before their time, and that mothers often throw up their hands in sheer desperation.

The urge to accumulate personal possessions is one of humanity's primary traits. This starts in days of our childhood and seems to gain momentum through the years. Many, in fact, collect so much that two lifetimes would not be enough to make use of it all. So, pack-ratting being the rule by natural edict, small wonder so few of us escape this basic proclivity.

Boys like to have things to keep, to hoard, to share and to swap. A pocketful of trinkets and gadgets gives importance and prestige to a boy. In this regard a few things of virtually no intrinsic worth can teach a growing youngster the value of many things, and he may even grow up an astute businessman because of his early traffic in these boyhood doodads.

As for me, I crammed the run-of-the-mill items and gadgets of many sorts into my pockets like most boys of my day—nuts, acorns, rabbit's feet, empty shotgun shells, horseshoe nails, string, and so on—and they all brought a pleasant sense of ownership in their own peculiar way. One prized item was the single-noted mouth harp that I usually carried in the bib pocket of my overalls—a better pocket for the purpose because it accumulated less foreign material to foul the delicate reeds. The harp, along with the other pocket treasures, helped while away many long hours while riding horseback to the village, going a rocky path to bring home the cows, or simply sitting out a rainy day.

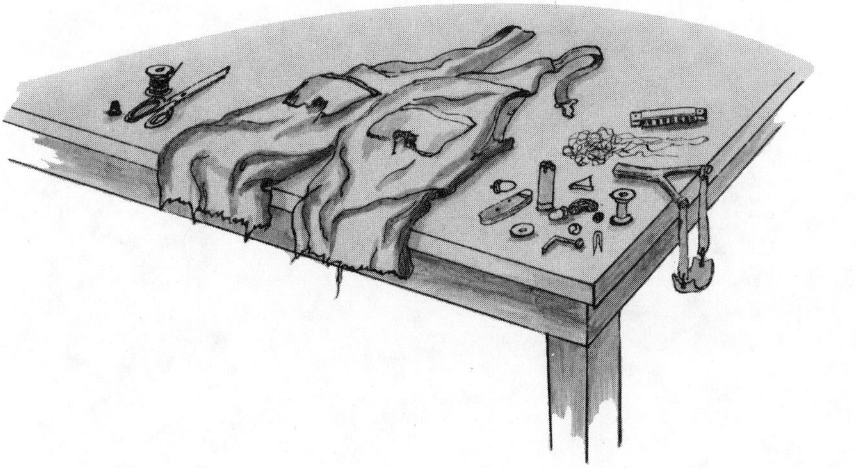

POCKETS

Pockets are so gosh all handy,
Good for just 'most ever'thing—
Shootin' marbles, rocks and slingshots,
Empty spools and scraps of string.

They are dandy for jawbreakers,
And that leath'ry turtle's egg;
Apple slices and the Barlow
That can beat at mumblepeg.

Crooked nails and ginger cookies,
Frogs and toads and lizards blue;
Rabbit's feet and lucky buckeyes
And the trusty French harp, too.

Pockets hold my earthly fortune—
Treasures all, a pride and joy;
These make up my stock for swapping,
And they make a wealthy boy!

THE FOOT RACE

A foot race is good for growing boys. Reasons to substantiate this statement are about as many as often there are boys in the race. Generally stated, country boys don't have need for seeking special outlets for any energy reserves, for theirs is an endless lot of chores that ever need attention. Fortunately, however, among the many exciting exploits and adventures they do find time now and then for a foot race, a corncob fight, stoning a wasp nest, or seeing who can chin himself the greatest number of times—even in the exercise known as "skinning the cat" from a low-growing limb in the apple orchard.

Winners come in all varieties, and any victory in the final analysis is after all only relative. Some of us feel that the cause is lost if we don't finish first; some have no qualms about conceding the number one place but still desire to be among the upper contenders; while others are content with coming in barely ahead of the last participant in the contest—or with even running in the race at all.

Whether in a foot race or in life's race itself, we know that we all cannot win the top place, and none of us would want it so. The effort, the cost and/or the consequences wouldn't be worth it for most of us. Every proposed race at the outset implies there will be a winner, but it also predicates a place for the loser—and of course all stages in between. Each position, each niche, is a place for someone whose will or best capability is suited to exactly that spot.

In the balance of things we should naturally aspire to the best of which we are capable, but at the same time we should not discredit achievements on the lesser planes. Each of us is called to fill a place of some order. We do well if we fill that place honorably and commendably. To strain for the impossible is only to invite frustration and despair—and only then history may write us off a failure.

THE FOOT RACE

Tired of mumblepeg and marbles,
All the guys sprawled near the stack.
John spat out a well-chewed wheat straw,
"Race you'uns to the barn and back!"

Lazy protests, grunts and mumbling
The suggested challenge met;
Few were really keen for running,
But with boys a bet's a bet.

Sam was much the most reluctant,
But they all got to their toes,
Brushing briskly chaff and fannings
From their tousled hair and clothes.

Glancing at the shimmering building
Full three hundred yards away,
Sam had half a mind to chicken,
But what would his buddies say?

At the starting line he rallied,
Made that high old "come-on" pitch;
Gave his shirt a final tugging
And his galluses a hitch.

"Ready, set, and go!" John shouted,
And the barefoot race was on;
Then he bounded o'er the rail fence,
Like a rabbit he was gone!

All were off and running
Much like cattle in stampede;
Walter, Brucie, Hank and Alvey
Were with John up in the lead.

Sam and Joe were lesser champions—
Maybe wiser than the rest.
It was only when things counted
That they gave their level best.

Fats was short and heavy,
Not a whirlwind on his feet;
Sam could not be sure of others,
But this Fats he had to beat!

These enthusiastic racers
Had now to the homestretch turned;
Sam was back, but not yet losing,
And so ran on unconcerned.

That the most had off and left him
Hardly would have seemed to mind;
He would watch before and after
Lest he'd end up plumb behind.

But when Fats came up a-puffing,
On the verge of being passed,
Sam began to put out effort
And he wound up second last.

Then the racers all lay panting,
Faces red and dripping wet;
John the most of all was winded,
But, by George! he'd won his bet.

Lose or win, they all had finished—
Every one had clinched a place.
This distinguished each contender
In that hard-run boyish race.

So with all the effort counted,
In a race that's finally done,
Maybe Sam was right to question
Who had really, really won?

PATHWAYS

Pathways are for dusty feet
   Skipping gaily high and low;
Sunbrowned, tough and calloused feet
   With really nowhere much to go.

Pathways are for grownup strides
   Hurried, climbing over stiles,
Seeking goals that lead afar
   On daily missions o'er the miles.

Pathways are important ways—
   Purpose surely makes them so;
All are trails to noted spots
   And ways where busy people go.

SPRINGTIME IN THE HILLS

For most of us spring is a welcome change from the unfriendly days of a blustry winter just past. No matter how many springtimes we have seen in our time, each approaches us always with a newness and a freshness that is most delightful. Whether we are aware of it or not, there is a masterful program at work in it all, for an ongoing scheme with never any changes would virtually frustrate mankind with gross boredom.

Responding to the functions of our seasons, we rejoice in the changes which are constantly coming our way. Each seems to provide us with an appropriate place in time to begin something or to end something. Changing seasons offer us the opportunity to assume new challenges and to abandon old ones. In this we experience a rebirth of ambition, new undertakings, new goals, and so are shaken out of the lethargy of repetitive routines before they reach serious proportions.

Being foremost of all seasons in bringing forth new life, spring has come to be recognized as the symbol of newness itself. Further, it inspires us with the desire to keep pace in a world of new activities. Then, too, spring erases most completely the characteristics of the previous season, and offers the most reassuring promise of great new bounties in the months ahead.

Springtime in the rural mountain areas is in a class by itself. Here indeed Nature does herself proud! With a profusion of delightful magistery she transforms the entire countryside, and with it the soul of man! What can surpass the heavenly beauty and fragrance of an apple orchard caught in a veritable avalanche of blossoms, the deliriously gay song of bustling birds as they seek new nesting places, and meadows and woodlands in life afresh that seem to roll on forever?

The mountain folks now busy themselves in making their seed catalogs come alive in their own fields and gardens. The old-timers faithfully heed the admonitions of the farmers' almanac so that their plantings are in keeping with the right-of-the-moon and the proper signs of the zodiac—and they swear by these!

So, springtimes come and go in their ordered cycle, and each in its turn is as new as though it were the first ever!

SPRINGTIME IN THE HILLS

'Tis springtime in the Ozark hills,
  For the wintry days are o'er,
And life is bursting out anew
  Where the snow had lain before.

A tapestry of tender green
  All bedecked with flowers fair
Heard the season's urgent calling
  And has spread out everywhere.

The stately oaks with tender crowns
  Now are nodding near and far
From the hillsides where the dogwood
  And the blushing redbuds are.

The apple orchard's breath is sweet
  From the trees in robes sublime,
And the bees are gay, rejoicing
  In this glorious blossom time.

Here the air is still and balmy
  When the sun has gone to rest,
And the sound of frogs is wafted
  O'er the pasture's slumb'ring breast.

Aye, springtime is a happy time
  When the evening shadows roam
And the whippoorwills are calling
  'Round my Ozark mountain home.

THE ANEMONE

Even while the last remnants of winter still linger on and practically the whole vegetable world is yet dormant, the wild anemone is already making way for its annual debut in the wooded areas of the Ozarks. It is refreshing to see those tiny blossoms peeping from protective covers of last year's weathered leaves, holding forth the promise of spring soon to come. Radiating its simple but uncontested charm in the unhurried scene around about, it makes no ostentatious issue of its presence, but pursues its purpose with unwavering dependability and a persistence great and admirable indeed for the tiny bit of creation it is.

On a leisurely early stroll through the woodlands one experiences a rapturous release of vivacity long suppressed through the sieges of wintry days. On such occasions our eyes are ever watchful for signs of new life and other welcome transitions the springtime always brings. Any signs of new life here can be quite noteworthy, for in these early days of sylvan awakening something versus nothing looms far more significant than something versus something in great abundance later on. In this regard the oft unheeded anemone stands out importantly despite its diminutive and retiring way.

The vernal season is the world coming awake—and the anemone is an abiding presence in this awakening. Its reassurance is welcome, warm and gratifying, with overtones of friendliness and the promise of exciting, new happenings ahead. We would surely lose considerably were the meek and lowly anemone left to go unnoticed and unadmired in our hectic workaday world.

THE ANEMONE

Where forests sigh in dormant sleep
  In sheltered margins 'round the lea,
There peeps through beds of weathered brown
  The modest, lone anemone.

Undaunted by the lingering chill
  That trails the hostile north's retreat,
It thrusts its friendly petals forth,
  The first a waking world to greet.

A wiry arm in meekness lifts
  That dainty star of violet white—
A harbinger by fairies sent
  To sip the springtime's early light.

Alone, it dares to grace the scene,
  Alone it sheds its beauty 'round—
Then, lo! it is forgotten quite
  When later verdure claims the ground.

You're great indeed while great you are,
  Anemone, it's just that way—
Then fickle eyes so quickly turn
  To those who steal your light away!

INGRATITUDE

Ralph Waldo Emerson, in his beautiful poem *The Rhodora,* penned the words ". . . beauty is its own excuse for being." To those of us inclined to a mind for the basic necessities of life, beauty as a very real essential might be easily overlooked or grossly discounted. However, since beauty itself is a non-material entity—it cannot alleviate hunger, shut out the rigors of a cold winter, or clothe the nakedness of our bodies —it must then take its place among the finer fringes that are ours to have and enjoy.

Fortunately, the Creator was wise in a concept of duality and multiplicity in His creatures in that while He created things of utility He at the same time made them pleasing to the eye and to other of our senses. Were it not so, the sky might have been something other than a deep alluring blue, the grass perhaps not the restful green it is, fire a drab and somber hue, and water the antithesis of crystal purity.

Man in his position can and does enhance, diminish and destroy the beauty of his world. Some of this he does of necessity, some inadvertently, and some wantonly. Yet, one can reason that if food nourishes the body, beauty ministers to the soul—and consequently to the mental well-being of us all. Everything else being equal, is it not better, more uplifting and inspiring to include beauty with the quality of usefulness? A tasty apple is more enjoyable if it is also a delight to behold; and a house can be warm and comfortable while at the same time intentionally beautiful by design and construction.

Scenes about us tell us great stories if we only have the faculty to see and to listen. And from it all we can learn a valuable, enduring lesson: With the same given quantities of materials a builder can fashion either an eyesore or a thing of beauty—and with approximately the same expenditure of time and effort. Each may choose according to his preference, but as for me, I shall take the things of beauty!

INGRATITUDE

We dwell in scenes of splendor
  Yet often see them not,
As though God has no purpose
  In things of beauty wrought.

The twining arms of wonder
  Our fleeting steps embrace;
A world of song and color—
  And all are commonplace!

Yet radiance of the sunset
  And glory of the dawn
He gave to make our burdens
  More lightly carried on!

THE OLD RAIL FENCE

The weathered old rail fence has always exemplified many notable things to our people. A gift from the past, it is a tribute to the character of the men and women who shaped the course of our country, and it constitutes a present-day remnant of something traditional in the rich and proud heritage that is ours. The rail fence was a "natural" for our early comers who were blest with an abundance of timber. All it took to produce it was determination and a lot of hard work!

Even children delighted in the rail fence. In days of my own boyhood we were often challenged to test our coordination by seeing who could walk the greatest distance atop the fence without falling off. The fence also provided other services, for leaves blown in by autumn winds collected in its corners and matted among the brambles and undergrowth. These proved a haven for wildlife, and here many survived the rigors of our Ozark winters in relative comfort and security.

But in spite of all the good the old rail fence symbolized, it was vulnerable to forest fires that ever threatened it. Never shall we forget the ominous scenes of a red night-sky in early spring to the south and east of our farm where stretched a vast expanse of wooded open range. On reaching the ridge top to the south, the scene we beheld was ever awesome, yet strangely beautiful, as great rings of fire fringed the distant hilltops and burned steadily toward our back forty and the tinder-dry rail fence that enclosed it. Incidentally, burning the woods was a "mysterious" annual occurrence which rather pleased cattlemen who desired woodland grasses to flourish unhampered by leaves for abundant free pasture in the summer months.

Whether we were tired or not after a long day in the field, the red sky meant the need for immediate regimentation of all available hands to man the pitchforks and rakes in the process of counterburning—fighting fire with fire! Along with this we invariably breathed a prayer that no wily winds would rise or perchance shift to blow embers in the wrong directions.

Hours later, our efforts apparently rewarded, with smudged hands and faces, eyes red and smarting from smoke, and muscles aching from long exertion, we retraced the fence rows for reassurance that it was safe to leave the scene—that no lingering blazes posed a further threat and perhaps render the entire evening's ordeal an effort of love's labor lost.

THE OLD RAIL FENCE

Along the byways and the trails
  That mark the Ozarks' pleasant land
Can still be seen the fence of rails
  Built long ago by calloused hand.
It stands in weathered zigzag row
  And leads away o'er vale and hill—
A relic of the long ago
  That grandly serves its purpose still.

This fence of old with lichened folds
  Speaks mutely of the yesterdays;
Its panels each a memory holds,
  Each rail an ancient scene portrays.
With wistful smiles old folks recall
  The rail fence in their fondest tales,
Yes, how they seemed accomplished all
  To proudly walk the topmost rails!

As settlers came with ox and plow
To claim these untamed rolling grounds
They built the fence in sweat of brow
To mark and keep the homestead bounds.
'Twas faithful shepherd, firm and neat,
Whose sturdy wall of oaken rails
Kept silent watch through summer's heat
And stood the gaff of wintry gales.

And when in glory's height it stood
It proved a home for feathered throngs;
It hid the nesting happy brood
That cheered the world with warbling songs.
Beneath the rails where briars grew
The Bob Whites made their secret runs;
They sheltered there when blizzards blew
And hid away from hostile guns.

A trellis rare, so rich in charms,
The rail fence by the country lanes—
The ivy here flung twining arms,
And grapevines wove their rambling canes.
So fine a landmark year on year,
With life so rugged, wild and free
When forests teemed with nimble deer
And turkeys called across the lea.

This fence, a gift from grandpa's day,
A time of life's unhurried mode,
When gallant lads and maidens gay
To gatherings in the saddle rode.
And still a symbol of that date
When stalwart men could swing the maul
Then later rise to men of state
And build a nation dear to all!

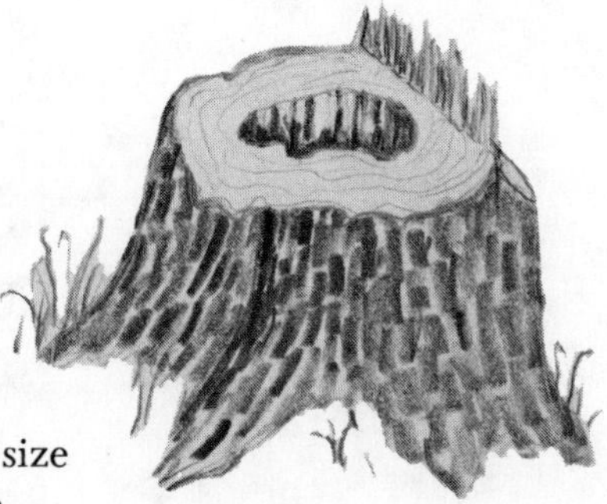

WARTS

Old ugly warts are funny things
  That come in every shape and size
And often when you're not aware
  A wart will take you by surprise.

They're found alike on man and beast,
  Yes, even on our hapless dogs.
And yet we're told by those who know
  That warts do come from handling frogs.

For just about most everything
  There is a remedy, we hear,
And there are secret things to do
  To make an old wart disappear.

But we have sworn to keep it mum—
  We crossed our hearts and hoped to die,
So if you tell someone we told,
  We'd simply have it to deny.

But take a dishrag, worn and wet,
  First rub the wart per mystic code,
Then bury it till full decayed
  At forks of some old country road.

Or take a grain of yellow corn,
  One per wart on face or hands,
And drop into a hollow stump
  Where stagnant, slimy water stands.

These tricks, with patience, time and faith,
  Work like a charmed phenomenon—
Before you know what's taken place,
  Every blessed wart is gone!

SWINGING ON THE GATE

Gates have always held an irresistible fascination for children. This may range from outrunning others for the dubious importance of getting to open them for passage of vehicles and livestock, to the thrills of sailing through space while swinging at their outer reaches.

Our farm gates were swung by various means. A simple method was to attach the gate to a tall vertical pole which pivoted on a base stone, preferably cupped, and at its upper end turned inside a forked branch, the two open ends of which were spiked to the top of the gate post. Sometimes a large horseshoe or bent piece of hickory served in place of the forked branch. Often, too, the thimble and hub from a worn-out farm wagon wheel were used for the lower pivot. Other hinges were leather straps, crudely fashioned wooden hinges, or metal ones forged in the blacksmith's shop from old wagon tires.

Those who have experience on the subject will agree that farm gates are not always in the best of condition. The weight of the gate bearing constantly on the hinges causes eventual sagging, so that opening one in this state of delapidation entails the tedium of dragging it open and shut. Such a gate unfortunately is never the one to bear small brown feet that come for a swinging thrill.

On the other hand, though, the added weight of gate-swinging youngsters hastens the sagging, and too often brings on the embarrassment of a sudden breakdown of the trusted old gate. At such times when a breakdown does occur, this results in other consequences, particularly when news of a broken gate reaches home; and more so if livestock gets out of the pasture and perchance into a field of corn or other crops.

But gates and youngsters make up a good combination! And barring a broken one now and then, gate-swinging shall always remain one of the joys of rural childhood.

SWINGING ON THE GATE

Each day brings on so many things
In childhood's carefree, happy state;
Among the joyous things to do
Is swinging on the pasture gate!
Swinging on the gate,
Swinging on the gate,
A flying glide, a thrilling ride,
There swinging on the gate!

O'er clover blooms and dandelions
And tufts of close-cropped tender grass;
Across the weathered wagon tracks
And hoof-worn trails where cattle pass.
Swinging on the gate,
Swinging on the gate,
Here to and fro we raptured go
While swinging on the gate!

These gates, we're told, on hinges hang,
And that our weight will make them sag;
That gates are hard indeed to move
When they are broken down and drag!
Swinging on the gate,
Swinging on the gate,
We bet our gold the hinges hold
For swinging on the gate!

But, lo! we'll never once forget
That battered knee and busted crown
When swinging extra fast and high
That loaded gate came crashing down!
Swinging on the gate,
Swinging on the gate,
With paddled rear we'll end it here,
This swinging on the gate!

THE BARNYARD LEAGUE

Was there ever a growing boy who got enough of playing ball? Though handicapped by too few to make up a team, boys usually manage to play at the game nonetheless. Where proper rules of the game are not too well known, or readily applicable, rules of sorts are made up on the spot—rules to suit the circumstances—or the owner of the ball!

In my earlier years, professional baseball was something we rarely heard about in the remote sections of the Ozarks. Aside from the barnyard games, or those played during recess at school, the big boys usually got together enough to play a Sunday afternoon game near the village center, usually boys from one community against those of another. A pasture field across the road from the blacksmith shop at Custer saw a goodly number of such gatherings. For most of the onlookers it was a place to go and something to do, but for the young men who played it was a very real challenge and they put their best into it. We smaller boys were justly impressed with the powerful swings and the long drives that stood out as phenomenal to us in those games, and we secretly resolved one day to emulate the feats of such sluggers as Tudor Bell, Wilgus Edwards, Andy Keithly and the Raulston boys.

Later as big-city newspapers found their way into our hills—the *St. Louis Post-Dispatch, The Kansas City Star,* and others—the major leagues began to come alive to us. Then with radio we began to hear play-by-play reports of baseball games in progress—and always we rooted for the St. Louis Cardinals! Moreover, the better known players of that time made lots of talk around the country stores, the grist mill, and the blacksmith shop while men waited their turns at getting their meal ground, wagons repaired, horses shod, or just waiting for the mail. Discussions included such as: which is the faster in base running—the "pull" runner or the "push" runner.

For us country boys all this spurred on dreams of careers in organized ball. Whether or not any of these dreams really materialized turned out not to be terribly important. However, the significance and the fun of the barnyard games have stood out as great as any of our early activities.

THE BARNYARD LEAGUE

Butch swings wild with tongue protruding,
  Gripping hard the broomstick bat.
We always lay his sloppy hitting
  To those gobs of pudgy fat.
Too, he never fails to argue
  On how many strikes he's had,
And we all give in to his tally
  'Fore he quits and goes home mad.

Steve, a better all-'round slugger,
  Hits the good, the bad, and all.
He puts such heft and steam behind it
  That we often lose the ball.
Then he'll run around the bases
  With a burst of breakneck speed,
While all the rest comb through the nettles
  And the prickly Jimson weed.

Bob and Smitty are the loud ones,
  Play the game with razz and shout,
And both are sure to have conniptions
  When they miss or make an out.
Quite a pain is giggling Hubert—
  Laughs aloud at every groan,
And, win or lose, our every heartbreak
  Somehow strikes his funny bone.

Nubbins always plays the outfield
  Near the wagon box in back;
Amazing how he makes those catches
  Dodging 'round the feeding rack!
Like a bolt of greasy lightning
  In he shoots that homing ball,
And so often holds the runner
  Based on first, the corncrib wall.

Shorty is our self-styled catcher,
  And we'll never know just why
Because he simply lacks the stature
  When the pitcher throws them high.
Every time a wild pitch happens
  And old Shorty goofs the catch
The game comes to a sudden holdup
  While we search the fennel patch.

Fun indeed, these barnyard leaguers—
  Each a corker, none the same,
And we have cried with belly laughter
  Over antics of the game.
But we all will long remember
  That glum look on Freddie's face
The time he tagged that half-dry cow chip
  That he thought was second base!

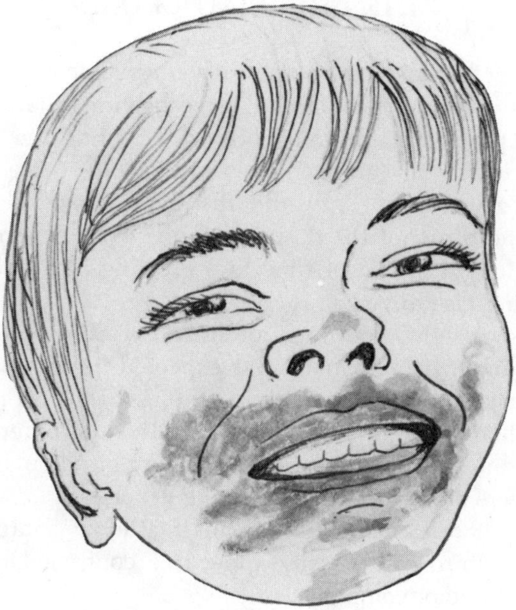

MULBERRY MOUTH

Mulberry mouth and fingers blue,
  O little man, how well you know
Up in the tree with birds so free,
  Just where the finest berries grow.

Mulberry mouth, contented lad,
  With telltale cheeks and purple grin;
There's not a doubt what you're about
  And ne'er a question where you've been.

Mulberry mouth, with boy to match,
  Unpurposed clown with impish face,
With stains and all, I'm wont to call
  Your world a bright and happy place!

Refrain:
Mulberry mouth and fingers blue,
Mulberry mouth, sir, how do you do!
  Up in the tree with birds so free
There's not a finer lad than you!

THE CHURNING CHORE

In former days some of the early muscular development in the arms of a rural youngster could well have been attributed, among other things, to the process of churning butter! Wielding the wooden dasher of the old three- or four-gallon churn could become quite a tedious chore any day of the week. Not only did the thick cream offer considerable resistance to the thrust of the dasher, but the process seemed to drag on for much too long a period of time to a growing boy who wanted to be doing something else anyway.

Most frequently churning butter was a Sunday morning assignment, particularly when company was expected for Sunday dinner—to us the noonday meal. Mother, anticipating the usual boyish protesting, tried to make the chore more inviting by placing the churn and a chair on the porch, away from the heat of the kitchen. Here on the porch of a summer morning we were always serenaded by the never-ending song of a catbird high in a walnut tree, mimicking all his feathered antagonists, and the rich-throated redbird in a nearby apple tree confirmed beyond a doubt the coming of Sunday company.

Mother had another purpose, however, in selecting the porch location, and that was so the spattering of the churn would take place where it could be more readily washed away. Being involved in the process, I always thought it short of miraculous how this cream could splash out through the small annular opening in the churn lid around the dasher handle. But splash it did! This despite improvisions used to stop it. Incidentally, one such anti-splashing gimmick was a cloth laid closely around the dasher handle; another was an inverted tin can with a hole cut in the bottom. The scientific reasoning back of this device was that a spattering gob of cream which finds its way through the first opening would not likely find its way through a second, and so would be trapped inside the can and ultimately drain back into the churn.

All the tedium associated with churning butter was not without reward, however. There was the welcome relief which the first particles of gathering butter brought, signalling that the process was nearly finished! Then there was that tasty piece of homemade bread spread with aromatic fresh butter, and that brimming glass of fresh buttermilk—a beverage that shall always remain a favorite of mine.

THE CHURNING CHORE

So often on a Sunday morning
  I must take a tedious turn
To wield the heavy wooden dasher
  Of the earthen butter churn.

With reddened hands nigh blistered,
  And with cream-bespattered floor,
It's easy for a guy to reason
  This is not my favorite chore!

The time just seems to drag on purpose–
  Long are hours devoid of joy;
As if it were to try the patience
  Of a work-bound hapless boy!

But the world perks up and brightens,
  And so sweet the catbird's song,
When at length, at last, and finally,
  Chunks of butter come along!

BLANCHE

The nearest village to our Missouri Ozarks farm was Custer, a wide place in the road, as an old-timer would describe it. Here stood the grist mill, the blacksmith shop, a few residences, and of course the grocery store with its canned foods, drygoods, and hardware, and with a small section in the fore part of the building officially barred off from the rest for the post office.

It was at least a once-a-week necessity to travel the four rather tedious miles to this hamlet for getting our mail and staple supplies needed back then even when hill folks lived in near self-sufficiency. At first the modes of travel were by horseback, wagon, or walking. Later the Model-T Ford relieved some of the monotony of those long country miles, and eventually better roads helped make the trip a bit more pleasant.

Always a bright spot on the way was the Walter Grogan place. Here warmth of friendly neighbors was ever exemplified by a greeting, a smile, or a spontaneous wave of the hand. Blanche was a flaxen-haired little girl who lived here with her fine parents and her older brother Hancel. Each member of the family was gifted with the spirit of neighborliness, but Blanche's sunny smile and hearty hand waves were especially refreshing as we passed, and this was noticeably lacking on occasions when perchance no one was at home.

As Blanche grew up and blossomed into beautiful young womanhood, these fine qualities of friendliness never diminished. Her innate radiation of sunshine and cheer undoubtedly contributed immeasurably toward making the world a better place in which to live. In any event, Blanche early had earned the affectionate title of "sunshine girl" from the warmth and sincerity which characterized her through her childhood and young adolescence—so much so that indeed the Grogan home itself had long ago taken on so much of the image of Blanche and her family that it seemed to have a delightful personality all its own. In the famous words of Samuel Walter Foss, here truly was a family "living beside the road and being a friend to man."

BLANCHE

Along a stretch of country miles
  A bright spot greets the traveler's eye;
Here warmth of hand waves and of smiles
  Help cheer the weary passer-by.

The place, a farmstead by the road;
  The radiant one, a child so fair
Who makes this friendly, trim abode
  Far brighter for her presence there.

A gift of sunshine unaware
  This winsome child with eyes of blue;
She, sunny as her flaxen hair,
  Makes all the world come smiling through.

So as we travel life's long miles
  We capture oft that needed ray
By smiling to the child that smiles
  For blessings rich along the way.

THE SCARECROW

The man who depends on his crops for a livelihood has his share of anxieties from day to day throughout the entire season. First there's having to know to plant in the right signs of the moon; then there are always the hordes of insects to fight; the myriad organisms that cause blight, mold, rot, wilt, and many other disorders; the voracious wild animals from the tiny field mouse to the fleet-footed deer; and by no means least, the birds of the air whose species are legion.

At corn-planting time we were oft reminded of the old chant:

One for the blackbird,
One for the crow,
One for the cutworm,
And two for to grow.

With the inference, of course, to put at least five grains of seed corn into each hill in order to ensure a full stand.

Most of the marauders are pests during only one phase of the growth cycle—either they dig up the seeds just beginning to germinate; feed on the tender shoots as they emerge from the ground; attack the stalk, leaves and other parts of the plant at midsummer; or descend upon the fruit or grain at near harvest time. The crow does double duty, however, in that he delights in digging up the newly-planted seeds, and also remembers to return for a goodly share of the ripening grain in the latter part of the season.

Very likely, because of him, scarecrows were invented, hopefully to keep away his kind and other pilfering birds. This makeshift device is designed to resemble a worker in the field, but more often looks like a farmer on the brink of economic disaster. Nonetheless, it dutifully guards over the fields at such times when the farmer has to be elsewhere. In truth, however, the scarecrow does a better job of imparting a false sense of security to the cropper than in scaring away the birds. Usually we find that the intended victims soon learn that the old straw man is really harmless, and they gather around in great numbers.

Having seen and learned much about scarecrows, I somehow feel that were I a bird I should seek out these men of straw and make their vicinities my headquarters—for a scarecrow advertises the fact that near him is something very special!

THE SCARECROW

Throughout the hours of night and day,
  Alone and staid, with raiment torn,
He stands there on a gentle knoll
  To guard the tender sprouting corn.

His outstretched hands so resolute
  Swing shiny tin foil in the breeze
To chill the hearts of thieving crows
  Who scold him from the nearby trees.

An unsung hero always there
  With watchful eye that never sleeps,
Through sun and rain without complaint
  He long the lonesome vigil keeps.

So, hearken to that saucy crow,
  Defiance in his every caw—
He's surely scared most half to death
  There perched atop this man of straw!

NATURE'S MELODY

Commenting once on my writings, Mrs. Lee Sanders, the then president of the Smoky Mountain Manuscript Club, said this one simply has to be her favorite of my poems. She explained that her position as teacher in the Tennessee School for the Deaf made her particularly sensitive to sounds. And a person in her capacity would understand best how much her pupils miss of Nature's gifts in the world of sounds that bless most of us every day.

God, with infinite wisdom, provided first the basic necessities for all his creatures, but He did not stop there. Knowing that all would have to share a more or less common environment, He added an all-pervading fringe of delightful extras to mutually flavor the daily existence of each. In this regard, all creatures by their very presence, their respective ways, and the pursuit of their activities, add materially and mutually to the harmony and well-being of the whole creation.

The need for man's working in the sweat of his brow is wisely assuaged by the presence of Nature's fringe benefits all about him. The hardships of the day's labor are always more bearable in the cool of a passing breeze, and more so when it brings the whispering of a fragrant pine, the laughter of children at play, the warbling of a song bird from a pleasant meadow, or the barking of a squirrel from a nearby tree! Many of these amenities are often taken for granted and are often discounted in the role of what we consider important things; yet even the most cantankerous among us would have to admit to a world of mediocrity were it not for these extras.

Yes, toil in quest of food and shelter God ordained a necessity, perhaps to teach us values. But He wisely spiced it with so many niceties, and crowned our efforts with so many rewards that each living hour becomes a privilege, and the entire creation, one great package of harmonious interdependence. Even if we were given the power to do so, I doubt that we would change a single chord in Nature's beautiful melody!

NATURE'S MELODY

There is music in the Ozarks,
  There is rhythm in the hills,
Now that restful summer's twilight
  Brings the call of whippoorwills.

Hear the sleepy owls awaking
  In the woodland here and there;
Croaks from frog ponds near the orchard
  Fill the pleasant evening air!

Hear the drowsy, lowing cattle
  Gathering 'neath the pasture tree,
Hear the tinkle of the sheep bell
  In the fold across the lea!

Harken to the clanking milk pails
  And the farm boy whistling, gay,
Hear the barking of the shepherd
  In a farmyard far away!

Yes, there's music in the Ozarks—
  Nature's sweetest melody,
And its notes will linger ever
  In the rustic heart of me!

THE DINNER BELL

Saved by the bell! This old expression is best understood around prizefighting rings, where it had its original significance. In a very literal sense, however, it also has a meaningful application to those who remember the delightful sound of the rural dinner bell at a time when it seemed that hoeing another row of corn or pitching another forkful of hay was beyond the capability of human endurance. Even the animals in harness would perk up their ears and pep up their strides at the summons of the dinner bell, for they, too, had long since learned that this sound means a welcome break in the day's labor.

Associated with the dinner bell are such pleasant things as sparkling cool drinking water from a deep cistern or from a gushing mountain spring; the divinely refreshed feeling after washing the dust of the field off one's hands and face; the tantalizing smell of food emanating from the kitchen; and that half hour or so sprawling in the cool grass, relaxing in the shade of the apple tree to let the hearty meal settle a bit before resuming the tasks that awaited for the afternoon stretch.

So, from the foregoing, it is understandable that through the years the sound of the dinner bell grows to fill a fond spot in the heart of everyone who labors in the fields. And it remains a cherished sound forever afterward!

THE DINNER BELL

The sounds of life we daily hear
Are part of one great master plan;
And country sounds that greet the ear
Are surely all a gift to man.
One, more than others, strikes a chord
That oft evades all words to tell,
For coming softly o'er the dell
There's one alone, the gentle tone
Of the good old dinner bell!

When field crops curl beneath the sun
And rows seem more than ever long,
The shimmering heat waves blur each one,
As man and beast both plod along.
Then comes the summons for a break—
A gushing well our thirst to quell,
A shade to pause and rest a spell,
As comes at last time for repast—
Bless that good old dinner bell!

So, little wonder that we all
Are partial to some special sounds,
For wrapped up in the bell's sweet call
Are things that know no mortal bounds.
That man who boasts he traveled far
And life has ever served him well
Has still, poor soul! not much to tell
Who's never known the happy tone
Of the good old dinner bell!

WADING IN THE POND

Boyhood in one of its most coveted dominions is wading in the old frog pond and feeling the cool mud oozing between the toes. Nature is alive here in many ways so vastly different from other haunts in the rural scene. Creatures of land, air, and water all claim a rightful domain at site of the pond, and here in detached manner they mingle in a unique sort of coexistence, each pursuing its native purpose in its own peculiar way.

Observing and pondering hours on end the behavior of the varied and many creatures in and about the farm pond is an experience second to none in its field. Unwittingly, these beings are both instructors and entertainers in their own right. Verily, there is never a dull moment as the parade of lowly actors goes through matter-of-fact routines, each thespian dutifully pursuing his continuing act with flawless expertise. And all this with unquestioned assignments, unerring performance, and without an obvious director. From any point of view, it is indisputably a superb production!

Yes, wading in the pond is a great pastime. Moreover, it is a childhood activity which early engenders a deep and abiding respect for our fellow creatures. In fullest appreciation of this we might observe: He who has eyes, let him see; he who has ears, let him hear!

WADING IN THE POND

Wading 'round the meadow pond
  With bare feet in the mud;
Dragonflies among the lilies,
  Hovering over leaf and bud.
Water-walking creatures show
  The surface firm and fine;
Dollar bugs in hurried circles
  All elude this hand of mine.

Frogs with loud protesting chirps
  Go leaping for the deep,
Then observe my bold intrusion
  As they from some vantage peep.
Ousels in the cattails perched
  To guard a nest near by;
Bristling bright-eyed from the rushes,
  Deep concern in every cry.

Polliwogs so newly here
  Enjoy the shallows warm—
Dots of black with tails a-wiggling,
  Thousands in my reach of arm!
Larger tadpoles and crawdads
  Are here in numbers, too,
And from clumps of reeds on farther
  Bullfrog eyes are peering through.

Wasps wing in to float awhile
  And drift as breezes blow,
While the singing daubers labor
  Then with fashioned mudballs go.
Algae, matted, soft and cool,
  Afloat at leeward side—
Carpet green for transient beings
  Here with fancied pomp and pride.

Wavelets rippling ever on
  Make fixed things seem to move,
Much like tiny vessels cruising—
  Which the hours at length disprove.
Here's a world of magic found,
  Alive at Nature's wand,
And 'tis boyhood's happy privilege—
  Wading barefoot in the pond!

BABY COTTONTAIL

There flushed out by the turning plow
  And caught beneath my daddy's hat,
He trembled in my eager hand,
  His heartbeats pounding pitty-pat!

To hold him was a boyish thrill—
  His fur so smooth and soft as down,
His tiny fluffy bunny tail,
  And plaintive eyes so big and brown.

So sudden this in his new world,
  And with no past to help him know,
He doubtless wondered very much
  Just was his captor friend or foe!

With thought of self, but good intent,
  I held this prize, one rare to get—
Resolved to seal him in my heart
  And make him my own cherished pet.

Then daily swamped him with my care,
  Caressed him, heart and soul and mind;
I fed him clover, tender buds,
  And morsels bunnies rarely find.

Untutored, both, with much to learn!
  For he was born to scamper free—
Too bad, alas! I found too late
  He could not live and captive be!

THRESHING TIME

Threshing wheat was once a special highlight in the year's activities. Even hearing that the machine was coming to our neighborhood, or hearing the piercing blast of the steam whistle in the distance, was enough to raise our blood pressure several points! Threshing time meant many things, especially to an excited youngster. Among them it meant seeing new people, doing unusual things, eating super-abundantly, and afterwards tumbling in the soft new straw. It also meant fresh village-ground flour for new batches of homemade bread, and newly-refilled straw ticks for the beds.

In my day, coming to our neighborhood were such fine threshermen as the Herndons, the Conways, and the Harrisons. During the season they gradually worked their way up through Gladden Valley, through the post oak flats in the Doss and Turtle communities, and eventually into the Dry Fork section of the county.

For many young men it was indeed a lark to follow the threshing rig from farm to farm, and often many horses were tied to fence posts near the scene of activity where these riders enthusiastically lent a willing hand to whatever task had to be done. For them it meant an ever-changing scene, and the best cooking anywhere—not to stress the chance meeting of new rural lovelies who helped with the preparation of the meals, waited on the menfolk at table, carried fresh cool water to the threshing crew, or just added to the occasion by their charming presence.

The advent of the combine and stepped-up techniques in agricultural methods gradually replaced the exciting old event of threshing time, even in the remote areas of the American scene. But progress so often is ruthless in its way, and many fine old traditions necessarily are lost in its wake.

THRESHING TIME

The early summer is upon us,
Golden bounties bless the year;
The spirit mounts in gay abandon—
Threshing time once more is here!
The pointed stacks of gilded treasure
Stand there glinting in the sun
Awaiting brawn and bright machinery
In a labor that is fun.

The massive steaming smelly engine,
Oily scents from here and there,
The shrill note from the blasting whistle,
Flapping belts that beat the air.
The wood pile for the hungry boiler,
Water barrels and odd supplies;
Aromas sweet from grain and wheat straw,
Puffs of smoke in summer skies.

From near and miles away the helpers
  Horseback and by wagons come,
And many long the thresher follow—
  Just like circus troupers, some.
And not a cent for compensation
  Is the purpose of a one;
In spirit neighbor helping neighbor,
  All for sake of goodwill done.

The girls in calico and gingham
  Come to see and to be seen;
They more enthralled by youthful biceps
  Than the mystic old machine.
They manage to get near the action,
  Stepping 'round the belts and hose,
And squeal when teasing males with hayforks
  Stab the ground around their toes.

The farmhouse, too, is all a-bustle
  With the women gathered in;
And each a master in her cooking
  For the tired and famished men.
They make great dishes all so tasty—
  Chicken, beef, and country ham;
Hot biscuits, greens, and red-eye gravy,
  Cakes and pies and luscious jam.

Then when the thresher, task now finished,
  Goes to serve another place,
It takes along some of our essence—
  Things resume a normal pace.
We cannot help but feel a let-down
  As we see it roll away;
But no event can last forever,
  Neither can our threshing day!

BIB OVERALLS

Bib overalls of faded blue,
Well worn and frayed, with patches, too;
  Hip pockets ripped and buttons gone,
  Bare puckered seams and stitches drawn.

Apparel's best with much to spare,
And softened well by wash and wear—
  Of all the garments one can own
  There's none of greater comfort known!

Such freedom at the waist and knee
For riding bareback, romping free;
  For climbing trees where warblers sing,
  Or flying on the grapevine swing!

Bib overalls, each precious pair,
Much more than simply rags to wear—
  With faded threads of denim blue
  Life's fabrics well are woven through!

WASHDAY BLUES

It is little short of ironical that a boy inclined to do virtually nothing about keeping clean and tidy would lament about the woes of washdays! But consistency never was a necessary ingredient in what it takes to make up a boy. And no boys among my early associates were particularly fond of washdays either. This, of course, was before the introduction of the modern washing machines, the piped-in hot and cold water that made them possible, and the miracle detergents whose enzymes and other additives virtually devour dirt and grime on contact.

For many today, washday as such has all but disappeared. Modern efforts in this area are a far cry indeed from the washdays we knew in the country a generation ago. There was always the never-ending need for what seemed volumes of water, and countless armloads of wood for the fire to heat it. In those days the only running water we had was the running we had to do to get it!

For many fine old mothers of the days of tub and washboard, the modern equipment affords a much-earned liberation indeed. But despite the hard work, wrinkled hands and bleeding knuckles that washdays entailed, there was commendably little complaining done on their part. In this regard, we hold those accomplished women of our early washdays in the very highest esteem, not only for the day-by-day dependability in their work, but also for their fortitude—that stabilizing effect in the family and on the growth of our nation.

WASHDAY BLUES

Seems washday comes one day too often,
  Though it comes but once a week;
Means toting heaps and gobs of firewood
  And a good part of the creek!

Those washday blues are never welcome—
  Rob the day of all its joy,
And everything is out of schedule
  That befits a growing boy.

Sounds of rubbing from the washboard,
  Creaking from the wooden stand;
Smell of soap, all brown and homemade,
  Piles of clothes at every hand.

The pan of starch, the tub of bluing—
  Same old washday sights we see;
The steaming boiler on the cookstove
  Where our vittles ought to be!

The call to stretch the sagging clothesline
  And to prop it in between,
For who would have the washed things dragging
  Once they're hanging fresh and clean?

The playful breezes snap the bed sheets,
  Try for size each pair of pants,
While sun rays bleach the waving clothesline
  (Or a shower comes up perchance!)

Somehow the blue jays and the blackbirds
  Are informed, as washdays go;
They fly o'erhead with colored berries
  And then blitz the wash below!

So o'er the gloom of all our washdays
  We are sure to air our woes—
Yet everybody loves the freshness
  Of the fragrant sun-dried clothes!

SMOKIN'

One might say that we in our growing years are imbued with a disproportionate share of curiosity. Later on as we experience more of life's events we seem to moderate to a certain extent the inherent drive to try firsthand each activity that comes our way. Too, the more experience we accumulate in some things the less we require in others, because degrees of similarity in activities and events carry over from those we know to those we don't. Experimentation, then, is the builder of the yardsticks with which we endeavor to gage and understand the world about us.

A good example is the shirt-tail boy with an opportune sack of tobacco, a pipe or cigarette papers, and a match. No amount of explanation, admonition or warning has ever satisfied a youngster's curiosity regarding tobacco. It takes personal experimentation, and then, whether for good or for bad, he knows—really knows for the first time—in his own personal way.

I shall always remember my first such encounter with some of my father's home-grown leaf. Because I had long helped in the planting, deworming and harvesting the small tobacco patch which served strictly for father's own use, a natural curiosity about the product developed and grew with me for several years. In due time and in line with usual developments one day I resolved to learn why tobacco figured so prominently in the daily necessities of our elders (mountain women in the neighborhood also indulged in its use in one form or another).

That was quite a day! Perhaps it was a day I can count as more significant than a great many others, for it taught me not only what smoking is like, but also what *not* smoking is like. The experience of "turning green around the gills," the terribly unpleasant aftertaste, the embarrassment, and last but not least the paternal chastisement which ensued, all were more than enough for one day—enough in fact to last a lifetime.

SMOKIN'

Good gosh a'mighty, who'd a' thought
As how we'd end up gettin' caught—
  There 'way behind the barn and hid,
  Just who'd get wise to what we did?

Our pipes were simply super jobs,
All made from big ol' fancy cobs,
  With punched-out twigs from elder limbs
  Or wicker-basket reeds for stems.

Our homespun 'backer crumbled dry,
Full strong enough to make you cry,
  We tamped in firm with much ado—
  Just like we saw the grownups do.

With lifted leg and sweepin' scratch
On seat of britches lit the match;
  Drew down the flame with man-size drags,
  Then reeled and coughed 'mid snorts and gags.

But we stayed on and puff by puff
Kept wonderin' when we'd have enough.
  'Twas nothin' great, but golly then
  All fellers have to prove they're men!

Then 'fore too long we understood
We didn't feel so awful good;
  The world got blurry, thick the air,
  And barn chased barn around us there.

All ghastly white and cold in sweat,
We found how sick a guy can get—
  For smokin' of all stolen joys
  Soon separates the men from boys!

Now ailin' kids can't hide for long,
And parents somehow guess what's wrong;
  'Twas then we learned our case for sure
  Was one a hickory stick could cure!

ROMPING IN THE HAYLOFT

Romping in the barnloft
  Where we come to play;
Climbing to the rafters,
  Tumbling in the hay.

Hay so soft and bouncy,
  Fragrant, fresh and clean.
Of our favorite places
  None is quite so keen.

Peering out the doorway
  High and open wide,
We can see forever
  O'er the countryside.

Yes, we'll take the hayloft
  For exciting play—
And it's really special
  On a rainy day!

THE WAY TO SCHOOL

Walking two or three miles to and from school was an accepted part of a country youngster's life in my grade school days in the Missouri Ozarks. Often the school roads were unpaved county roads except where "short cuts" through fields and trails through wooded areas enabled us to shorten the distance a trifle. Our trek to South Ozark and Victory schools led mainly along such county roads. These often were dry and dusty in late summer and early fall, and so muddy when the "bottom dropped out" during the spring thaws that the weedy and brush-grown banks on either side proved to be decidedly better walking. South Crossroads, the one-room school in our home district, was an exception, however, as no county road led schoolward from our farm. Here our way to school took a course through cornfields, down the meandering dry bed and the sand bars of Halbrook branch, over fences, along hilly farm trails which edged cultivated crops and led through marginal upland pasture fields where clumps of oak sprouts, poor joe grass and red sorrel abounded.

To one inclined toward the sequestered trails and nature's unspoiled beauty, the latter doubtless would have been the preferred school road. Here gray limestone cliffs flanked our path along the lower slopes, and jutted out at intervals farther up the hillsides on either hand. Too, here and there mountain springs spilled their crystal waters down the face of a bluff or poured from overhanging ledges. Columbine and wild ferns adorned these rugged formations, and growths of ivy climbed in profusion and draped their lengths over the crags and trees in the valleys.

Here the sunny mornings and evenings, seasonal thunderstorms, chilly set-in rains, and the blustery days of winter, all presented a variety of conditions for us on the school road. When heavy rains brought the dry creeks to raging torrents we either had to miss school, or be taken across the swift waters on horseback, often with the water so deep that it lapped at the saddle stirrups and even our feet!

If the foregoing rings of schoolday hardships, then perhaps that is what they were. But when these things are part of one's everyday existence, and when circumstances offer no alternatives, they are taken in stride and with little or no complaint.

THE WAY TO SCHOOL

When September brings the Ozarks
  Autumn days bright, crisp and cool,
Then excited rural youngsters
  Walk once more the ways to school.

Paths now rank from growths of summer
  Edge the cornfields and the leas;
Ferns and ivy in the low ground,
  Clustered wild grapes in the trees.

Gentians fringe the rustic wayside
  Where the woodland creatures play,
And the goldenrods so heavy
  Hang their heads across the way.

Over boulders gray and weathered,
  Past thick hazel bushes brown,
On where limestone ledges greet us
  With clear waters tumbling down.

All along the sandy creek beds
  Now devoid of summer's heat,
Through the gap and o'er the fences
  Go our bare and nimble feet.

Arms embracing books and tablets,
  Pencils clipped to garments new—
Young folks feel the hand of fortune
  Surely blest them through and through.

From the lunch pail full of goodies
  Come rich odors strong and clear—
Smells of apples, bread and cookies,
  And that sumptuous roasting ear!

All these hold a lot of promise
  For a day that's hard to beat;
These with study, fun and frolic
  Make our every joy complete!

SCHOOLDAY AUTOGRAPH VERSES

Our school days are so dear to us
  And far too soon, alas, they end!
But they will linger to the last
  If I have gained you for a friend.

* * *

When you've wed your fellow
  So handsome, tall, and true,
Don't forget this scholar
  Was one who loved you, too!

* * *

When fleeting time has drifted on
  And you recall this happy year,
May you remember me as one
  Who truly held your friendship dear.

* * *

May all the years that beckon now
  Bring naught but happy days to you,
And scores of friends your life endow
  With love and sunshine ever true.

* * *

When marriage begins to go sour
  And your woman gets hateful and rants,
Just let her take note of the fact
  That it's you who is wearing the pants.

* * *

Sparkin' you is such a thrill;
  There's magic in your eyes.
Holdin' hands peps up my heart
  And gives my tummy butterflies!

AUTUMN IN THE OZARKS

A teenage effort, the accompanying poem was first published in the *Missouri Farmer* after the publisher, the late William Hirth, first sent it back with the request that I include something about the quail and the possum.

The poem, however not in the best literary form, portrays a scene which attests that life always takes on a new dimension with a change of seasons. With autumn there is a new burst of excitement in the air that banishes the lethargy of a summer's hangover. This is marked by a sharp change in pace, a whole new line of goings-on, and new anticipations. Verily, a sort of unexplained restlessness pervades the bright golden days that bless this season.

Among the highlights, of course, are the shift of interest to the various school activities, the many facets of harvest rich with new bounties, the kaleidoscope of colors that presents the far-flung hills and valleys in the rarest panoramic vistas, the busy wildlife creatures obeying that compelling impulse to lay away a goodly store for inclement months ahead, the season's final pageant of wayside blossoms, the depth of azure in the skies, the haunting blue haze of Indian Summer, and the great friendly harvest moon that lingers on at night.

Fall is the payday of the year, and a time when we in receiving take time to humbly acknowledge the Giver. A time when our grateful eyes drink deep of autumn's golden light and our hearts sing with the exultant mockingbird and the jay. Yes, autumn is a time for counting our blessings and rejoicing in the sheer delight of being alive!

AUTUMN IN THE OZARKS

Now it's autumn in the Ozarks
And beauty dwells in this land of thrills;
The sunbeams play throughout the day
While the sky sweeps down to the colored hills.

The countryside stretches far away
Like a wrinkled quilt of red and gold;
And farm homes peeping here and there
Nestle snugly in each tinted fold.

The magic touch of Autumn's wand
Has made her call known everywhere,
For summer's green of the rolling hills
Has turned to colors strange and rare.

The dogwood's garb has changed to red
And spreading oaks are turning gold;
The walnut trees have shed their leaves
And ripened nuts have lost their hold.

The grass is brown by the cobble fence,
  And yellow are the buckbrush hedges;
The trailing ivy in crimson robe
  Climbs o'er the rustic limestone ledges.

In pasture lanes where cow paths go
  Nods the goldenrod in faded gown;
There the sumac stands in garnet red,
  And buckeyes show their glossy brown.

There's buried wealth in the garden plot
  Where amber vines lie on their bed,
And farther up on a sweeping slope,
  The drooping apple boughs are red.

The pumpkins all sun in the fields,
  Where stately corn shocks stand,
And o'er in the dell the hazelnuts peep
  Through windows made by Autumn's hand.

Up in the oaks where jay birds cry
  And under load each twiglet droops,
There's where the rambling grapevines run
  And swing their crop in purple groups.

On zigzag rails along the road
  The squirrels are busy all the day,
Carrying nuts and acorns brown,
  To store for winter's use away.

The sharp, clear note of the calling quail
  Is heard near ricks in the meadow field,
And down by the creek goes the possum's path
  Where persimmon trees lay off their yield.

Yes, it's autumn in the Ozark hills—
  I know these words are true as true,
For smoke steals from the chimney tops
  And curls so high into the blue!

THE RABBIT TRAP

O little rabbit, won't you come,
Hop into my rabbit gum?
From the apple take a bite
To stay the chill this frosty night.

Signs are fresh on matted grass
In the orchard where you pass;
Nibble marks on brambles show
Where your favorite runways go.

Long you've scampered wild and free,
Now I want you all for me–
O little bunny, brown and white,
Come into my trap tonight!

THROWIN' ROCKS

Whatever city kids fight one another with is one thing, but in the country they throw rocks. As a matter of rhetoric, in many localities the word *stones* would be more appropriate here. Not so in the Ozarks, for we were not overly obsessed with particulars, and so we simply threw *rocks*.

Although a dangerous practice, when one is at odds with an adversary skillful rock throwing can make up for any and all deficiencies in stature. Too, rocks can easily overtake a fleeing opponent who might have scored somehow with a sharp bit of name-calling, a sneak blow, or whatever, and then is in the process of "retreating" to a safer distance.

We often threw rocks more as a bluff than real intent to do bodily harm. On at least one occasion, seeing that a missile released with mayhem aforethought was about to hit an off-guard schoolmate, the hurler frantically cried "Look out!" and was much relieved when his throw went amiss.

Throwing rocks on our school grounds was strictly forbidden, though now and then in a fit of temper a thrower dared to test the validity of the rule—usually coming out the worst for the infraction. Conduct on the school road, either to or from, likewise came under the jurisdiction of school authority, though here out of sight of the teacher, more throwing went on. When rock throwing on the school road was reckoned with later it was always because someone "told" on you.

Throwing rocks is a builder of biceps—and here practice makes perfect in such areas as distance and control. Boys become accomplished in years of this exercise, throwing at random things at hand such as trees, wasp nests, tin cans and the like. Prowess in throwing also carries over in such activities as corncob fights around the barn, hurling sticks and stones at squirrels in the tall timber, in throwing contests at county fairs, and pitching baseball. Throwing rocks, moreover, is a step-saver, as for keeping in line those stragglers when driving home the herd of cows, ridding the garden of roguish livestock, or discouraging the family dog who persists in following when he is not wanted.

Not always a commendable thing to do, rock throwing is nonetheless part of rural boyhood. Show me a mountain boy and I'll show you a rock thrower.

THROWIN' ROCKS

We country boys would lose a weapon
  That sustained us quite a while
If someone messes up all nature
  And throwin' rocks goes out of style.

It's just a way of self-defendin'—
  Fellers have to hold their own!
And if it's known you're good at throwin'
  You're apt to be left well alone.

The bully can be quite a terror
  And he'll often "fix our clocks,"
But little guys can still get even
  When it comes to throwin' rocks.

We've got to know just where to catch 'im,
  And to keep clear out of sight.
It can't be on the reg'lar school road,
  For then teacher gets uptight.

You keep a watch for when he comes,
  Best to have some others there,
And make it sure no victim sees you,
  For that would mess the whole affair.

Then when he comes along a-saunterin'
  Proud and smart-like, actin' cool,
You let the rocks fly out in volleys
  Then watch him go, the runnin' fool!

CIDER TIME

What country boy or girl has not thrilled over the exciting time of year when cider making is the order of the day! This is when the golden autumn sunshine has given the luscious apples that finishing touch of honey-rich ripeness as they hang in great bounty from the sagging trees.

All related tasks somehow lose their drudgery and everything seems fun—turning the handle to make the huge flywheel spin around as the apples are pulped and made ready for pressing, tugging at the sturdy lever to turn the pressing screw, and even toting the marc to the feed lot where the pigs squeal in constant anticipation of each new batch that is brought them.

In the round of a year's activity on the farm, few tasks indeed surpass cider time. For the labor that is entailed there awaits not only an immediate reward as one samples this "nectar of the gods," but also this delightful event serves as a memory-maker which promises to linger on and brighten those many years ahead!

CIDER TIME

How good to be so privileged
  When in childhood's pep and prime
To frolic in the apple orchard
  In gay cider-making time!

To breathe the rich aroma
  Of ripe apples everywhere—
The red and yellow luscious beauties
  That perfume the orchard air.

To climb the towering ladder,
  Up to reach that largest one
That always hangs the very highest,
  Blushing in the autumn sun.

Butterflies and yellow jackets
  Winging in the gentle breeze,
Rejoice in harvest's sweetest bounty
  Piled pro tem beneath the trees.

Grimes Golden and red Winesap
  Blend this favorite annual swig,
With Maiden Blush, delicious Staymans
  Jonathan and Limber Twig.

The groan, the creak and clatter
  Of the busy cider mill
As first it crushes, then it squeezes,
  Juices flow the pans to fill.

Then toting pails so full and foamy—
  One of many happy tasks!
The pathway leads us to the cellar
  Where await the wooden casks.

Gay times like cider making season
  Bring our days a rosy glow;
They round out thrills of happy childhood
  And the finest years we'll know!

BUSTER'S COMEUPPANCE

"Boys will be boys!" is an old excuse that has been used rather defensively so often and so long it has earned a well-deserved place among our most familiar clichés. From time immemorial boys have always been just that, and a safe prediction is that they will always remain so. Men, too, having only recently been boys themselves, tend to shield their younger facsimiles in many of the wayward and erratic involvements in which they find themselves.

Naturally more venturesome if not to say more foolhardy than their sisters, there is little wonder that the mortality rate for boys is correspondingly greater than that for girls. Small wonder the female population exceeds the male! Barring an occasional tomboy, boys can be expected to make headlines almost any day, often doing things that make one's flesh creep.

Back of many antics of a boy is a near inexhaustible store of energy, and then there is that desire to be very much on the stage of action. So, understandably, we will have boys hanging by their toes from fences and trees, clowning for a laugh, slopping through water puddles, or perpetrating some sort of prank just for kicks.

Some boys are a bit slow about learning the principles outlined by the Golden Rule and so are inclined to let a series of successes at forward tactics take over to the point of making them tyrants and bullies. Fortunately or unfortunately for them, there has to come a time when a lesson must be learned at the price of much pain and humiliation. But a lesson learned the hard way is the one best remembered!

"Buster's Comeuppance" here portrays boys generally—boys that you and I have known firsthand. The poem relates an incident that really happened in days of my boyhood, but has doubtless happened dozens of times in many places, before and since. It portrays both sides of an everyday picture—the one who is overdue a lesson on general demeanor and those who find it necessary to play the role of teacher.

In our world, however, no one situation is permitted to last for very long, and in the check and balance of things it is necessary to have some of both extremes, for to quote another cliché: "It takes all kinds!"

BUSTER'S COMEUPPANCE

Old Buster always was a bully
  O'er the meek and younger guys;
He picked on first one then another—
  Never one of his own size.
He called the shots out on the playground
  Used the kids like they were tools,
And pushed in where he wasn't wanted,
  Played most games to suit his rules.

When Buster said, "First bats!" regardless
  All the others would kowtow,
And if a one was heard to grumble
  Bus was sure to clean his plow!
At times the gang got good and fed up,
  Tried to put Bus in his place,
But wound up with a bunch of shiners
  In about just every case.

Now this went on for several seasons;
  Fellows somehow kept their cool,
Till plans one day in whispered secret
  Went the rounds of Barker school.
The plan was centered 'round the outhouse;
  Only trusted ones were told,
And even these stood quite aghast
  As they heard the plan unfold.

'Twould take a bit of timely action,
  Nothing should come up alack!
There was a button latch on outside,
  And an op'ning high in back.
A forked stick was first positioned
  Through the hole and laid just so,
And long enough to serve the purpose
  From a safety point, you know.

Assignments were then made of duties
  So that all would come off right;
A group of guys would relay signals
  To the key men out of sight.
A cross-up here could well be tragic
  If a sentinel failed his post;
With fingers crossed and tense the planners,
  No one knew who trembled most.

Then came the time, the hour of zero;
  School let out for late recess.
That Buster would head for the privy
  Was more sure than just a guess.
So, there he went, just as expected!
  Everyone must now be strong.
Two guys were hid behind the building,
  Others passed the code along.

Pretending everything was normal
  So that Bus would never know,
The planners were about to even
  All the scores that vexed them so.
At signal, when old Bus had entered,
  One then quickly latched the door;
The other manned the stick with gusto
  As was never seen before.

Now pandemonium rent the silence
  As though Hell had broken loose—
The tearful cries, the shouts and cussing
  Proved they'd cooked old Buster's goose!
This seemed to last for many moments
  Till the battered latch gave way,
And Buster darted from the outhouse,
  Leaving early for the day.

Well, Bus somehow survived the torment,
  Though for days he went unseen.
When he came back, reserved and silent
  Things went on a new routine.
Like other youngsters on the playground
  He would wait and take his turn—
Such a shame it had to happen
  Life's important ways to learn!

But things went on with best relations,
  Now a different game of ball!
The end for victor and for vanquished
  Proved a lesson good for all.
No one was proud of the adventure,
  Though it worked out good as gold;
And which one poked that fateful wasp nest
  Was a secret never told!

MOLASSES-MAKING TIME

One of the many extras of autumn is golden molasses fresh from the new crop. For generations in rural America molasses making was an event that always received a special rating.

In my boyhood there was always an air of excitement on this occasion. But there was work, too. First came stripping and topping the cane stalks, then cutting and hauling them to the cane mill where the denuded stalks were fed, butt-end first, into the rolls to squeeze out the juice. Then, too, there was getting wood for the fire under the 'lasses pan, and so on. The mill was turned by a patient, plodding horse or mule, self-led, pulling the sweep around and around in a great circle, while the "pummey" pile grew larger and larger as more and more cane stalks passed through the mill.

The foaming green juice ran into a barrel through a covering of cheese cloth or piece of an old bed sheet, used to keep out the frenzied bees, wasps and yellow jackets. A second juice barrel, also covered, was positioned atop the cold end of the evaporator; it maintained a desired level in the "pan" through a wooden spigot opened to let out the right amount of flow. As the juice progressed through the channels, side to side, moving ever toward the hotter zone in back, the "skimmin's" were removed, and all the while the color gradually changed along the way until at the "finishin' end" near the flue it was drawn off into lard stands and other containers, a rich golden amber product ready for the most discerning appetites!

It was a special delight for little folks on the school road homeward to stop and sample the hot molasses by means of swabs improvised from joints of cane stalks, chewed or otherwise frayed at one end into brush-like implements. And no one seemed concerned about the possible lack of sanitation from the repeated dipping of the swabs into the golden channel, for we know the heat immediately dispatched any germs that came into the stream.

The real reward came afterward, however, when molasses and fresh butter, blended into an emulsion, was spread over hot biscuits or corn bread. A rare way to top off any meal!

MOLASSES-MAKING TIME

With the tang of autumn on us
And the cane full in its prime,
On the list of fall agenda
Now it's sorghum-making time!

Nuded stalks in piles for squeezing
Juice the foaming barrel to fill,
Dobbin, lazy, bored, and patient,
Plodding 'round the old sweep mill.

Piles of tacky pomace growing,
Yellow jacket, bee and gnat
Drawn by luscious juices flowing
Visit barrel, pail and vat.

Wood fires in a rustic furnace,
Turning juice from green to tan
As it moves through devious channels,
Browns and thickens in the pan.

Expert eyes upon the process,
Hands with skimmers play their role,
Feet that move in shoes bespattered,
Step around the skimming hole.

But, withal, the scene that lingers:
When from school the homing clan,
Books aside for cane stalk swabbers,
Stops to sop the 'lasses pan!

HALLOWEEN

Halloween is definitely for the young fry. As special days go, it has a color all its own, and by its very nature is uniquely different from all other days.

Halloween in the Ozarks, as in most other places, has always been regarded as an auspicious time for pranksters to try their ingenuity at mischief of one sort or another. At this time young folks in particular feel they can do their deviltry with special impunity, as they help goblins perpetrate strange and unheard-of shenanigans.

In the Ozarks, however, our nocturnal Halloween doings always seemed rather tame compared to those which many of our predecessors boasted about. It was nerve-tingling to hear old-timers tell of the wild and wooly pranks they pulled off in their earlier years. One favorite among them was taking a buggy or wagon apart and then reassembling it on top of a neighbor's barn roof. Another was to set back by a distance of about six feet the outhouse at a public meeting place so that during a nighttime gathering, as a revival or the like, a hapless person visiting the privy could see the building only dimly outlined in the diminished light at this distance, and on approaching it could not see the newly-exposed pit that lay open between him and the building now in its new location.

Somewhat less drastic pranks perpetrated by the spooks of former times were relocating porch swings to the cowshed, interchanging front and rear wheels of a farm wagon, setting a hayrake in someone's front yard, or placing the hog troughs in a chicken house.

Around the stove at the country store it was a treat to hear the former Halloween goblins recounting the consternation of their hapless victims, and their tales never failed to elicit guffaws of laughter and hearty thigh-slapping. It seemed, too, that the tales got better as one teller inspired another. And if belly laughs are good for what ails us, Halloween pranks might have served their purpose as good old mountain therapy for our forebears.

HALLOWEEN

Goblins, spooks and vampire bats,
Pumpkins, owls and yowling cats,
All in hordes are on the scene,
For, lo! tonight it's Halloween!

Shadows in the creepy night
Cast by wisps of lunar light
Make the stumps and logs appear
Like crouching evil witches near.

Apparitions flying high,
Mounted brooms across the sky,
Jack-o-lantern's eerie grin,
To try the very souls of men!

'Tis a night for creatures rare
Man and beast to haunt and scare!
As the world holds grim and black
Goose pimples creep up every back!

But you know, we're somehow glad
That the goblins, good or bad,
Come and do their weird routine
To chill our spines on Halloween!

NOVEMBER RAINS

There is nothing like a persistent rain to dampen the spirits of a youngster so recently spoiled by a bright sunny autumn and long hours of carefree outdoor playtime. Indeed, the continued confinement of a long rainy period soon exhausts the resources of pent-up little folk. Longingly, they peer through the water-stained windows at the drenched playground, the drippy swing, and the other playthings now saturated and enveloped in a gray world of falling rain. Parents, too, with more than usual patience must rise to the challenge of keeping peace on the home front, and seeing that there is something constructive and entertaining to maintain the enforced togetherness at a tolerable level.

When the chill of late autumn comes to the Ozarks with a set-in rain brought by an easterly wind, and a falling barometer indicates no letup in sight, there is reason enough to bring on a sense of rainy-day blues.

For one thing, the condition is worsened psychologically by the distressing knowledge that the pretty days of the recent past have ended. Already most of the crop of autumn leaves have drifted hither and yon, many of them matted in fence rows and thickets, and the season's winded chant of wild geese flying has once again come and gone. Ahead now is a store of ever more inclement weather for the late fall and winter months —a period that seems an eternity to energy-packed little tykes.

However, nothing comes our way that is without purpose, and the old consolation that "on every life some rain must fall" is ably substantiated in more ways than one. At least, we learn patience, resourcefulness, and see the values at the other end of the measure. Thus, in time, we learn to take the rainy days and so appreciate the sunny days all the more.

NOVEMBER RAINS

November rains, November rains,
  Pattering down on faded leaves;
Falling with a grave persistence,
  Dripping, dripping from the eaves.

November rains in country lanes,
  Empty fields and woodland nigh;
Falling, falling, cold and somber
  From a gray November sky.

November rains, November rains,
  Coming down the livelong day—
Tidings of an autumn gone
  And a winter on the way!

THE WASHTUB BATH

The sight of the washtub on top of the cook stove on a Saturday evening always held an ominous significance to us of rural vintage. It meant unmistakably that a bath was inevitable. Being born some years too soon, or living in the wrong places, we with no indoor plumbing did not exactly relish these Saturday night events, but rather put up with them as a necessary inconvenience. It wasn't exactly fun to draw water from the cistern or to carry it some distance from a mountain spring, but we somehow gave in to the philosophy that it was important to look presentable on Sundays for whatever transpired on that day.

With the tub of warm water placed on the kitchen floor near the stove and presumably away from drafts, all other members of the family politely abandoned the kitchen in deference to the bather. So in the security of this rather precarious privacy the soap and washrag went into vigorous action, all the while the bather kneeled or squatted in the tub. After a quick rinse (which was merely a second pass with the washrag, this time without soap) the towel was a delightful finale to the process, and we felt almost triumphant in that this chore was overwith for another week.

Putting on the napped cotton "long-handle" drawers, or "long johns" (our facetious terms for the suits of long underwear) felt snug and delightfully comfortable after that invigorating interlude in the tub. Perhaps this warm snuggy feeling was a reward of sorts for dutifully pursuing the weekly ordeal. Incidentally, the clinker about this long underwear was that after repeated laundering the knitted fibers lost their elasticity and then the close fit became a loose excess of material which had to be folded over itself and held in place by long stockings pulled over these "lumpy" folds. Ah, yes! Those washtub baths! Although nearly a tradition, we were grateful for one thing—they generally came only once a week!

THE WASHTUB BATH

Life has its roses and its thorns,
  Its dark spots and its light;
There's joy and fun the whole week long—
  Then washtub baths on Saturday night!

But who said life was meant to be
  One continuous primrose path?
For good things have to end, you see,
  When comes our time to take a bath.

We boys were made for fun and play—
  All other doings to deplore;
So soap and water, we might say
  Were surely meant to be a chore.

The world and all may click along
  Till comes the old familiar sight—
The washtub on the kitchen stove
  Takes down our crest on Saturday night.

"But playtime makes for grimy boys!"—
  Such sayings really gripe and hurt;
And moms see knuckles "black as coal"
  While we can't see a speck of dirt!

And so with all red-blooded folk,
  There's naught provokes a boyish wrath
Like on a blooming Saturday night
  To have to take that washtub bath!

CHRISTMAS

Early impressions of Christmas shape our Christmas spirit forever afterward. Some subscribe to the philosophy that children should not be deceived by the myth of Santa Claus, and while they may have reasons for taking this position, I emphatically disagree. Personally, I would not take anything for the thrills and excitement we as children experienced in those wild anticipations at every Christmastide. Even the disappointment in what we learned in later years could not offset the memory of the happy Christmases past.

Our Christmas in the Ozarks was observed more along the customs known to my parents in their own childhood rather than those that prevailed among our neighbors. Items of decoration on our tree were strange, too, for many were fragile glass ornaments of various shapes, colors and sizes. One old-timer, fascinated by the beauty of them, walked up for a closer look. "Is them apples?" he queried of one round red glass ball, and before we could answer, his inquiring finger had poked a sizable hole in one of them.

Unlike native customs, we were roused at midnight on Christmas Eve by calls from our elders to "come quick—Santa is here!" We jumped up instantly and staggered into a transformed living room, but not soon enough to get a glimpse of the jolly old fellow. Somehow he always eluded us by a matter of seconds; however, once or so we even thought we saw him moving away as we were held up to a window, our eyes eagerly trying to follow a wildly pointing finger.

At any rate, we remember the bright scene he left behind. The glittering evergreen tree ablaze with fragrant wax candles, the rousing beat of a new record playing on the tin-horned talking machine, the new things by the tree, and that all-pervading scent of oranges. Oranges! I was well along in manhood before I stopped associating oranges with Christmas!

By present standards our Christmases were far from anything lavish, for not only were the gifts fewer—and many were homemade—it just seemed to take less to make a child happy back then. Christmas was Christmas to us because, among other things, it brought a change from everyday things to eat, to do, and to wear. Based on this premise, our children today have "Christmas" every week, and in greater measure than we dared hope for even that one time a year.

CHRISTMAS

That jolly season is upon us
  And the signs are everywhere;
Rich smells of spicy goodies baking
  Are now special in the air.

All day there's traffic, fuss and mystery—
  Lots of bustling going on,
And even after it's come bedtime
  Busy feet move here and yon.

We hear a lot of stir and whispering,
  Paper rustling in the night.
The clank of hardware, muffled tapping,
  And then stretches long and quiet.

We find our parents acting strangely,
  When we catch them by surprise.
They do some odd communicating
  With those shrugs and rolling eyes.

And funny things are with the house—
  Wish we had the honest scoop;
But certain places are off limits
  And we're not supposed to snoop!

We can't be taking chances;
  Better watch as things unfold—
Don't know much about the others,
  But for me, I'll do as told!

With evergreens, soft snow and candles
  And excitement running high
We'll just keep watch for sleigh and reindeer
  In that pregnant Christmas sky!

THE CIPHERING MATCH

The old one-room country school! One of its memorable highlights was that occasional change from routine study—the ciphering match. In larger schools this was a full Friday afternoon's activity, but in schools with less enrollment usually the last session of the day—after the last recess—was devoted to this purpose. Even those who were not the strongest students welcomed the change, for each in taking his turn had the privilege of calling out the exercise he could do best. Too, the very smallest pupils could score for their respective sides as significantly as did those in the higher grades, even though they did so by making the most marks in a given period of seconds.

Naturally the contest knew no bounds; brother competed against sister, pal against pal, and blushing Sue against that "special someone." All entered the contest with enthusiasm, and the outcome was always taken in good spirit.

Variations of the ciphering activities were geography matches and spelling bees. In the geography match, members of the two sides each vied first to find, on selected maps, the cities, rivers, and lakes called out by the teacher. The spelling bees took on various forms, but mostly it was a contest in which each individual fended for himself—all pupils standing in one huge circle around the schoolroom. The teacher selected words commensurate with each speller's grade level, and so it was fair to all in the match. As a speller missed his word he sat down and observed the progress of the remaining contest, leafed through a reference volume, or tried his hand at sketching or coloring. The last one standing was the "champion."

If nothing else, the Friday afternoon ciphering matches taught an element of good sportsmanship. They prepared most of us for the continuous contest that life in later years sets for each of us, for both successes and failures are essential to meaningful growth and development. Moreover, we learned that all cannot be winners in every undertaking, but that usually we can choose and play our best odds and wind up winners some of the time at one thing or another.

THE CIPHERING MATCH

The bell tolls end to late recess
  On a hard-played Friday afternoon;
The playground games and shouting cease—
  'Tis time for study all too soon!
The flush-faced panting pupils all
  File past the bucket on the bench;
Each takes the dipper quick in turn
  And gulps a drink his thirst to quench.

As books takes up, each in his seat
  With backs of geographies for fans,
In subdued tones and whispers loud
  All make their plea per prior plans.
"Let's cipher! Cipher! Cipher, please!"
  Large and small in unison begin;
Then eyes are all on teacher fixed
  For hopeful signs that she'd give in.

They dare not much too boisterous be,
  Nor to push the teacher's patience far,
For oft in past high pressure failed,
  And none would now their chances mar.
"Let Sam and Bessie choose up sides!"
  In a new approach implores Marie.
All sensing teacher's fleeting smile
  In one accord renew their plea.

For what seems eons teacher waits
  While the outcome one can scarce foretell.
She ponders all the lessons past,
  Then reasons they were done quite well.
As all sit tense she gives the nod
  And a bunch of hearts leap high that day.
Then with relief and hushed applause
  The ciphering match gets under way.

With school in even teams divided,
  Side for side and graded, two by two,
Both strive at chosen exercise
  Each other soundly to outdo.
The winner takes the next in turn
  And two best out of three is scored;
Thus lowest to the highest go
  So resolutely to the board.

Progressively up through the age groups
  Goes the test of speed, of skill and brains,
Then after all are finally down
  The grinning victor proud remains.
With mixed emotions, friends and kin
  Each would win with great dispatch,
But all come out with better views
  At close of every ciphering match!

Part II

Adolescent Ado

PITCHIN' HORSEHOES

Pitching horseshoes in mountain country is natural as cornbread for breakfast. Youngsters learn early from the inveterate old-time "champs," and the games are usually in order whenever time permits, and two or more pitchers get together. At the village blacksmith shop the game of horseshoes is a serious matter to the "regulars." Once one establishes an enviable record he guards it with much pride and determination. This of course is reason enough for any and all comers to try their hand against the "champ." Many a "sody pop" is bet, won and lost over some of these close-pitched games.

Amazing it is how proficient some of the pitchers become after several seasons' practice! They are the ones that show up at rural gatherings with horseshoe pitching foremost in mind. Onlookers, too, turn out in numbers to watch the more contested games. Here one hears a lot of good-natured bantering, razzing, and bragging, much of it over a pipeful of "homespun terbacky" or a sociable plug of Log Cabin twist.

But pitching horseshoes is by no means limited to the village area, nor to public places, for most farmyards are frequent sites for this sport. All that it takes is a couple of pairs of horseshoes (often those only recently worn by old Dobbin), and a couple of iron stobs driven into the ground the proper distance apart. Then a couple of players are off to try to outdo each other.

The rules we played by varied somewhat from those used by professionals, but one thing was always the same—we played with honest-to-goodness horseshoes—none of the simulated shoes the big-timers use. Only those shoes that were no more than a shoe's width from the stob counted points for the pitcher—though younger players often counted points for the nearest shoes no matter how far afield they strayed. One point was counted for one shoe closest; two points if both were closer than the opponent's, and so on. A leaner netted us three points and a ringer five points. For a full game the players getting twenty-one points were always the winners, unless it was a "quickie" which ended at eleven points.

PITCHIN' HORSEHOES

Pitchin' horseshoes in the mornin'
(Dew's still heavy on the hay!),
Workin' up some needed practice,
Gettin' better ev'ry day!
Throwin' straight with some perfection,
Yes, and throwin' wild ones, too.
"Better watch those roly-polys. . . .
Put a cowbell on that shoe!"

Pitchin' horseshoes in the noonday
(Horses need a bit more rest!),
Time for maybe one more quickie
Now that pitchin' is the best.
Pitchin' horseshoes in the evenin'
(Just about too dark to see!),
"Watch that toppin' out my ringer. . . .
Better leave my leaner be!"

Pitchin' horseshoes by the millpond
(While our corn a-grindin' goes!),
Puttin' on a bit of show-off,
Pitchin' 'gainst the village pros.
Throwin' for the stob with purpose,
Scorin' close with lots o' pressure;
"Hold it just a dog-gone minute—
This is one we've got to measure!"

Countin' points with quick addition
(Makin' cracks to hold our own!),
Dodgin' when a shoe comes glancin',
Hearin' players moan and groan.
"That, you say, was sloppy throwin'?
Well, we'll take it just the same;
Looks as though we've got you bested,
And this ringer takes the game!"

JUST WHO AM I

"Judge not lest ye be judged" is an oft-quoted Biblical admonition. Most of us agree that in principle it is a good one. However, in the light of human shortcomings it is also one very difficult for day-to-day living, for even when we make the judgment that we are not judging, we *are* judging!

Allied with the foregoing is the notion that somehow we are qualified to render judgment on occasions where we think our experience, age, or innate wisdom justifies it. Yet many with virtually none of the stated three bases constantly indulge in the forbidden act of judging, while a sage with every apparent qualification will prudently refrain from the action. It is simply the nature of man to exalt the value of his capacity in this regard, and as Shakespeare so aptly put it, ". . . he plays such fantastic tricks before high heaven as make the angels weep." We for the most part are inclined not only to judge, but to do so in haste—before we have all the facts and even the necessary qualifications—if indeed we *ever* have such qualifications.

On this the Scriptures remind us first to remove the beam from our own eye so we can better see the mote in our brother's eye. This is tantamount to saying that if we are critical of our brother we have not yet removed our own beam—our own shortcomings; that we have not refined our own being to the extent of being graciously tolerant of our brother's failings. So it appears we do well when we keep ourselves above reproach insofar as that is possible, and stick pretty much to minding our own business.

This poem was written when in a mood of soul-searching, with the ultimate realization that all are lacking in capacity when it comes to judging, regardless of how long and valuable the experiences in our past. Worse yet, if the act of judging others adversely is motivated primarily by a desire for self-exaltation then we really are giving in to an act of self-incrimination.

Lest the wrong impression is herein conveyed, I hasten to make the confession that despite the thoughts set forth in this commentary and the poem, I have not been able always to put to practice the ways I know to be best. For most of us *knowing* what is good and right, and *living* the principles of this knowledge are two entities oftentimes worlds apart.

JUST WHO AM I

Just who am I that I should see
But fault in those who walk with me;
  That I should say from day to day
  The men I meet along life's way
Are not the type they ought to be?

Just who am I that I should share
No part of life's besetting care;
  That I should go this road below
  Apart from all, and never know
The grief that oft my neighbors share?

Just who am I that I should sneer
When fortune greets a fellow near;
  That I should hate those high and great
  And, envious, seek to underrate
The steps that led to each career?

I know, thank God, it's all His plan
And knowing, I can understand
  'Tis base and weak for one to seek
  The laurels of perfection's peak
By trampling down his fellow man!

THE STREAM OF LIFE

Written in my teens, this poem reveals a contemplation which every young adult sooner or later undertakes. Understanding the processes of life and the purpose of our individual being does not come to us easily, nor in a complete package with all the mysteries neatly cleared up.

Rather, bit by bit our realm unfolds, each bit often a disjointed, apparently unrelated segment of an unknown whole. Eventually, when there have been a sufficient number of the scenes revealed to us we suddenly grasp what seems to be the entire picture. Certainly, we see that there is an interrelationship among the bits, and that there is a composite entirety—a beginning and an end—to the processes of life we know.

Observing that the waters in a stream undergo the sequences in a cycle not unlike those of each living being is not necessarily unique with any one person, nor any particular generation, but it is indicative of the mastery of some phases in our understanding. There seems to be a sameness in the patterns of many things we encounter along the way. An example is the structure of the atom, the molecule, and the universe itself. Another example is the pattern of cycles in which so many of our living creatures of flesh and fiber unerringly operate. It goes without saying that knowledge gained in the function of one therefore helps us understand the functions of others.

As there is merging of stream after stream along the course of a river, even so our lives merge with many, many others as the years, like miles for the river, go irrevocably by. And as the destination of every river is the sea, so the stream of life is ordered to flow unmistakably to an eternal sunset, that one common sphere that, like the wide mysterious ocean, may ever hold our admiration, but in this life will always elude our complete understanding.

THE STREAM OF LIFE

Life is like a winding stream
   That courses through the years;
Its waters catch the sunlight's gleam
   Yet oft are drenched in tears.
The current is life's main career
   And ever onward rolls
While eddies are the hobbies dear
   That swirl along the shoals.

It issues forth from mountain springs
   Unstained as dawning's dew,
There lulled by songs that Nature sings
   And steeped in heaven's blue.
Here babbling on in childhood glee,
   While cradled by the hills,
It lingers long in rhapsody,
   And tarries in the rills.

But ferny dells are left behind
When brooklet days are o'er;
Its waters, fresh and surging, find
A broader vale before.
And nearing now, those glories fade
That far so rosy glowed,
While many erstwhile hopes are stayed
As ever grows the load.

It wends its way through vales of sun
And where dark boulders lie;
The rapids loom up one by one,
And fast the miles go by.
Through fertile green and desert brown
The course leads day by day,
Not once to pause, but ever down
Along that destined way.

And then at last it nears the sea,
A placid stream, and slow;
With burdens laid off by degree
As currents feeble grow.
Its waters stained along the way
Now whisper half asleep
As softly steal they to the bay
To blend there with the Deep.

SMILE AWHILE

When your life's a chain of troubles
And your dreams, all broken bubbles,
While your woes recur in doubles,
    Simply pause and smile awhile!

When your friends all seem to fail you
And your past mistakes assail you,
Ever haunting, as they trail you,
    Simply pause and smile awhile.

When the skies look dull and dreary
And the days grow long and weary,
Aught seems everything but cheery,
    Simply pause and smile awhile.

When the future days are seeming
To have lost their former gleaming,
And your work seems unredeeming,
    Simply pause and smile awhile.

Though life's cares be irritating
And your routine not elating,
There's a world of sunshine waiting
    For the one who smiles the while!

THE LOVE OF MOTHER'S

Whether we are aware of it or not, much of what we are is instilled in us at mother's knee in the tender years of our childhood. True, the father makes his contributions, too, and these nurture principally the masculine side of our make-up. Both are acknowledged to be vitally important in the development of our offspring, with no disparagement intended to either.

Mothers, however, teach more of charm and grace, patience and understanding—the virtues that tend most to refine the character of her progeny. Much of our basic gruffness, the rough edges of a man's nature, are removed and smoothed by maternal admonition and example. Tenderness is not usually thought of as a dominant masculine trait, but show me a man totally without it, and I'll show you a tyrant and a despicable person. Without tenderness there is little understanding and consideration of others. Lack of it opens the door to myriad kindred negative qualities such as selfishness, greed, deceit, infidelity, and criminal tendencies.

Proud indeed is the man who had the blessing of a good mother, appreciated that fact, and was intelligent enough to garner in the priceless treasures of her influence and training. Certainly he goes forth better equipped to make a commendable husband and father, a better helpmate, a more reasonable fellow being.

Though a man has the courage of a dozen lions, the capability to move the proverbial mountain, and the power to command legions, he is not a man at all unless he has within him the love of God, respect for womanhood, and compassion for his fellow creatures. These latter are the virtues that invariably are traceable to the love and training of a devoted mother, and largely to her must go the credit and the praise.

Pictured are the author's mother, the author, and sister Anna.

THE LOVE OF MOTHER'S

O boundless main whose vast domain
   Has long claimed penly glory,
And whose enfoldment's oft retold
   In stanza and in story,
I know a sea surpassing thee,
   And like thee many others—
A sea replete with love so sweet,
   The boundless love of mother's!

From every side its sweeping tide
   Engulfs the infant's pillow;
And deep, caressing tenderness
   Bestrides its every billow.
Through wayward ways of childhood days
   And slips the years betoken,
In golden sands or murky strands,
   Its bonds are never broken!

Oh, blest is he who sailed this sea,
   And knew its surging passion!
Its lasting force will steer his course
   In upright, noble fashion.
A love more true man never knew
   This side of heaven's portals,
For God above made mother's love
   The sweetest love of mortals!

MAY BASKETS

Hanging May baskets for that special someone is a widespread old custom. It serves to give May that extra dimension which makes it a month of months. In the Ozarks region we especially needed this as most of us wanted for extra social activities during the years I was growing up.

Doubtless the custom was conceived by a very reserved person who lacked in particular the courage otherwise to make known the heart throbs caused him by some unsuspecting, irresistible fellow creature of the opposite sex. We have the courage somehow to manage the most difficult undertakings when most of the details are smoothed by established convention, and here the most timid can come forward with impunity and be counted among the courageous.

May basket hangings, however, were not necessarily limited to those young adults with serious intentions, as many mere youngsters also enjoyed this method of expressing feelings of warmth, friendship and neighborliness to others roundabout. Anyway, it was something to do, and something special at that. Besides, there is only one month in the year which provides us the opportunity to give expression to that secret passion smoldering so long in our hearts!

To the best of my recollections, smoldering passions or not, I don't think I ever passed up the call to join a group of merry May basket hangers. Tired after long hours in the field, yet it took a remarkably short time to be ready to go, and away we went! In many instances we even went without baskets for those we called upon. It was the fun that it afforded us rather than executing the custom in its last fine details. Moreover, it didn't seem to matter to the would-be recipients either that no basket was actually hung.

After the sudden call at the gate announcing our presence and our purpose, we usually hid behind the shrubbery, a nearby tree, or whatever came handy. If we were lucky and managed to get caught, we got a kiss or two for our efforts, and after all that was all right—for the custom of May basket hanging is an accepted and established convention. And that made it all legal and proper!

MAY BASKETS

"May basket, May basket," he cried at the gate
Then scurried for cover to breathlessly wait.
  The subject inside full enthralled by the shout
  Slipped on her best gingham and came running out.
With heart all a-flutter she, emotional and tense
Then stole down the pathway and dashed to the fence.
  In dusk of the eve of a day nearly gone
  She searched out the pickets, both hither and yon.
At last in the grayness her peering eye caught
The form of a basket, the prize that she sought.
  All neat and so pretty, with a ribbon hung there
  She saw the dim outline of a masterpiece fair.
She sensed its firm contour, its May roses grand—
Exceedingly fine for a masculine hand!
  A slip she withdrew from the fragrant bouquet
  And squinted to see what the note had to say.
The message she read nigh gave her a start:
"I love you, my darling, with all of my heart."

Here scrawled in bold letters, no doubt of intent
The words so obviously said what they meant.
Then casting about shyly she hoped she could see
Who might this painstaking mysterious one be.
She lifted the latch and swung the gate wide
To search the deep shadows just on the outside.
With caution and prudence she peered here and there
But spotted no mortal, no soul anywhere.
Then standing in stillness, her heart bounding free,
She heard a twig snapping behind a huge tree;
Approaching with daring and half in cold fear
She spotted a figure as she lightly stepped near—
And then she saw Johnnie, so handsome and strong
Who secretly had dwelt in her heart for so long!
He made as to run, as if tardy to leave,
But easily she caught on his flying coat sleeve—
For races are never successfully won
When heart is not in it for racer to run.
Without any words they both understood,
Both grateful for customs so fine and so good;
Then blushing unseen in the darkness of night
She felt him embrace her so pleasantly tight.
Reward for the basket must not go amiss
And so she then gave him a tender sweet kiss.
And years that since blessed them, all happy and bright
All had their beginning that May basket night!

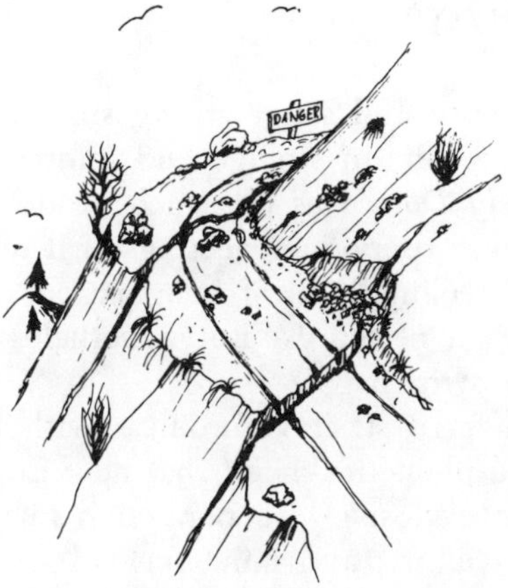

THE TREACHEROUS ROAD

The road was narrow, rough and steep
  And every washout threatened woe;
An idle glance could well bring on
  A crash into the depths below.

Each driver made it foot by foot
  With bated breath and grave concern,
And then, perspiring, sighed relief
  When he had cleared the final turn.

Then looking back from whence he came,
  With shaking head he'd grimly cry
That lest this hazard be removed
  Somc hapless soul will surely die!

In time the road was fully changed
  To one so straight, so smooth and wide;
The grade was levelled all the way
  With massive rails on either side.

And now no driver under stress
  Sweats out the way as in the past;
No man sees need to hold his speed,
  And traffic's moving on at last.

But woe, alas, no happy end
  Can now conclude this episode,
For scores of crosses mark the way. . . .
  Since man remade the treacherous road!

LONELY DAYS

Puppy love and the yen for poetry and song writing simply go together. Oftentimes this combination results in strange and unpredictable end products. At any rate, *Lonely Days* was one such product I came up with during my early "romantic" period. Reflecting on it now, I would say it portrays a bit of actual feeling, a lot of imagination, and a good deal of mechanical manipulation of words. But nonetheless it was fun and something of a challenge to write it.

After putting the words together in strict accordance with the rules of English, meter, alliteration and phonetics, I felt that now Edgar Allan Poe no longer could hold claim exclusively to perfection in this field. The only difference between his efforts and mine seemed at the time that his were published and mine were not yet discovered.

One of our nation's honored writers, tells of a question put to him once by a would-be poet. In substance, this fellow wanted to know just how does one go about writing a poem. Apparently the man felt there must be a guarded secret, and once informed on the know-how, everything from thence forward would be a simple routine of writing and rhyming.

In my humble way I have always felt that an acute sensitivity is a basic requirement in this endeavor; and next, the specific inspiration which exhilarates and motivates one with a desire to capture on paper and share with others the thoughts and feelings that come to the one inspired. Critics agree that there usually is a noticeable difference in product quality between work resulting from "grinding out a rhyme" and a truly inspired piece of creative writing.

Regardless of which of these *Lonely Days* might happen to be, its words unfortunately have never had a tune, and therefore have never been sung—or even heard beyond the confines of my own household, for that matter—but then to the best of my knowledge *The Raven* was never set to music either!

LONELY DAYS

When you were here the skies were clear,
The moments fleeting, gay;
But slowly, oh, so slowly go
The days when you're away!

Chorus:
The only days that are lonely days
Are days when we're apart,
For it only seems that lonely dreams
Bring yearning to my heart.
But oft of old you softly told
Of love so sweet and true
So to the end I'll truly spend
These lonely days for you.

Oh, must I wait and trust to Fate
The dawn of sweeter days,
When golden years will hold no tears,
And never part our ways?

A TRIP TO THE SAWMILL

Togetherness among members of my family was achieved in my growing years without conscious effort—it was just there. Working at tasks great and small from day to day invariably involved parents and progeny together. These contacts were priceless, not only from the standpoint of learning firsthand the best methods of doing the work at hand, but importantly, too, the reasons for doing each task. Then there was ever the windfall opportunity of absorbing a bit at a time the knowledge and philosophies our elders had gained in half a lifetime of living, learning, working and reading. We never knew just when these morsels of wisdom were imparted to us, but their sum total undoubtedly amounted to a sizable education not attainable in any classroom, and I am sure all proved worthwhile goodies in our duffle bag for the ways of life ahead.

A trip to the sawmill was an example of doing things together. The unusual things are always delightful—and trips to the sawmill were a bit out of the ordinary in our daily fare, so they thrilled us no end. Early recollections were the morning drive on the old Eminence Road, south across Gladden Valley past Standing Rock, then over winding dirt trails to John Swiney's noisy, busy and exciting sawmill. Here was a world of activity so much apart from the quiet days between rows of growing corn, or in the meadows, even at haying time! Seeing the heavy slabs as the saw sliced them off great virgin logs, the roaring steam engine with the flyball governor going mysteriously around, the huge stacks of lumber air-drying there, and the logging teams of oversized mules with near human intelligence—all were a treat, and we took them in with wide-eyed wonderment. But seeing my dad laboriously haul two half-loads of lumber up the steep road, and then make up the full load for the trip home made me wonder why sawmills always locate in some deep hollow. Later I learned that it is easier to skid logs downhill to the mill and then haul out the product than it is to do it the other way around.

Later in young manhood it devolved upon me to make such trips on my own. At one time a portable sawmill even located at our farm and sawed our own timber for a contemplated dream house. While the lumber was gradually used for other things and the dream house remained only that, the fascination of the sawmill has survived the passing years.

A TRIP TO THE SAWMILL

When the corn is laid by in the summer
And the meadows are clean of their hay
Then we come to a lull in the season
For those jobs we have had to delay.
One is building the needed new structure
For the storage of harvest in fall.
This betokens the need for new lumber
And those trips to the sawmill and all!

It is fun on the jolting old wagon
As we ride on the bare running gears;
Empty standards and coupling extended
In the ways of the best mountaineers.
With my dad in command of the horses,
Gripping firmly the pair of check lines
And me manning the rope to the brake pole
As we come to the sharper declines.

Many ridges and vales crown our journey
And the trail so exciting and new
Leads away through bright sun and deep shadows
Where majestic pines reach for the blue.
Then our road plunges over a ridge top
And we go down the narrow ravines
Whence come sounds of a puffing steam engine
'Mid the clank of the other machines.

Up and down the whole valley re-echoes
  As the carriage flies forward and back;
This with screams of the saw through the timber
  And the clap of new boards on the stack.
Dulled in all of the noise and confusion
  And so nearly drowned out by the din
Is the thud of the logs on the mill ramp
  With occasional shouts of the men.

We see cant hooks and skids for log handling
  And conveyors take sawdust away;
The log wagons with chains and load binders,
  And the mule teams that pull them all day.
Aromatic sweet scents of pine rosin
  And the sharp acid tang of the oak
Here all blend with the smell of hot journals
  And the hint of a pleasant wood smoke.

Every man with his given assignment
  Helps the mill to keep running in style—
The block setter, the sawyer, the tender,
  And off-bearers bear slabs to the pile.
Here is one good example of teamwork
  Where the workers all strive to excel.
Makes us glad for such things as the sawmill
  And for lumber that serves us so well!

PLOWIN' NEWGROUND

I'll swear I took the darndest beatin'
And am sore and achin' still
From wrastlin' that ol' bull tongue colter,
Plowin' newground on the hill!

The nags that pulled it kept me cussin',
Had me yellin' morn till night;
They didn't like the job much neither,
And their triflin' was a fright.

We'd move along in sort o' fashion,
Then would snag a pesky root.
The handles jerked my weary shoulders
And then whacked my ribs to boot!

Just when I'd think the goin' better
Up would come another stump.
The sudden stop would jolt my gizzard
And I'd take an awful bump.

We hit a rock without no warnin'
Broke the doubletree right now.
The plow line 'round my middle yanked me
Headlong over the blasted plow.

One thing that's sure to get my nanny—
For here no plowman ever wins—
Is when the blade cuts roots in tension
And they slap me on the shins.

I know that most jobs dare our manhood
And we take them on the run;
But this here plowin' in the newground
Is a job I'm proud is done!

RUNNIN' OL' BLUE

No one ever grows up in the Ozarks hill country without becoming well indoctrinated in the fine points of running the hounds in a pastime known as fox hunting. In the scene around a mountain cabin hounds play a role of prominence—often lean, "gant" and rawboned from constantly being on the go. A favorite with hill country men is the blue tick hound, but acceptable and proud performers also are various and sundry other strains, crossbreeds and genetic combinations of just plain dog. And it is indisputable that the best performers make "proudful" owners. In fact, it has been said in a more-or-less facetious vein that the mountaineer values his hound, gun, mules and wife as his proud possessions—and generally in that order. Whether or not this is true is incidental here, but in just about every instance a good hound never lacks the love and loyalty of his owner. Perhaps more over this particular possession than the others, bitter confrontations and even lawsuits have resulted when mayhem befell a dog at the hands of a spiteful or thoughtless neighbor.

It is a common occurrence on a clear, still night to hear the "music" of the mountains—the baying of hounds somewhere in the distant hills and hollows. When, along with it, one hears an occasional note from a horn (often fashioned from the horn of a steer) echoing from a ridge top, then it is a sure bet that this is more than hounds merely foraging for a luckless rabbit, but that a sure-enough fox chase is in the works. Much like fishing, fox hunting can become a very compelling activity once it gets "in a feller's blood." So much so that sometimes the usual responsibilities of providing for the family fall into a subordinate category, and here the wife and children have to make up the deficiency.

Among the many fascinating aspects of fox hunting, however, an interesting note is that the hunters rarely ever bring in a fox. To the uninitiated this may seem strange indeed, but to those who know, it is the chase, and not the prize, that makes the sport what it is. To take the fox would at best yield only the fleeting worth of a pelt; to let him run free is to ensure more future runs for dog and man, and with them the continued resounding of the traditional music of the hills.

RUNNIN' OL' BLUE

Jed was a cuss who'd lay around—
  To him all work was nigh a sin;
His fav'rite was Ol' Blue, the hound,
  A critter just 'bout next o' kin.
A fox chase was his great delight;
  There's nothin' more he'd rather do
Than j'in the gang and set all night
  Out in the hills to run Ol' Blue.

It mattered not the time o' year,
  Nor even whether night or day,
But when the night was still and clear
  Sound carried better, bay by bay.
Around a fire each hunter strained
  To hear the run with much ado;
Jed really had his sharp ears trained
  For ev'ry sound from good Ol' Blue.

"The dogs hit 'long 'bout ten o'tlock—
  On Windom Forks took up the chase;
They topped the ridge 'bove Standin' Rock
  And circled way 'round Jones's place.
With buglin' notes, Blue in the lead,
  The hounds kept chase on through the night
Till change in voice let know they'd treed
  In Brumley's Gap just 'fore daylight."

To Jed no hunt was ever bad—
  Relivin' them, he'd talk for days;
He'd tell of all the fun he'd had
  And give his hound nigh all the praise.
So Jed's big moments were the thrills
  With lantern, jug and twenty-two
To hear the music of the hills
  While out all night to run Ol' Blue.

CAVES

I'll take you to my favorite cave
  Back in the mountain not too far,
Where up a hillside rough and steep
  Outcropping bluffs of limestone are.

The trail near hid by tangled vines
  Leads from a winding creek below;
Here weeds up to a horse's head
  Help keep the secret that we know.

The entrance to the cave itself
  Escapes so oft untutored eyes,
But crawling inside for a ways,
  It opens up to goodly size.

Our pine-knot torches show the way
  'Round breakdown slabs and boulders near,
And darkest darkness seeks to hide
  Its mysteries from intruders here.

At length we come to where a dome
  Goes arching up some forty feet–
As though it once a gallery was
  And ancient gods came here to meet.

No palace born of wildest dream
  Could boast of charms, of grander sights–
Those rich formations, columns tall,
  Those stalactites and stalagmites!

One passage right, another left,
  It seems that ever on they go,
And every turn anew reveals
  Of Nature's silent grand tableau.

So hidden these, superb and strange,
  Creation's rare phenomenon.
Yet caves afford us ways to glimpse
  The Master's work still going on!

A FAITHFUL HORSE

One of my earliest recollections was an event which occurred a short time after our family moved to the farm down near Gladden Valley in the Dent County Missouri Ozarks. I remember an early morning hike in which I toddled after my father, mother and sister over what seemed a stony and difficult path. I could not understand what prompted this unusual outing, but despite my mere three years I sensed somehow the pronounced air of excitement and urgency which prevailed as we hurried along. Father led the way a few paces ahead and conversed breathlessly over his shoulders with mother, who followed next.

The way led first along a well-worn path behind the garden pickets, next across a sand bar and stony bed of a dry creek, and then finally up a rough access road which led to the grassy upland atop a ridge ranging across the south side of our farm. (Mother called this ridge the "berg"—reminiscent of the mountains of her native Switzerland where she spent her early childhood. This stuck through the years, and there never was a question on what part of the farm the "berg" was.)

After what seemed an endless climb up the wooded slope we at length emerged into the open pasture land which seemed to me a vast expanse indeed. Still winded from hurried climbing, we paused a moment and then proceeded to the place over the brow of the ridge where father somehow knew to take us.

Then, our eyes following the proudly pointing finger of my father now many yards ahead, we beheld the object of our urgent mission. We saw an awkward but beautiful newborn colt making his way around his gentle doting dam. Instantly the mystery cleared up and the early morning hike began to make sense. A tot remembers best another tot; and here indeed was another tot—a baby horse! Mother and father promptly named him Hans. And because it was a case of love at first sight for this bright-eyed newcomer the "y" was added. So we called him Hansy all the days of his life.

A FAITHFUL HORSE

I saw him first in June one morn—
  A June that I then thrice had seen,
An awkward, bouncing colt just born
  And stumbling 'round the pasture green.
His dam, a gentle plodding bay,
  Might well have been concerned to see
That, pausing in his circle-play,
  He nosed his early love to me.

Throughout each golden childhood year
  Did friendship true our hearts entwine,
And memories that I now hold dear
  Include somehow that pal of mine—
In sunny fields and creeks near by,
  In meadows where we children played,
He cropped the fragrant grasses nigh
  Or dozed in summer's noonday shade.

But passing years brought tasks in truth
  And one by one our duties grew;
When teens brought on the cares of youth
  I trailed all day the share he drew.
Yet how I thrilled with boyish pride
  When evening shades began to roam
To throw my brown, bare legs astride,
  In knightly pomp to ride him home!

Though life for me had just begun
  And still withheld the most my tears,
This partner of my boyhood fun
  Was living out his sunset years.
And though my tribute humble be,
  It voices heart's sincerest source—
None ever in a score and three
  Served nobler than this faithful horse.

BRINGING HOME THE COWS

Through my boyhood years on the farm an almost daily chore was bringing home the cows for milking. This was a requirement early in the drippy mornings and again in the evenings when the day's work in the field was done.

In general, finding a grazing herd was not too difficult, for at such times the animals were more or less out in the open expanses of the pasture, and here they were readily spotted from one vantage point or another along the way. Also, when one animal was seen, it was a sure bet the rest were close around—except when a maternal member of the herd might have sought seclusion at calving time.

The difficulty that plagued me most was trying to find these bovines when they were lying down in hidden nooks, such as where underbrush grew thick, or in the fringes of densely wooded areas. Moreover, when this chore got off to a late start—like after a long day behind the turning plow or the double shovel—the gathering dusk of a summer evening compounded the problem quite considerably. I shall never forget the moments of encompassing solitude at such times out in the wilds of the back forty. Pushing through the thickets, I would halt my steps at frequent intervals where tangled growths and interleaved forest vegetation permeated the air with strong smells of hickory leaves, sassafras and pennyroyal. Here I would stand very still, holding my breath, trying to listen while the persistent mosquitoes and gnats "yin-yin-yinned" again and again in my ears, and the only distant sounds that came back were those from neighboring farmsteads a mile or so away.

Belling one or more of the cows proved a tremendous aid in finding them, but this was not always as reliable as one might suppose. Some of the more accomplished animals learned to maneuver surprisingly well without sounding the bell—this particularly at such times when they wanted to escape detection. Then, too, a sleeping cow ringeth no bell!

Yes, bringing home the cows was an accepted part of our day—a real institution in the rural America I knew. Admittedly, it was not always a chore that was welcomed with an excess of enthusiasm then, but now I see it filled a very necessary place in the order of things that fell to our lot.

BRINGING HOME THE COWS

'Tis touching hands with God and nature,
  Bringing home the herd of cows,
Here sensing full the native grandeur
  That so well the trail endows.
The burst of morning's early freshness
  Or the lull at eventide
Quite oft compels a resignation
  To a world of peace inside!

The laden dew-drenched wayside grasses
  Nod to greet the newborn day,
And crystal-studded webs in numbers
  Sagging, drape across the way;
Or fogs like thick and downy blankets
  Tuck away the vales from view,
To hold until that ball of pallor
  Comes at last to burn them through.

When springtime's sun has bowed to twilight,
  Blurring paths where hoofbeats fall,
The peep of frogs in marshy lowlands
  Sounds the note for evening's call.
The cows in single file and silent
  Every turn and footway know;
Their breath so fresh from new-cropped clover
  Fills the air as forth they go.

Then looms the barn lot in the grayness
  Where the milkyard kittens play.
Here comes at last the passive plowman
  To his final chore of day.
And through it all he feels a kinship
  With the beasts his lot allows—
A closeness born of patient living,
  And from bringing home the cows!

OZARKS RENDEZVOUS

Remember the city fellow who could not sleep in the country because it was too quiet? The reverse can also, but more understandably, be true when one who is accustomed to the quiet of rural ways goes to a large city. Naturally, much depends on the things to which we become accustomed.

This poem was inspired when returning to the hills of home after a short stay in St. Louis. The peace of the rural scene loomed as a marked contrast to the continuous, unnatural sounds one hears in large metropolitan areas.

But psychiatrists point out that for some the noise, hustle and bustle of busy places serve as an escape from boredom, and from having to come to grips with the kind of person one really is. On this premise, we might say that those who see noise as an essential requirement in their existence are admitting to an inherent need for a purposeful distraction, a positive means for avoiding the reality of close contact with their inner selves. And for persons so inclined it becomes self-evident that the sheltered rural areas may best be written off as a no-no.

For others, however, who start sufficiently early in life and have adjusted to its ways, the hill country can be a great conditioner. Its therapeutic effects can overcome many ills of body and mind. Perhaps, then, there is a deep underlying reason for the great expanses of wilderness on our continental masses. The natural environment may thus be medicine for the human species—a builder of stalwart bodies, strong characters, and stable minds. This seems to be attested by the ways of men and women who in the past, and in the face of grave adversities, hewed mighty civilizations out of primitive hinterlands.

Today, life in the sequestered hills may well be the very therapy our hectic citizenry direly needs to combat its hypertension, heart disease, and nervous breakdowns, to name but a few. In the light of the foregoing, few can dispute that the absence of pell-mell activity and confusion leaves one pretty much in the relaxed position where he must face himself squarely; where he might search the depths of his soul, reflect on his own personal being, his purpose in it all, and on the God of his wonderful creation!

OZARKS RENDEZVOUS

I have found a place in the world's wide face
Where the skies are of a deeper hue,
Where the hills at play steal so far away
They hide beyond horizons blue,
And the wayward streams far surpass our dreams
In nature's rarest rendezvous.

Where the moon at night gives a softer light,
The stars wink from a closer range;
Where the whippoorwills from enchanted hills
Their happy notes of love exchange,
And the night sounds call to the souls of all
In whispered ways so sweet and strange.

This abiding calm is to me a balm—
A sweet retreat from fret and woe,
Where the cares of life and the scars of strife
To deep oblivion quickly go—
And I find anew in my rendezvous
The peace that few will ever know!

THE OLD COUNTRY STORE

To me country stores were always sort of special. Here was usually something of interest, and always there were people. Country merchants, too, usually contributed much to the pleasure of a trip to the village. Many were the times these kindly storekeepers would slip a stick or two of peppermint candy into our bag of groceries, and what a treat that was!

While there were several country stores within a reasonable radius of our farm, really only two of these figured with any degree of prominence in my childhood—the E. R. DeWitt store on the old Eminence Road, and the Jadwin store at Custer. Gene, as Mr. DeWitt was called, with his wife Mary ran a good country store. I always thought that E. R. had the best merchant image—a congenial person, rather portly with neatly trimmed mustache and beard, and gold-rimmed eyeglasses that grooved his temples. He was natively a Quaker with really a quake, and always jovial with a twinkle invariably lurking in his eye. His khaki pants and wide, heavy suspenders were a contrast to the blue denim overalls most men wore, and his pockets always jingled with an overflowing handful of assorted coins.

The Jadwins also were fine storekeepers. First, Ida in her quiet way gave the store an atmosphere of warmth and dignity. Later Jim and Nan took over and carried on the business. Jim with his cigar, whistling nostrils, and characteristic limp, in his turn became a favorite merchant.

Country stores were usually complemented by the proximity of the village smithy, the old grist mill, a tie yard or the like. Activities were many and varied, but mail time was when most folks liked to be there. Also, since this was the time before established rural eating places, many drummers, hunters, and travelers would stop at the country store, buy cheese, crackers, cans of sardines, mustard or tomato sauce, and together with a bottle of soda pop made out an enviable meal.

Village life went on at its pace for many years, and fortunate indeed was he who was privileged to include in his adolescent years the blessings of having known this colorful experience. In time, however, better roads and rapid modes of transportation brought the more distant towns within easy reach, and so eventually the villages waned and many of the old country stores began to pass out of the picture. Unfortunately, Custer and the DeWitt stores both have gone with the years.

THE OLD COUNTRY STORE

So dear to us always is the old country store
With walls hung with posters and its rough battened floor,
Box heater and nail kegs and the cane-bottomed chairs
Where denimed philosophers settle all big affairs.

The checkerboards ever cause a lot of ado,
For village champs often have to prove who is who.
But "chaws of terbacky" from a twist passed around
Makes everything social and good feelings abound.

The open salt barrel and the cracker barrel, too,
Stand alongside the counter near the Buster Brown shoe.
Cob pipes for the smoker, chewing plugs by the bar
Piled next to cough syrups made of honey and tar.

The smell of ground coffee and of spices galore
Are all a part parcel of the old country store;
And Wrigley gum flavors, stocks of peppermint sweet,
Bonbons and gum slices, make the layout complete.

There's gingham and organdy stacked neatly in rows,
With overalls and jumpers and the other store clothes.
The rickrack and ribbons and the bright spools of thread
Compete with the canned goods and the shiny new sled.

In back are the plow shares (known as plow points to some)
With twine and axe handles and the kerosene drum.
The barrel of molasses near the vinegar cask,
New boots and much hardware for most any farm task.

One corner, off limits, barred to look like a jail
Is for the post office and Uncle Sam's mail.
Here daily there's action and excitement revives,
As everyone's stirring when the mail hack arrives.

The store's the center for so many miles 'round
That grownups and youngsters here can always be found.
And through the glad seasons that betoken Time's race,
That store will hold ever a revered special place!

THE TOILER'S TRIBUTE

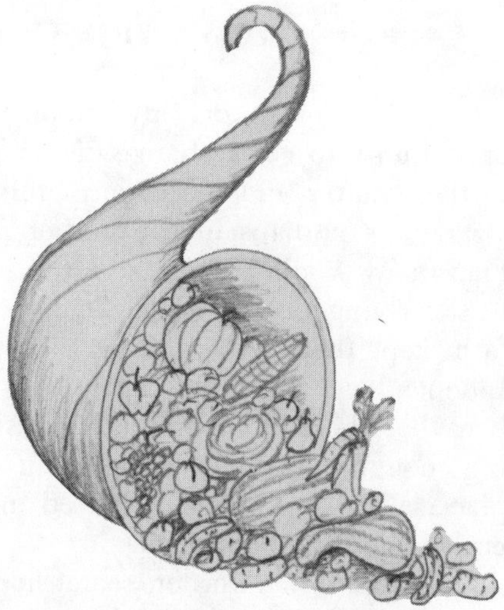

Turnin' sod and sowin' seeds,
Cuttin' sprouts and pullin' weeds,
  Cultivatin' hillside ground,
  Helpin' make the world go 'round.

Clearin' newground, splittin' rails,
Cuttin' hay and tyin' bales,
  Rakin', diggin', grubbin', mowin',
  Helpin' keep the ol' world goin'.

Stackin' clover, threshin' wheat,
Raisin' hogs and smokin' meat,
  Sweatin' hard with spade and hoe,
  Helpin' make the ol' world go.

Shuckin' corn and pickin' beans,
Cannin' plums and turnip greens,
  Usin' prune hook, plow and churn,
  Helpin' make the ol' world turn.

Plantin' orchards, sortin' fruits,
Findin' herbs, and diggin' roots,
  Makin' sales by peck and pound,
  Seein' that the world goes 'round.

Workin' long in patient toil,
Year on year with sun and soil;
  May we say when he is gone:
  He sure helped the world roll on!

TOWN PICNIC ON THE FOURTH

The Fourth of July, among other things, affords everyone the opportunity to get a change of scenery, for on this day the city folks go to the country and the country folks go to town. In our section of the Ozarks, as perhaps in most other places, the foregoing was more true than many would care to admit.

Young people in particular felt utterly defeated if work on the farm kept them from getting to go to the town's annual celebration of Independence Day. Having to get newmown hay into the stack or the barn before that impending rain storm, having to plow the corn now big enough for laying by, or doing any one of dozens of jobs around the place, all in good time thwarted many youthful plans and brought unconsolable disappointment.

If truth is in order, secret hopes were not unknown that a drenching rain would terminate the haying operation, or render the cornfield too wet to plow. Moreover, reported broken doubletrees or other breakdowns in farm equipment are remembered that strangely coincided with farm activities on this date—and of course these necessitated the consequent drive into town for repairs or replacements.

For dating-age farm youngsters who on this day were missing the excitement of the goings-on in town, the very thought that perhaps someone else was riding the Ferris wheel with that special person was utterly devastating. This assuredly brought the conviction that here Fate not only was dealing a bad hand but was openly cheating. The only consolation in this case was the thought that hopefully the wrong could yet be righted and the damage somehow repaired at the next opportune meeting. But in the meantime the injustice of it all hung heavy over the rural scene.

Whether jubilance or frustrations, or shades between, the Fourth came once a year for us, and I suppose that most of the time we were fortunate enough to observe it pretty much as desired. Thrice blest, however, seemed those who had their work well enough in hand that a day of celebration made no real difference in the schedule of farm duties. After all, every good American should pause and be mindful of the significance of the day, and watching a good patriotic ball game never hurt anyone!

TOWN PICNIC ON THE FOURTH

Sody pop on ice and people millin' 'round,
Chewin' gum and candy wrappers litterin' up the ground;
  Ice cream cones and popcorn, cotton candy, too—
  All concessions busy with a humpin' lot to do!
Tasty hot dogs here 'mid pickle-lovin' gnats
Served by local Legionnaires in wilted paper hats.
  Wailin' toy balloons and squawkin' kids galore,
  Swingin' fiddle tunes and cloggers dancin' on the floor.
Men clean-shaved in fresh, clean shirts and overalls,
Makin' with the banter and good-natured smarty calls,
  Standin', squattin', whittlin', sprawlin' in the shade,
  Talkin' crops and weather while a-sippin' lemonade.
Women folks a-fannin', bound in friendly chats,
Tots on laps a-sleepin', gettin' tender lovin' pats.
  Pushin' through the crowds in gigglin' twos and threes,
  Gals in ruffled ginghams and in see-through organdies.
Shyish bigger boys with pocket change to spend
Eye the lovely chicks with hopes to treat a special friend.
  Poppin' firecrackers heard most every place,
  Runners puffin', sweatin' in a wild three-legged race.
Ticket takers' booths and barkers for the rides,
Young 'uns ever waitin' turns to get to swing and slides.
  Glider flyin' high, excited youngsters squeal,
  Callyope on merry-go-round and creakin' Ferris wheel.
Crack of hard-swung bats and all the baseball sounds
Comin' from the ball field in one corner of the grounds,
  Shoutin' fans in bleachers, cookin' in the sun,
  Cheerin', booin', yellin' for that needed winnin' run.
Double Eagle soundin' from the swelterin' high school band,
Orations by the speakers on the podium at the stand.
  Then at last at evenin', what a dazzlin' sight—
  Shootin' off the finals—grand ol' fireworks in the night!

PICKING BLACKBERRIES

"I'll declare, th' berries ain't no good atall this y'ar," lamented "Aint" Emmy, our good neighbor up the valley, one dry day in early July. "With no mite o' rain lately they jes' didn't plump out like they orter. But ah reckon we'll have to pick what they is, shrivelly or not, for it looks like thar won't be much else, less'n it goes to rainin' right shortly!"

And "shrivelly" indeed are the wild blackberries after a dry spring. However, with abundant rainfall they turn out beauties and a delight to fetch home.

Picking blackberries was always an important item in the early part of summer in our mountains. Outfitted with big straw hats to make the summer sun a bit more tolerable, and thrice-patched garments which could not come out any the worse after continued encounter with the uncooperative briars, we would sally forth and a-berry picking go. Usually we went out in the early morning so as to beat the heat of the high sun. We'd seek out the best berry patches, usually around the fringes of the pasture fields, the site of an old house place, or fence rows along the bottom land.

Preparation oft included old stockings on the arms as a safeguard against excessive scratches. These we pulled up to the shoulders and fastened with safety pins. Wrists and ankles were usually rubbed with sulfur, coaloily rags or bruised pennyroyal leaves to discourage chiggers and wood ticks which are present on every berry outing.

Our eyes had to be necessarily alert, not only to spot the best berries, but also to discern the most plausible ways our bodies had to contort in order to move in to get them. At the same time we had to keep alert for snakes that seemed to prefer life in the berry thickets, hiding in the weathered layers of last year's leaves entrapped among the brambles.

In my stained-finger and blue-lipped berry-picking days, tedious and tiring though they were, an effort was by no means without compensation. The jams, jellies and cobblers that eventually graced our table were delightfully rewarding in the months long after the briar scratches had healed and the chigger bites had ceased their plagued itching.

PICKING BLACKBERRIES

Come don your rags and high-top shoes,
  Then grab your pails for off to go
With broad-brimmed hats and bonnets, too,
  To where the luscious berries grow.

Repellents dabbed on here and there
  To ward off tiny thirsty things
That lie in wait for vital blood
  Each passing homo sapiens brings.

Long stocking-arms help guard the flesh
  That fiendish briars prick and tear;
These, too, deflect the infrared
  Our solar rays are known to bear.

Such charms the males may have to boast
  And beauty maidens may possess
Are well concealed and fairly lost
  In berry-picking garb and dress.

Defensive thickets rampant grow
  Like barriers 'round a hoarded loot,
And oft they tax both mind and frame
  To probe the ways to guarded fruit.

Here fur and feathers feast and sing
  In rightful course of free domain,
Resenting now invading feet
  That come their treasured fair to gain.

And all the while time drags its feet—
  The pails so slowly, slowly fill;
Temptation ever calls to seek
  Those better vines just up the hill.

But perseverance is the key
  For most achievements on our way,
So brimming pails and fingers blue
  Reward our berry-picking day.

OUR PARTY LINE

Before the telephone system reached the highly complex stage of commercialization we know today, there were no ready-made telephone lines in the rural countryside to which one could hook up his "new-fangled" telephone. Moreover, because no one alone could afford to build and maintain his own line those many miles into town, a telephone line had to be a cooperative project in which some twelve to twenty farmers pooled their resources for purchase of the wire, brackets and insulators. Each member was called upon to furnish a specified number of poles (cut in the woods at no cost), and each was expected to do his share of all work entailed in building the line.

When time permitted between farm tasks, the farmers and their older sons cleared the right-of-way, set the poles and stretched the wire. Once this party line was tied to the telephone company's line at the corporate limits of the county seat, it became functional with all other similar lines in the network. One long ring reached the operator at the central switchboard. "Central" made the requested connection and rang the long and short combination of rings on the desired line to complete the call.

Building our telephone line took place during my early teens, a time when it was flattering indeed to be doing a man's job in a work so technically foreign to the routine of plowing corn, cutting sprouts, or weeding the garden. There side by side with my father and the neighbors, mile by mile, we progressed from Gladden Valley along a devious route, picking up a farm house here and one there, on into the county seat.

Doubtless this was doing it the hard way, but in those days no one really minded. However, a new telephone line completed was only the beginning. Maintenance meant frequent treks over hill and dale to trace out the cause of a dead line. Often this meant removing a fallen tree or limb from the line and splicing the wire if broken. Excessive weight of ice on the line or a bolt of lightning were other enemies to rural telephone service. Trouble-shooting was done in a sense of duty by members nearest the problem area, with no compensation asked or given. Really no one expected pay for a cause that might save a life, as for example to summon a doctor in the dead of night. It was in this regard that the rural party line gave its subscribers an earned sense of security.

OUR PARTY LINE

When telephones came to our hills
  They brought our lives a new dimension—
And who'd have known that Graham's phone
  Would arouse so much attention!
That ringing bell, a bright new sound,
  Was something near divine;
We'd talk in style across the miles
  There on that brand-new party line!

Each ring that came, no matter whose,
  Would bring down every last receiver—
For listening in was not a sin,
  And all were taken with the "fever."
A talking circle, new each day,
  Made every local action known;
And many a one left work undone
  While hanging on the telephone.

Subscribers on the party line
  In due time would remember
That code of sorts, the longs and shorts,
  Assigned to every member.
For other lines, one long-cranked ring
  Got "central" at the county seat.
With skill and ease, her "number, please?"
  Soon had connections all complete.

The phones were like all man-made things,
  With service oft erratic;
We'd often squawk at loud "cross-talk"
  And deafening summer static.
But good or bad, 'twas all we had—
  Still quite a nice machine;
And best of all, as I recall,
  Was three short rings on Line Eighteen!

THE SUNSET

Doubtless since his most primitive days man has been moved by the splendor of a colorful sunset, and perhaps for nearly as long he has attempted to express his feelings regarding it in one way or another. In fact there is hardly a poet or author who has not written in some measure concerning the sunset—all of which bears testimony to the impact of this phenomenon on humanity. And certainly our literature has been enriched greatly by these efforts!

To me the beauty of a sunset is more than merely a tableau staged by Old Mother Nature as the grand finale of another day. It seems to have a significance beyond this in that it exemplifies to mankind how forcibly some things can be brought to a close; how a crescendo of light and color can encore the brightest of days, witnessing that the end can be beautiful and even triumphal to the last detail. For in what ways more ceremonious can a busy world be brought to cease the activities of its wakeful hours—to be brought to a time of restful, well-earned repose?

For us in the Ozarks there were always the ageless hills around and about, and when the sinking sun set the sky ablaze at eventide, despite the simplicity of an otherwise uneventful day, we all shared in something that neither wealth nor power could produce, hoard, or subdue. All this a serendipity at close of day, a fringe benefit for the serenity of mortal minds, and for the peace of man's physical well-being.

High from a ridgetop in these Ozarks a colorful sunset can be breath-taking indeed. Here moment by moment the distant hills undergo a succession of transformations, each more gorgeous than the last, until finally they are silhouetted a deep purple against the fading light in the western sky.

With grateful hearts we take the gifts of a masterful creation, knowing that the close of day might easily have been drab and uneventful were it not for the grace of an abundant Provider. What is even more significant is that sunsets, like all other things on earth, are unique, each being one of a kind—never two exactly alike! Fortunately, because of this, sunsets will continue to come and go in their infinitesimally different ways, and being privileged to observe them will never grow commonplace!

THE SUNSET

The sun this evening sank in splendor
  Far beyond the purple hills
And sent the evening shadows stealing
  O'er the sleepy woodland rills.
She deftly draped her farewell portals
  In ethereal robes so grand,
And with a symphony of color
  Made our world a wonderland.

She beckoned to belated sunbeams
  Lagging in the leafy gold,
Much as a mother sheep at nightfall
  Calls her lambs into the fold.
She softly bathed the summits flaunting
  Lofty pines and oaks, and then
Caressed them with a touch of crimson
  Ere the darkness tucked them in.

The sun in setting seemed to tarry
  With a slow departing glow—
Just like a playful child at bedtime,
  Seemed somehow quite loath to go.
Perhaps she shared my thought so timely:
  'Tis but Nature's fleeting game,
And though this scene be grand tomorrow,
  It will never be the same!

THE PLAY PARTY

After weeks of uninterrupted work on the farm a break was always welcome. Of particular delight was the news that a cake supper or "play party" was to be held on a coming Saturday night at one of the homes in the valley. With this to look forward to, the days passed quickly, and before we knew it, Saturday had come and the party was excitingly near.

In sheer anticipation of the coming event the mothers and daughters invariably found time to bake a cake for the occasion, and to see that the best gingham, calico or organdy dresses were washed, starched and ironed crisp and pretty. The boys planned their work so they finished a bit earlier on Saturday afternoon, did ahead of time as many of the chores as possible, and then took a quick dip in the pond or the old swimming hole before "dyking out" in their clean jeans. The man of the house usually found it sufficient, after a cleaning up and a shave, to don a clean chambray shirt and his best pair of blue denim overalls—both fragrant from the smell of laundry soap, and the freshness of having dried in the bright sunshine and aired in the summer breezes.

The hostess, too, had the house spick-and-span, her work done up and put away, and had a pot or two of coffee on the kitchen stove. During the evening the grownups chatted, exchanged their versions and comments on the latest happenings, and on some occasions gathered around the old pump organ for a bit of homespun harmony. The tiny ones eventually fell asleep on mother's lap or were laid across a bed until time for the trip home hours later.

Meanwhile, the teen-agers gathered out in the moonlit summer night and engaged in the memorable old singing games that were perpetuated generation after generation down through the years. Hilarity and good wholesome fun held forth as these youngsters strove to outdo one another in humor, song and in going through the figures and capers that characterized these traditional old party games.

Woven into the history, customs and traditions of these good country people were many such gatherings, and verily these social hours enriched our heritage and served to make for good relations among the families of our day.

THE PLAY PARTY

Happy voices, clear and vibrant,
  Rang out in the bright moonlight
As the youngsters in the country
  Gathered on a summer night.
Lads and maidens paired in couples,
  Hands outstretched in line or ring,
Put their best in all the figures
  As they'd blithely skip and sing.

"Old Jim Price," "The Old Brass Wagon,"
  Then the favorite, "Skip to Me, Lou";
"Dusty Miller Boy," "The Mush Pot,"
  And "The Thread That Runs So True."
When you'd swing those lovely misses
  'Twas a thrill you'd never tell;
More so when the girl in secret
  Was the one who rang your bell!

Oldsters on the porch and inside
  Talked about whatever came;
Seemed they were not even watching,
  But were watching just the same!
They'd get ready cake and coffee,
  For the stalwart and the sweet,
Then those present of all ages
  Paused the while to take the treat.

At these parties there were bonded
  Many fond and lasting ties—
In those handholds love was tendered,
  And by careless telltale eyes;
Tied together years and memories,
  Made for smoother married ways,
And so many knew one reason
  Was those grand play party days!

THE QUILTIN' BEE

In early days the well-known quilting parties were get-togethers that afforded a bit of needed social contact for the fair sex at a time when the duties of the household permitted few diversions. Here was principally an activity which made no inroads in work that had to be done, yet one that provided pleasant hours while work was in progress.

Preparatory to the actual coming together of the women at the quilting bees, many hours of painstaking work were generally done in the individual households. When the more pressing duties of the day were done, and often in the hours of long winter evenings by the fireside, the ever-busy hands of the good housewives were at such tasks as cutting out salvable pieces of cloth from otherwise worn-out family garments, selecting and arranging them for piecing together successively larger patches, usually in accordance with some handed-down design or pattern. These doings in the "leisure" hours were referred to by some of the old-timers as "settle work."

Either at home or at the quilting gatherings these patches or blocks were in due time hand-stitched together to make bed-size quilt tops. In some instances these tops were put together from so many small pieces that the stitches themselves nearly outnumbered the threads in the assembled scraps! "Crazy Quilt" was the name generally given the random hodgepodge of sewn-together pieces of any and every kind, color and texture of scrap material.

At quilting bees, even to the present day, these quilt tops, together with equal-size plain linings, are stretched on quilting frames with a likewise bed-size spread of cotton batting (or some old frayed quilt of previous vintage) laid in between. These composite layers are then stitched through to hold fixed their relative positions, the stitches again following an ornate pattern of spirals, compound curves, squares, obliques or other. The edges, too, are finished so that the completed product is a joy to those who produced it, and a treasure to the proud owner for a long time to come.

Through the years the lovely pieced-together quilts have come to be prized possessions—each with a value and sentiment all its own. And proud indeed are the women when they air these masterpieces out of doors, so to share with the admiring passers-by the exquisite beauty of their handiwork!

THE QUILTIN' BEE

When it comes to social doin's
All our women folks agree
Nothin' much in these h'yar mountains
Beats a good ol' quiltin' bee!
At some farmhouse in the holler
They all up and gather in,
Spend the day with thread and needle,
Neighbors, friends and kissin' kin.

'Round the frame swung from the rafters
Busy hands make stitches fine,
Quiltin' battin', tops, an' linin'
In some fancy done design.
Things move on in reg'lar order—
Pot o' coffee on the stove,
Workin', eatin', laughin', tellin'
All the latest 'round the cove.

Quilts in turn o' one or t'other
Are affixed onto the frame;
Patterns passed down mom to daughter
All are called a certain name:
"Jacob's Ladder," "Broken Dishes,"
"Weddin' Ring," or "Irish Chain";
"Garden Basket," "Duck and Ducklin's,"
"Crazy Quilt," or "Window Pane."

Friendship quilts make prideful owners,
Get more wu'th as time goes on;
'Broidered names on blocks are special
Whether donor's here or gone.
Then there is a mem'ry version
Pieced from bits o' treasured cloth—
Danny's rompers, Grandma's aprun,
Or from gowns o' plighted troth.

Seems this quiltin's quite th' ringtum—
Pleasures women young and old,
And them quilts do make us cozy
When th' wintry winds blow cold.
Quilts are all a thing o' beauty
Hangin' in a mornin' breeze;
Shore would lose a proud tradition
If we had no quiltin' bees!

O ROBIN FAIR

Your eggs of blue, O robin fair,
  Are good, so good to see,
And though I would so much
I know I must not touch
  Lest there no baby robins be!

Your world of sunshine, mother bird,
  Must have dark moments, too,
As you perch tensely nigh
To watch with anxious eye
  What this intruder's here to do.

Most mortal men have lived in doubt
  And I myself have known
What joy must fill your heart,
When I at length depart
  And leave your precious eggs alone!

THE GIFT OF WEALTH

The writer who penned the words "The best things in life are free" might well have been a country boy with an acute sense of values. Whatever prompted it, that statement could be applied to many things that are frequently overlooked or discounted as things hardly worth having—and this generally because they are categorized as commonplace things.

In the accompanying poem, the subject gifts are of more than passing value because they are basic in our creation. Moreover, because they are basic (and if man does not devise means of destroying the order of things) they promise to endure unspoiled as long as the old world itself endures.

Alternatives to these gifts are by definition artificial in nature—fabrications which depend on the gradual but sure exploitation and eventual depletion of irreplaceable resources. The gifts enumerated here, as well as many others of a similar nature, may be simple in character, but who can deny that they all are wholesome, delightful, and refreshing? And they bid fair to enrich the life, the physical and mental well-being of every person fortunate enough to be, or to have been, their direct recipient.

In the haunts of my boyhood in the Ozarks we sort of took these gifts for granted. Personally having known only life as a country boy, there was little else against which to measure the values of what we had. In the ensuing years, however, my horizons broadened to include many other facets of life—in cities and other places around the country. As these presented themselves it was rather in retrospect that I could at last compare the worth of the earlier gifts with that of the latter. As a consequence, then, those we earlier took for granted have in the process come into their own as worth considerably more than we thought—as the man who lost his health realized for the first time what he had had before his loss!

THE GIFT OF WEALTH

O country lad, so brown and freckled,
  A picture from the book of health,
You're blest with Nature's rarest fortune,
  The finest gifts in terms of wealth!

By this we speak not here of money,
  Not things of gold, nor mansions grand;
But, lo! a bright and boundless treasure,
  The priceless gifts from Nature's hand.

To know firsthand the simple bounties,
  Delightful things that thrill us all—
Those fragrant orchards in the springtime,
  The aromatic grapes in fall.

Gooseberry pies of pleasant tartness,
  Those wild strawberries in the lane;
The sight of golden clouds at evening,
  Or robins in a gentle rain.

The creek of babbling crystal waters,
  Its bridge, a weathered crossing log;
The grassy field for running barefoot
  That losing foot race with a dog.

To thrill o'er calves newborn and wobbly,
  Or walk behind a homing herd;
To know the smell of new green acorns,
  Or see the first flight of a bird.

The call to romp in pleasant meadows,
  Those outings with a line and pole.
The sand so warm and smooth, the pebbles
  Down at the world's best swimming hole.

What more than these could mortals covet,
  What greater treasures can there be?
And all are more than simply priceless
  Because they all are ours for free!

SUMMER AFTERNOON

When dog days come to an Ozarks summer they virtually draw a curtain of inanimation over the passive hills. Fortunately, it is a time of year when little is demanded of man or beast in the way of exhaustive effort. Long since, the corn is laid by and is now in the stages of silking and tasseling; the hay is put up in stacks settled and browning in the sun; and threshing time is well out of the way for another year.

For a country boy these are good days in that the lull is a welcome opportunity to get that "second wind" before work entailed in the autumn harvest begins. They are also not-so-good days because the heat of the day goes into three figures, and this essentially saps all desires to engage in any strenuous undertakings—even play.

The thoughts in this writing are based on observations of events lived firsthand and many times over when the Ozarks drifted into the doldrums of summer inactivity. Calling one Sunday afternoon on such occasion on Mack, my neighborhood playmate who lived on the next farm a mile or so down the winding Halbrook valley, I found the place practically abandoned of all semblance of activity. Even Mack, who had earlier suggested that I come over on Sunday "evening," had given me up and had gone elsewhere. "Evening" to him, as well as to most of the hill folk 'round about, I learned later, meant that time of day beginning immediately after the noonday meal.

His father, alone in the house, trying to relax and perchance catch a summer afternoon nap, apologized profusely for Mack's absence and, thinking that he might return shortly, suggested that I tarry awhile. Accordingly, I sat in semisilence and rather awkwardly in a chair much too large for me in the huge living room of the Bridges' farm house. But Mack failed to show, even after what seemed an eternity. Meanwhile, none of the characteristics of a summer day escaped my attention—characteristics known so well and understood by every boy who grew up, lived, worked and played in the Ozark hill country summers. In those constrained moments of waiting, however, all loomed especially prominent, and thus made more than passing impressions on the mind of a sensitive country youngster.

SUMMER AFTERNOON

Summertime, parched and languished, stands still
On a breathless afternoon, the sun
Hovering high o'er browning pasture fields,
And ridge tops shimmering like hot new loaves
Fresh from some infinite oven.
Beneath the drooping lilac bush and untrimmed shrubbery
Where kindly shade abounds, the dust-bathing fowls,
Sprawling in abandon, pant open-beaked;
The while waves of chirping sparrows in needless effort
Bristle and flock in repeated sorties from woven wire fence
To the garden shrubs and back.

The indignant cry of a lonely jay
Comes from the distance, muffled and unanswered;
While circling high and swooping low, the graceful
Chimney sweeps make their unending rounds,
Winging and wheeling, trilling and twittering–
Until on occasion one breaks away to flutter down
A somber, sooted shaft to ease at length a pair
Of spent and weary wings.

Oaks and hickories swelter in silent resignation,
Their leaves limp and exuding honeydew,
The aromatic scents diffusing through the motionless
Atmosphere encompassing the scene.
Here dozing on foot in the stagnant shade beneath,

Side by side and head-to-tail, an equine pair mutually
Fends away pestering vermin persistently and intrusively
Bent on marring their peace.
And barnyard weeds, rank and minty-smelling,
Wilt and droop over newly rusting farm machinery
So lately abandoned for another time.

The rambling old house exhaling hot vapors of seasoned pine,
And yawning drowsily behind its add-on porches, sits resting
Through the hours as if spent from too many summers.
It holds totally impassive to the wavering monotonous drone
Of a hornet intent and uncompromising in pursuit of
Unwary prey as it doggedly plies the length of the porch
Rafter by rafter, ever on and back again.

Indoors, the living room portrays its own version of lethargy,
Breathing out musty scents, dry and old-housey. The wall
Clock with half a mind to stop, seems to pause now and then
As its tired pendulum completes each swing with
Only enough momentum to release another hushed tick or tock.
Somewhere in the depth of resonant timber
The lonesome cadence of a dauber's song tattles
Of a project hard under way.
And a frantic fly buzzing from its place of tacky entanglement
In desperate effort at extrication, pierces the calm as it
Sounds its own requiem in one last doleful moan
And joins its other hapless fellows in eternal rest.

Immediately outside, close against the stoop, lying
In comfortless shadows, the resigned shepherd
Whimpers in a troubled sleep, twitching tail and paws
In response to some mental chase of great promise.
A high-pitched hum announces a newsbee hovering for a trice
Outside the screen door. He lingers long enough to relay
His undeciphered message, then zooms away suddenly
And is lost in the distance.

Thus the summer afternoon tucks away
A world, unhurried, unworried, and yet charming in its torpor;
The lagging gait of Time marking another unseen step,
Immeasurable in the immutable ways of an ongoing creation.

WORKIN' OUT THE POLL TAX

Workin' out my daddy's poll tax,
Handlin' now a man-sized load,
Payin' off this year's assessment
As we work the county road.

Proud to be considered grown-up—
Pick and shovel, and the likes;
Handlin' timbers for the culverts,
Drivin' all them heavy spikes.

Walkin' big behind the grader,
Throwin' loose rocks to the side;
Cuttin' brush and droopy branches,
Takin' all in manly stride.

Cleanin' out the weed-grown ditches,
Fillin' ruts and washouts, too;
Carryin' on in dusty britches
Same as older workers do.

Sittin' in the shade at noontime,
Eatin' from a gallon pail—
Chicken, beans, and hunks o' cornbread—
Portions for a grown-up male.

Keepin' at it till it's evenin'
And down low the summer sun;
Glad in secret to be finished,
Happy for a man's job done!

REVIVAL MEETIN' TIME

There were no regular Sunday church services in our immediate Ozarks community during my years of growing up. For one thing, few communities supported even a part-time minister, and quite often those we did hear were self-ordained preachers who were also neighboring farmers. Sunday school, though, was held in our schoolhouse, where the younger groups read Bible stories while the grownups read from the Bible, then discussed to the best of their understanding the content of the scripture passages. Not infrequently a lay leader, and on more rare occasions, an itinerant man of the cloth present at the Sunday gathering, would bring a message to the assemblage.

To make up for the lack of regular weekly services, it was deemed necessary for the spiritual well-being of our rural folk that a protracted revival be held once or twice a year. These were nightly gatherings, usually for a week's duration, often conducted by a self-invited preacher, and assisted by a faithful complement of local leaders. For miles around the folks, young and old, families together and individuals, came to these revivals. All available transportation was employed, including walking. The services were moving evangelistic experiences with much hymn-singing, testimonials and prayer.

Following the close of each "meetin'" the night was astir with sounds of hoofbeats, the jolting and clucking of farm wagons bearing cane-bottomed chairs and children on pallets of hay, the staccato of automobile exhaust on winding county roads, and gay voices shouting, talking, singing and laughing until all gradually died away in the distance.

On the Sunday following close of a successful revival a baptizing was held in some convenient pond, creek or river. This always brought a sizable gathering at the water's edge. The services were impressive in their native simplicity—much, I fancied, as Jesus was immersed in the Jordan. To the tune of an appropriate hymn the minister and converts, each in turn, and all in their Sunday go-to-meetin' clothes, waded into waist-deep water where was performed the ritual of baptism.

Thus, the good folk of our mountain community kept their covenant with the Father, Son and Holy Spirit in the fine old tradition of their forebears—perpetuating the principles of Christianity through the generations by simple devotion and fine exemplary ways of living, loving and caring.

REVIVAL MEETIN' TIME

The old schoolhouse is full to bulgin'
  And the lamps are lit up bright;
There's even Arnett's Coleman lantern,
  For revival starts tonight!
There's nary spot that isn't taken
  By all ages, short and tall,
And tots are perched on every desk top,
  Lanky standers, backs to wall.

The playground's full of cars and wagons,
  Ev'ry tree's a hitchin' post—
(When man and beast do double duty
  It's the plowhorse does the most!)
Outside the windows youths are gathered,
  Each one egged on by his pals,
And covered by the shield of darkness,
  Steals sly glances at the gals.

The air inside is warm and stuffy,
  Kids are fussin' here and yon;
Bedraggled mothers busy fannin',
  Try to hear what's goin' on.
The elders, deacons and lay leaders,
  Free with handshakes and a pat,
Are standin' by so to be ready
  When comes time to pass the hat.

There's Sister Lotus at the organ,
  Drops of sweat upon her face,
Her feet a-pumpin', fingers flyin',
  Soundin' off "Amazin' Grace."
While Uncle Charlie, hymn book wavin'
  Leadin' off each rousin' song;
And Marthy Halcomb, crisp in gingham,
  Singin' alto loud and strong.

Then Brother Logan brings the message,
  Gatherin' steam, he sheds his coat
And mops his face while scorin' sinners
  Till the veins swell in his throat.
And while in turn he shouts and whispers
  Of the sins and Noah's ark,
Resoundin' "amens" from the corners
  Signal that he's hit a mark.

And when at last good Sister Hattie
  Takes her turn in lengthy prayer,
She's joined by scores of other saved ones
  Gathered 'round the lost ones there;
Then all in all, there's much rejoicin'
  When a soul grasps the sublime,
And all are grateful for the blessin'
  Of revival meetin' time!

BIG BRITCHES

When a feller feels good and is
clippin' along,
Thinkin' that life is a breeze
and a song,
Sure that nothin' can now make
him fail
And at last he has got the world
by the tail.
That's the time that he'd better
watch out,
Take another good look around
and about–
For Fate sees him takin' the line
and the lure
And is waitin' to crumble his
cookie for sure!

You take for example the case of
Big Joe,
For so long he had a hard rough
row for to hoe;
Had so many troubles he couldn't have more
And day after day was the wolf at the door.
Then it all happened when the rocky old soil
Way in the back forty began to spout oil;
And came so much riches he knew not what to do;
Got too big for his britches, got everythin' new!

Now rid of his poverty, he put on the dog
Spendin' money like water, livin' high on the hog;
Figured now and forever there's honey and pie,
And then he got a shockin'–the oil well ran dry!
So, as I was sayin' that come as it may
There's always for sure that ol' reck'nin' day,
And lest we get carried away, I have found
It's better to always keep a foot on the ground!

TWILIGHT SHADOWS

Often after a long day of working on the farm for a more distant neighbor, there was still that long weary walk home at eventide. As yet uninitiated in the ways of later industrial trends, country folk knew no fixed time, no blowing whistles to mark the beginning or end of a workday. Usually the dragging of hay shocks, pitching hay or stacking it, cutting or breaking out corn, sawing wood, or whatever, continued until sundown, and often after shadows had fully lengthened across the valleys.

On the homeward way on such occasions it was usually my preference to take a shortcut rather than trudging the long way around on county roads or the more frequented open trails. This of course meant going cross-country in the proverbial beeline, at times through open fields and grassy meadows, but in Ozarks terrain, more often roughing it over hill and dale, fallen trees, cross and perimeter fences, through brambles, weed thickets and great expanses of wooded areas.

Relaxing now, in a manner of speaking, from the day's labor, it was times of solitude like this that gave me moments for soul-searching thoughts—moments that seemed to release an exultation, indescribable but vastly reassuring and delightful—and this despite tired and aching muscles and the moisture of a sweaty shirt on my back. Here it seemed that the wayside trees virtually listened as I walked past. With something akin to a sixth sense I somehow felt more than merely their presence there in the stillness of the evening, for their nearness and their splendor communicated something beautiful in our wide and wonderful surroundings.

Many times things in combination complement one another in an unspoiled rustic scene such as this, and all is peace and harmony when one permits himself to relate favorably to them. This combination can include joys of youth, the satisfaction of a day's work done, the consistency in the ways of nature with her scented breath of woodland herbage—this topped by the last rays of the retiring sun touching at the darkening fragments of clouds in the western sky, and twilight encroaching everywhere on the trail. To me this all seemed a reward of sorts for some undefined deed of the day, of the past—or a promise of some good to come in days ahead.

TWILIGHT SHADOWS

Twilight shadows tiptoe softly
  Through the wildwood in the vale,
Hushing all the notes diurnal,
  Save my footfalls on the trail;
Shadow fairies bent on mission
  For a Master out of sight,
Stealing slowly 'round the ridges,
  Off to meet the coming night.

Twilight shadows whisper softly
  To the trees, the hills, and me;
Whisper things of peace and beauty
  Deep in Nature's mystery—
Things that find their voice in stillness
  When the evening shadows roam,
And they bring me sweet contentment
  On my twilight roadway home.

THE DROUGHT

Only those who have experienced the heartbreak and despair in seeing their crops burning up in continued dry weather can fully grasp the pathos in this writing. Eyes are constantly on the sky in hopes that a kindly cloud will shape up and bring blessed relief before all is totally lost. And such clouds as do form, some even with audible rumblings of thunder and every indication of a sure rain, seem simply to evaporate, or to go around—and then nothing! Disappointments such as these only deepen our already frustrating concern, for in hill-country farming, just about everything depends on the outcome of the growing crops.

On these dry summer nights the family sits in darkness on the porch—sort of keeping a vigil until bedtime. Meanwhile the unconcerned katydids are loud in the trees, and the impassive lightning bugs silently flash their undulating progress through the night. Again, we watch the far horizons of the night sky, searching for the hint of a distant storm. An occasional flash faintly lights up a remote remnant of the night.

"That's *heat* lightnin', they say!" father volunteers, lest we get encouraged by prospects of a coming rainstorm.

"Anyway, all signs fail in dry weather," responds one of us resignedly.

"Besides," puts in another, "they say it never rains in the nights of July!"

As a drought continues, the damage to the crops and livestock worsens with each passing day. Assessing the status quo tends only to banish hope and bring on a feeling of utter resignation. When leaves of forage crops twist and shape themselves into rolls (to minmize evaporation of tissue moisture) this is regarded a danger signal, but there is still hope of resurrection by a timely rain if these leaves unroll in the late evenings after the direct heat of the sun has gone.

In prolonged dry periods we saw the usually trusty spring dwindle to a trickle and then cease entirely, and with this the watering hole for livestock dried up. This meant additional chores night and morning driving the farm animals over hill and dale to a neighbor's spring where water still flowed—and toting back a pail or two of drinking water. This continued until those much-looked-for rains finally came to our hills and to its long-suffering inhabitants.

THE DROUGHT

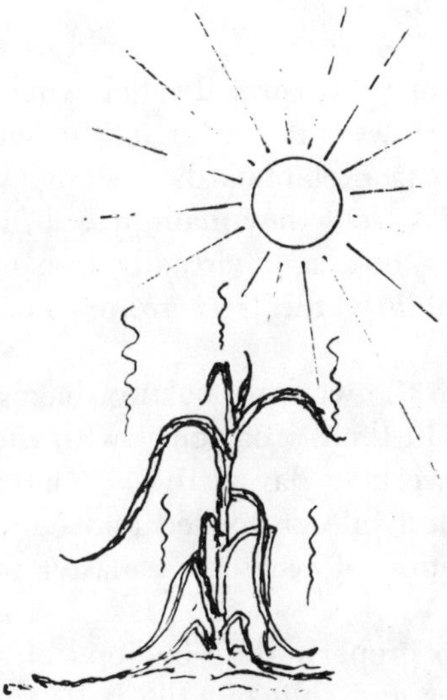

Thirsty hills so parched and dry
Search in vain a blazing sky;
The grasses brown and brittle lie
Where ridges once were green.
Fields with withered corn leaves rolled,
Leaves that nights no more unfold,
While men in prayerful ways behold
The heartbreak of the scene.

Clouds that come from day to day
Blithely go some other way—
Avoid, alas! our dusty clay,
The while we watch them go.
Matters worsen, days drag by,
Springs now trickle, ponds are dry
And driven cattle must rely
Where distant wells yet flow.

Water hauled in barrel and tank
Drawn by horses lean and lank;
The worst concoction ever drank
When cooked by solar fires!
Then ill fortune, on her heels
Comes a Fate that double deals,
And this with shrunken wagon wheels
That throw expanded tires!

Break, o break, ye drought, tonight
Ere we lose our pittance slight;
Rain, please come in midst our plight
And ease our current grief.
May we hear that pleasant roar
Of a long-due drenching pour,
Gushing from both roof and door
To bring us sweet relief!

OAKEN SHAKES

Before days of ready-made roofing, many a rural dweller would have been hard pressed for means to keep dry were it not for split oaken shakes. These shakes, also known in many areas as clapboards or shingles, were made by hand from suitable timber. The roof they made was a bit rustic in appearance but was a long-lasting one, and virtually free of cost except for labor, the nails, and the value of the trees from which they were made.

A long-cherished art was embraced in the work of making shakes. Many old-timers greatly prided themselves in their proficiency with the frow. Quality of product and quantity per working day were two marks of expertise, but minimum waste—the smallest pile of spoiled and damaged material—was always a telltale indication of whether a master or a novice was at work.

Before my arms were long enough to properly drag one end of a crosscut saw, I helped my father cut timber and split out the bolts for making these shakes. It was an early education not only in working with timber, but also in resourcefulness. This has been useful in a number of ways in the ensuing years. As I grew to young manhood I enjoyed wielding the frow myself and making the shakes along with my father and later with others in the neighborhood. Laying and nailing down the shakes to cover many a rural structure, too, proved a pleasant and challenging kind of work, for a roof well laid served unsurpassed through the rigors of time and weather.

When an extra touch of workmanship was desired in the shakes, it was customary to smooth their surfaces with a drawknife. For this operation a rig was improvised in which the shaver clamped one end of each shake in turn, held the clamp firmly by a thrust of his foot while drawing the knife over the shake. The soft sour-smelling shavings accumulated in sizable piles around the shaving rig, and this was always a delightful place for little folk to play.

Making shakes is no longer as popular as in the past, but is by no means a lost art, for deep in the mountain sections of rural America, the art and mastery of the frow and mallet still hold forth, and so carry on a proud tradition in this field.

OAKEN SHAKES

When comes the need for roofing new
  For cabin, barn or outside shacks,
Then off we go where tall trees grow
  In finest mountain timber tracts.
Here expert strokes fell mighty oaks
  With trusty crosscut saw and axe.

We cut the logs to lengths of shakes,
  Remove the bark and heartwood so
The wedge we drive the blocks to rive
  Splits with the grains that radial grow;
Then subdivide with skill and pride
  To make bolts ready for the frow.

We next set up the needed rig–
  A jack made from a forked tree,
With poles crossed right to give it height
  And help attain rigidity.
We set its frog on stump or log
  And slope it for the right degree.

From chunky sticks of hickory wood
  We fashion mallets firm and sound.
One end we chip to fit our grip
  For sturdy handles smooth and round.
We then find rocks and unfit blocks
  For weighting stacks of shingles down.

Now comes the call for arts of old,
  The skills hill folk have long applied—
Soft mallet blow, light thrust of frow
  And cautious eye where grains divide;
As fibers bend in sections thinned
  We shape a shake of joy and pride!

For many tasks we yield the toll
  That unavailing labor takes.
The jobs that earn us no return
  Demand excessive, unfair stakes.
But from this task none more could ask
  Than half-a-lifetime oaken shakes!

NEWFANGLED CHANGES

In all my ramblin's and my rangin'
I can see in ever' way
That things are shore to be a-changin'
'Cause thar's somethin' new each day.

It's apt to get yer brain all tangled
'Bout those gadgets and the like;
We cain't keep up with things newfangled
That keep comin' down the pike.

We've talkin' boxes, and by doggies!
Now I've heerd of ridin' plows,
And, too, they're makin' horseless buggies,
And a thing that milks the cows!

We soon won't speak of walkin'
And, no work, we'll have a ball.
It makes a whole new way o' talkin'
When you keep up with it all.

Just t'other day a guy lamented
That these changes have to be;
If cars had never been invented,
Said we'd still the changes see.

We'd have windshields on ever' saddle,
And we'd figure out some way
To rate the output of ol' Dobbin
By the miles per bale o' hay!

COUNTRY SINGING

Fortunate indeed is that community in which talented persons reside. Particularly, when these persons are so good as to share their talents with whoever desires to profit from them. A bit in the category of special were the nights when our old schoolhouse was lit up for a Sunday night singing.

In my teen-age years we enjoyed these singing classes and song fests at South Ozark school. Those who generously shared with us their knowledge of music were able leaders like Web Arnett and Uncle George Halbrook. We were grateful for this opportunity to learn the rudiments of written music, for this kind of training generally was not included in the curriculum with the three R's in our Ozarks country schools. Infrequent though these opportunities were, the gems of melodic wisdom we picked up here opened for us a greater appreciation for musical composition and they served us well ever afterwards.

Farther from our immediate neighborhood, but equally fascinating, were such occasions held now and then in the Jadwin community. Here Willie and Otto Schafer were the teachers and leaders. It was not too far for a number of us young men to ride horseback the six or eight miles of a Sunday evening to attend these "doings"—even when our mount was a farm animal that doubled as best he could for a riding horse.

The first time I heard here the sung notes, *do re mi . . .* , in place of the more familiar words, I thought I had strayed into a new and strange world indeed. Heretofore I had always heard the syllables *la la la* substituted when one could not readily recall the words of a song, but these notes, never! In due time we learned that sight reading of these notes was readily accomplished by observing the shape of the notes appearing on the lines and spaces of the bass and treble staffs. For many, shaped notes are considered a shortcut to note singing, for with their use one is not required to learn a more tedious way to sing the names of the notes as determined by the signature and their staff positions. Primarily for this reason most hymnbooks purchased for country religious services in our years were invariably specified to be printed in shape notation.

COUNTRY SINGING

There's a lot of heart and soul
When hill folks gather in to sing.
Here the schoolhouse is a-throb
As its very rafters ring!

Melody and harmony
To charm an Ozarks summer night,
As the singers read their scores
By an oil lamp's yellow light.

Leaders teach of clefs and time
In ways the group can understand.
Tuning forks then set the pitch;
Time and beat, by wave of hand.

Keynotes given to each voice,
And each singer sounds his note—
Prolonged hold of blended tones
As from one great golden throat!

First the notes and then the words,
In clear, true tones the leader starts:
Mi re do, do la do sol,
While all voices sing their parts.

At the place where songs are heard
The world seems great in everything,
And it's fine, so fine indeed
When good folks come in to sing!

AUTUMN WANDERLUST

What is more refreshing than a bright October day out with nature in the hills? Rambling unhurriedly through the painted woodland and climbing on the lichened, weather-pitted crags that jut out on the hill-sides, all can bring a brimming sense of elation to the rambler.

Many times we feel a compelling urge to yield to the "call of the wild" and to forget the rat race that our mode of life has thrust upon twentieth-century man. Doubtless, we were made to live more in accord with natural laws, pursue our ways more leisurely, and to drink deeply of the charm and abundant beauty around us. And while we know we were meant to take and enjoy these priceless gifts, we know, too, that we are to leave some—yes, to help perpetuate a goodly share for the generations to come.

Basking in the autumn sun in a veritable Garden of Eden makes us painfully aware that many such scenes have, necessarily or otherwise, yielded to the blade of the bulldozer, and the arm of commercialization has reached in and transformed them to something second-best. We like to think that built into our world is a store of resources meant to serve man and all other living beings forever. This, of course predicates they be taken at a natural rate and in reasonable proportions. Now it is apparent that we have accelerated both the rate and the proportions without heed or concern about doing a proportionate amount in return. We, therefore, hear alarming cries of exhausting and despoiling those natural resources we had taken so much for granted. Moreover, we are "soiling our nests" with a wake of waste and refuse created in the process—depletion, erosion, pollution and contamination! All are by-products of our accelerated existence—a tax that nature levies to halt the imprudent ways of man.

There are those who would impute these woes of ours to the rise of science and technology. Those more discerning, however, would point to the fact that science and technology also have shown us how to control our waste and safeguard our resources. This we have tended to ignore, for alas! controls such as these are costly; they decrease drastically the net profits otherwise there for the taking. So the practice has been to take the goodies, let nature take care of the garbage, and the next generation find its own resources.

AUTUMN WANDERLUST

What a pleasure to go tramping
  Through an Ozark mountain fold
When gay autumn in her glory
  Turns the leaves to red and gold;

When the gentian fair, unrivaled
  Mocks the azure of the sky
And the ramblers on the ledges
  All in velvet crimson lie;

When the rod of radiant sunshine
  Nods a welcome by the trail;
And the blue of Indian summer
  Lurks in every distant vale;

When the bright-eyed woodland creatures
  Steal in silence to and fro
As they take the gifts of autumn
  And with treasured bounties go;

When the freedom of the open
  Leads me onward with its call,
Like the carefree roving chieftain
  Once the monarch o'er it all!

Oh, it's pleasant to be living
  In a wealth of autumn thrills,
And to go on idly tramping
  Out with nature in the hills!

THE PIE SUPPER

In the long crisp evenings of mid or latter autumn it was a frequent occurrence for pie suppers to be held here and there in the one-room schoolhouses in the rural Ozarks. The purpose was twofold, for pie suppers were an exciting event, usually with a program of humorous dialogs and country music, and also they provided a means for raising money for additional needed books, items of furniture, curtains for dramatic programs, or playground equipment.

The schoolhouse on such occasions was all a-bustle with young and old gathered in from far and near. The girls brought pies packaged in unidentified boxes which were artistically decorated with ribbons, lace, rickrack, and brightly-colored crepe paper. The adolescent youths had saved their money for some weeks in advance and "blew it all" for the pie belonging to that special girl. Rivalry over a popular girl's pie often ran the cost up to a ridiculous figure, and it was not uncommon for a number of boys to pool their financial resources in order to outbid a fellow who was going "serious" with his lady friend. Sometimes this conspiracy resulted in the fellow failing to eat pie with his sweetheart, or else made him "pay through the nose" to get it.

Additional excitement and humor highlighted the evening when nominations were made for the honor of prettiest girl present, the man with the dirtiest feet, the most lovesick couple, and/or certain others of some notable distinctions. At a cent a vote the money would come rolling in, and at times the contest progressed to a high pitch. Whatever it proved, besides furnishing hilarity to the gathering, at length the winning beauty, the honored man, and the outstanding couple received respectively the cake, the bar of soap, and the jar of pickles.

After the event drew to a close the dating-aged youth frequently walked home the girl whose pie he had bought. And country roads and trails being what they were, it was not unusual for the girl to excuse herself a short distance from the schoolhouse to retrieve her everyday shoes from a fence corner where she previously had hid them. This change not only made walking the homeward miles more comfortable but also saved the better shoes for other special occasions.

THE PIE SUPPER

Poor Nancy wriggled, blushed and pouted—
  Her pie at last was up for sale!
The box adorned with bows and ribbon
  Was fashioned for her special male.
But where was Joe who should be bidding
  If he this morsel is to win?
And now it seems that goony Harvey
  Would be the one to bid it in!

"We've got the forty, now the fifty"—
  Squire Halbrook served as auctioneer.
The youths were packed into the schoolhouse,
  Some standing, pushing from the rear.
Each feeling handsome and so grown-up,
  And bidding up with confidence—
Some high-pitched voices, others breaking,
  Calling out their quarters, dimes and cents.

"Why doesn't Joe get with the bidding
  If he's the one to get my pie?
And if that Harvey is high bidder
  I know I'll surely up and die!"
Then as more tense now grow the moments
  And bidding slows as sale is near—
"It's going once, and twice, young fellers,
  Speak up or miss this goodie here!"

Then, lo! a clear new voice is bidding
  Just when it was about to go.
And Nancy heaved a sigh, so grateful,
  For, yes, at last it's really Joe!
He paused to count it all together,
  His total lot of worldly cash,
Then held his own against his rival—
  A showdown in financial clash.

When all was going hot and heavy,
  And figures reached a new high score,
A panicked voice squeaked out the final—
  For Joe was done—he had no more!
Then Harvey bids another nickel
  And flashed a fiendish victor's grin;
Joe slunk away to friendly darkness
  Escaping Nancy's upturned chin.

To highest bidder went the booty,
  But Harvey paid a tidy stake;
The hope to beat Joe's time with Nancy
  He felt 'twas worth the risk to take.
But triumph for a social moment
  Is, alas, a pittance small,
For Joe it was walked home fair Nancy
  And bested Harvey after all!

EGOTISM

A man of the world he claimed to be
  And boasted day by day
That none of the great were great as he
  Nor meet to go his way.
A sneer of contempt had he for those
  Who held a role of fame,
And ever was he high on his toes
  Besmirching honor's name.

At work or at home, at church or square,
  No mortal stood his test,
And vainly he'd say that everywhere
  He ranked above the rest.
But great though he thought himself to be,
  He fooled himself alone—
For humps on his fellows' backs saw he,
  Yet could not see his own!

THE SHIVAREE

When a couple marries in the rural mountains of Missouri it is a pretty sure bet that there will be a shivaree soon afterward. In this event the tranquility of the honeymoon abode is suddenly disrupted some late evening or in dead of night by a thunderous outburst of ear-splitting noise at the hands of well-wishing friends, neighbors and relatives. This old custom not only conveys a message of love and esteem to the newlyweds, but it sets things in order for the marriage to get off to the right start. Usually, the more prominent or popular the matrimonial partners, the more sure the occasion, and the greater the gathering—also perhaps louder the noise!

In return for generosity of their efforts the nocturnal serenaders expect a reward of cake, coffee and other treats that the serenadees know to have ready. When these are not forthcoming a penalty is imposed, and this varies with the will and imagination of the intruding visitors. Taking the "love birds" out to a pond for a ceremonial ducking has been a favorite penalty. Others are: riding the groom on a rail while toting the bride in a washtub partly filled with water; covering the couple under a pile of loose hay or straw; or subjecting them to an enforced hike of a country mile or two, the groom at times carrying the bride piggyback.

There have been times when the enthusiasm of the revelers unfortunately got out of hand and tragic consequences resulted, like inadvertently injuring the hapless couple, drowning the bride who could not swim to safety after being tossed into the water, and other heartrending incidents. Fortunately in my personal recollection nothing so drastic ever happened in our locality, and we are grateful indeed that it has not.

When things are at a norm, however, the gathering is invited inside and the evening turns into a delightful fest of chatting, eating, good-natured jesting, and playing games or music.

Once shivareed, a couple breathes easier for knowing this is over with. Now the marriage moves into the more daily routine which is characteristic of staid married folks. Henceforth, living happily ever after is up to the individuals concerned and the circumstances that Fate bestows upon them through the years.

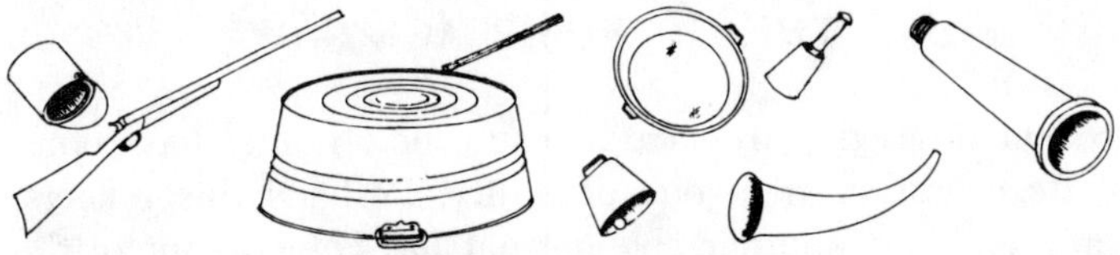

THE SHIVAREE

All slinking in the veil of darkness,
  Gathering quietly as per plans,
We came with buckets, tubs and cowbells,
  Shotguns, horns, and old dishpans.
In quiet, breathless stealth and caution
  Back of hay rack, shed and log
We waited in the utmost silence
  Lest we rouse a barking dog.

When all at length were there and ready
  And the zero hour at hand,
We rushed as one the nuptial dwelling
  At a hushed but firm command.
Then in that peaceful slumbering farmstead,
  Startling filly, cow and goose,
We pierced the very realm of stillness
  As all Hades then broke loose.

The bedlam held in height of frenzy
  While the minutes slowly passed;
Then deep inside a lamplight flickered,
  Signalled they were up at last.
The rousing serenade continued
  As we shouted, banged and cheered
Until the cabin door swung open
  And the newlyweds appeared.

Now came the threats of dreadful mayhem
  Lest we all were given treats.
Then lingering long, the friendly throng
  Played games 'mid sumptuous drinks and sweets.
But none of us would leave the couple
  Till we saw that public kiss,
Ensuring thus the gods would yield them
  Years of love and wedded bliss.

THE OL' FIREPLACE

In recent times the fireplace in many new homes has come to be an item of decor rather than one of utility. Perhaps this reflects more than anything else just another change that has come about in the span of a few generations. However, there are those still among us who knew the fireplace when it was the only source of heat in the house. In days when firewood grew in great abundance only a few paces from the door, the fireplace very conveniently and economically filled such requirements as existed. But then, too, no one expected the house to be uniformly or even comfortably heated throughout. Seeing the condensed vapors of one's breath even near the fireplace was not uncommon, for loss of heat through the walls and the uninsulated, often bare ceilings was great indeed.

Sitting by the fireside was not only a sociable thing to do, but more a necessity in order to keep reasonably warm. In those early times whenever one called upon a neighbor during a spell of very cold weather he simply joined the entire family at the hearth, for that is where they were huddled most of the time during their waking hours—this along with the family pets and certain household commodities that were brought in to prevent freezing.

Nonetheless, the fire blazed beautifully, sputtered and popped as it played around and over the logs. Besides furnishing some semblance of physical comfort to the household, the old fireside was an ideal place for pondering the events of the day, the past, and the future. Many were the hours spent gazing into those cheery flames and watching the glowing chunks and embers shift and fall, the while a galaxy of sparks joined the shimmering waves of heat and wisps of hickory smoke as they disappeared up the chimney! Somehow we feel it a privilege to have known the romance and quiet of that day, to have enjoyed the prevailing simplicity of life, and the togetherness in the family circle. For these and other reasons, therefore, we now regard the old fireplace with more than passing consideration!

THE OL' FIREPLACE

Most folks are fond o' things old-timey,
  Things that hit a special key
And, yep, I've got some, too, I reckon—
  One 'ats been plumb close to me—
For 'way back yander man discivvered
  Fire could sarve the human race;
Then took it with him in his dwellin'
  Inventin' so the first fireplace.

Through all o' histry's misty ages
  We are more than apt to find
The indoor fires of ev'ry nation
  Done their good for all mankind.
They sarved our country in good measure,
  The savage, then the pioneer;
They held at bay the cold of winter
  And brung to all a mite o' cheer.

Our settlers shore could not a-made it
  Through the rigors o' their lot
'Thout that great ol' hearth a-blazin'
  'Round that cast iron cookin' pot.
It riz the bread for next day's bakin',
  Soured the cream to he'p it churn;
It roasted brown them lushus ches'nuts,
  And cooked the hoe cakes to a turn.

The fireplace was the household center,
  Cookin' place and where folks sat;
'Twas even sought out by such critters
  As the family dog and cat.
Old-timers watched the changin' embers
  While they would old stories tell,
And passin' men dropped in for warmin',
  Pulled up a cheer to set a spell.

But I rec'llect some shore 'nuff failin's—
  How it pulled drafts 'round the door;
And gettin' in those gobs o' firewood
  Got to be one awful chore!
It sucked that heat right up the chimbly
  In full many a mountain shack;
You well could roast yer blasted shinbones,
  And all the while you froze yer back!

SELF GRATIFICATION

It matters not what comes to pass,
Nor whether there is justice done
With those who rank their ego first
And live for personal credits won.

Thus order is so oft misplaced,
With purpose and real values lost,
For many would exalt themselves
Without regard who pays the cost.

No treasure house, despite its hoard,
Outlasts man's greed for all the best.
Too late the thoughtless all will find
That they too lose with all the rest!

THE POSSUM HUNT

Among the nocturnal activities of hill country folks in the fall must be listed the old special outing, the possum hunt. Mr. Possum, for his escapades to those favorite haunts as the persimmon grove or the remains of harvest in the apple orchard, prefers the chilly, clear nights, preferably with no wind blowing (certainly no wind from the east).

The usual garb for a possum hunt is necessarily something that will keep the hunter warm and comfortable, but nothing that must be spared from snagging in the undergrowth, the saw briers and blackberry thickets. Heavy shoes or boots are a must for walking over rough and rugged terrain. Minimum equipment, besides a hound or two, should include a coal oil lantern, an axe and a flashlight. Incidentally, carrying the lantern may be a responsible chore, but the warmth from the flame is usually a welcome compensation for having to carry it. The lanterns push back only enough of the darkness to enable one to see where to go—or not to go. Stumbling along is often more the order than the exception.

Every now and then it is necessary for the hunters to halt for several minutes to permit the baying hounds to thoroughly flush out the surrounding area. When Mr. Possum is apprehended a decided change in tone of the hounds' baying will clearly make this known to the ear of the experienced hunter. The flashlight is the best source of light for spotting the animal in the tree. The particular tree is the one up which the dogs are barking and snarling, about which they are circling, clawing the bark and gnawing at nearby grapevines that get in the way—a sure sign the possum is there! Two beady eyes beaming back at the light confirm his presence beyond all doubts. If the tree happens to be a sapling then the axe is brought into play. Otherwise, climbing, or a shot with a twenty-two caliber rifle is in order, but it is always desirable to take the animal without any shot punctures in his pelt.

Mr. Possum has two special characteristics. One, when cornered, he pulls back his lips in a grin-like act of defiance—from whence comes basis for the expression "grinning like a possum." The other, when taken, he likes to play dead, presumably hoping his captors will give up and go away. So, one feigning sleep or inattention is said to be "playing possum."

THE POSSUM HUNT

Over hills and through
the valleys,
We with feeble
lanterns go,
Searching out the
wily possum
Where wild grapes and
'simmons grow.

Hear the trailing hounds
a-baying,
Down below the pasture
pond,
Chasing through the brushy
thickets
And the grassy slopes
beyond!

Echoes from the dogs resounding
As they circle left and right,
Answered by a distant hoot owl
In the crisp, still autumn night.

Soon the baying gets more constant
As the hounds on course are bent,
Heading down a wooded hollow,
Where they picked up Possum's scent.

So with hastened strides we follow,
Lanterns swing, our breathing fast,
And our ears our chart and pilot,
Catch up with the dogs at last.

Baying, clawing, snarling,
'Round a crooked, vine-grown tree;
Dogs and man in semidarkness
Straining hard the prize to see.

Then we spot two gleaming signals
Flashing back from out the dark—
Proving that our hunting partners
Once again have scored a mark.

THE TIE HACKER

Tie hacker, tie hacker, the best in the mountains
  Where you work in the oak and the pine.
Here your heart's in accord with your labor
  And your hands always hew to the line.

Tie hacker, tie hacker, your efforts are ever
  To the good of both nation and state,
For in helping to fashion our railroads
  You are helping to make our land great.

Tie hacker, tie hacker, your work is important
  For your loved ones are counting on you;
They have need for both food and for raiment
  And the money for taxes is due.

Tie hacker, tic hacker, you swing a mean broadaxe,
  And it's great how you make the chips fly;
Here we see a refreshing example
  Of the things we can do if we try.

Tie hacker, tie hacker, endowed with hard muscles,
  With the choice of good timber tracts near,
And the mountains so good and abundant,
  Tie hacker, you're full in your sphere!

O WINTRY WIND

When a wild nor'wester bears down on the Missouri Ozarks and the mercury hovers around zero or below, the comfort level has long since become a nonentity. Often such a wind reaches gale proportions, roaring through the trees, whistling through the draws and chilling the very marrow in one's bones! To breast it for any length of time not only requires special effort in order to make any progress at all, but any exposed flesh soon becomes numb and leathery to the touch. Just where all this violently transient atmosphere comes from and where it all goes has always evaded the understanding of a country boy—especially one with a variety of chores that have to be done regardless!

This cold intruder often blows for days together, persisting with wild abandon as if to try the very souls of men. Snow so cold it is virtually dry and brittle is driven along and drifted in its wake. In the constant turbulence the flakes are broken down and carried in dust-size particles through tiny crevices in the walls, through the clapboards on the roof and around doors and windows.

Many a night, when a boy in half-wakefulness, I felt that just at any time the cabin roof would go when under sustained thrusts the rafters creaked as they yielded a bit, and creaked again as the thrust momentarily subsided and they moved back. In the mornings after such wintry tirades we often found tiny pyramids of fine sifted snow inside on the window sills where the relentless wind had driven through the crevices. These were the mornings, too, when we found the dipper frozen solid in the water bucket on the kitchen table, and the window panes opaque with sheets of frozen condensate done in weird and wonderful designs.

We know that seasonal changes have a purpose in the great scheme of things—and so do the violent winds of winter. It is even short of miraculous how well man and beast adjust to the demands of ever-changing weather, and how well both come through it. Doubtless all are better for having weathered the extremities nature imposes upon us, for a continued sameness would afford little or no real challenges, and no one would be prepared for unexpected contingencies. So, wintry winds and all their discomforts, in the words of Robert Burns, make us better men for a' that!

O WINTRY WIND

O wintry wind, why all your fury
As you across the Ozarks blow?
Here sweeping in from open prairies,
Unbroken miles of driven snow!
Perhaps you've gone too long unchallenged
And now the mountains rile you so.

O wintry gusts, your piercing thrusts
Come hurtling o'er the frozen miles,
Refining snow as on you go
To drift it in artistic piles.

You roar untamed through brush and treetops
Shred the lone, last-clinging leaves,
Then whistling through bleak fields and feedlots
So rudely ruffle shocks and sheaves;
And yet there's naught can better fashion
Grotesque ice monsters on the eaves!

Your blasts so bold, your biting cold,
With snow and ice your coat of mail,
You take your posts like conquering hosts,
Invade defenseless hill and vale.

Our friends afield in fur and feather
  Are snug in shelters tucked away,
Surrendered they their haunts and freedom
  Till better times this foe allay,
For nothing well can stay invaders
  That know no rest by night or day.

O wintry wind, we'd have you end
  Your hostile siege of field and door,
And with the dawn we'd have you gone
  To leave our hills at peace once more!

SLIDING ON THE ICE

Our seasons all bring special sports
   Which we consider very nice,
But winter is the only one
   That features sliding on the ice.

This sport takes place in many ways
   And each with many thrills and spills.
There's sliding on the old millpond,
   And sliding briskly down the hills.

A running start or belly slam,
   And off we go at breakneck speed,
While trusting none to block our way,
   Lest both should wind up sore indeed.

The sliding's great on sled and shoe,
   And dishpans, too, will do perchance,
But when we slip and get upset,
   We even slide on seat of pants!

TO A DYING YEAR

Everybody pauses to observe the passing of the old year and the advent of the new. To a varying degree we customarily engage in some New Year's Eve activity in which we give more than a fleeting thought to the stroke of midnight. We are aware that this is not just the end of another day, but that it is one that marks a sizable division in the flight of time.

Often with mixed emotions we go from one year into another. The events of the departing year, both the good and the bad, are all irrevocably gone into the past and thus have become history. We regard them with joy, tears, or relative indifference, depending on how these events affected or afflicted us personally. But the new year knocks at the door of everyone and everything, and always with a store of undisclosed offerings for each of us. To find out what they are we must proceed to meet them head-on, one by one as the days come and go. We cannot hasten a single day, and desirable or not, neither can a living creature avoid any part of it.

Time in its broadest context embraces an ongoing process lost in the infinite past, and obscured in the interminable future. No man ever has anything but the living present in which to pursue what he is about. He is part of this process and yet is also pitted against the benevolent or inexorable role it holds for him. Time even sets the circumstances that help or hinder man in his daily pursuits.

In the light of this we must glimpse the thought that the significance of the individual is as a particle of the proverbial dust from which he is made. It is only in working *with* the forces of time that a degree of accomplishment is ever attained—and even the term *accomplishment* is vague in that its definition must remain a questionable quantity.

In this poem I attempted to present the fleeting thought that came to me on a youthful turning of time at New Year's that the glory man claims for himself in pursuit of his mundane affairs is ill-conceived and misappropriated—that the events which occurred really belong to the increment of time in which it took place, and if noteworthy at all will be so recorded. Remember, not man, but *time*, continues on!

TO A DYING YEAR

We hailed your coming broad and far
With wild, tumultuous cheer,
Accorded you with din of war
A welcome good to hear;
And with resolve and much ado,
Upon your midnight stroke,
We in our aim to start anew
Cast off our spotted cloak.

We early saw your plans unfold
When you in youthful days
Bedecked our orb with wealth untold
(And gained a fleeting praise),
And then with shower, shade and shine
The summer tasks pursued
To grant to mortal man his wine,
His raiment and his food.

Abundance owned your every field
  When slowly, meekly, you
A season's work at last revealed
  Beneath your autumn's blue;
Then gave with passive hand away
  Those fruits of labor grown,
And man gave you the credit—nay!
  He claimed it for his own.

Now came this day in crowning white
  To mark your end of time—
The grandest in your certain flight,
  Most august and sublime.
Aye, counted is your final day,
  And loath we see you go,
For glorious was your fleeting stay
  And great your work to know.

Unselfish year, you well have taught
  A lesson to our kind,
For sages more could teach us not
  Than did your days unwind.
O dying year, may I achieve
  Your record closed today—
A trail of worthy deeds to leave
  The while I pass this way!

Part III

Adult Agenda

THE SQUARE DANCE

Recreation is the salt that spices the ways of labor! And one of the most delightful means of social recreation for country folks has long been the old-time square dance.

Square dancing is a term loosely applied to various forms of moving through certain established patterns. One form, known as mountain style, is done in a circle made up of couples. Here at direction of the caller the dancers do the figures with successive partners, the males usually progressing counterclockwise and the females clockwise. Another form, the reel type, has two lines, the males in one line facing their partners in the other, and again, the dancing partners at head of the lines perform the called figures with each successive couple, progressing towards the foot of the lines where they take their place, as the next couple, now "head," continues as the first had done.

However, the true *square* dance (known as western style) is where four couples make up the four sides of a square. The first couple forms the side nearest the caller with backs to him and the music. With numbering counterclockwise, the third couple stands opposite, facing the first; the second and fourth face each other across the square.

Couples, with girls at the fellows' right, start the dance with bows to partners, neighbors and those across the set. An introduction may take the form of a ring as dancers join hands, circle to the left, then break with a left allemande, and go into any number of figures as chanted by the caller. All the time the participants step to the beat of the music to execute the figures gracefully and in unison. In the finer state of the art the dancers clog as they go through the figures, the music virtually moving their feet.

As an early fascinated onlooker, later as a participant—even on occasion in the position of "wielding the bow"—I would agree that square dancing is great fun. More than that, it is therapy for those who are tense or reserved. One evening of "cutting the capers" may send one home physically spent, but the mental relaxation and the exhilarated spirits more than compensate for any weary feelings. And, as one inveterate dancer put it, "Thar jist ain't nothin' else whar a feller can kick up his heels ary higher nor hold hands with more purty gals than at a rip-snortin' country square dance!"

THE SQUARE DANCE

In dusk of the evening, the last fading light,
They came to the dance on a Saturday night;
The oldsters and young ones, the meek and the game,
With laughter and song, in high spirits they came!

From hills and the valleys, from near and afar
They traveled on horseback, by wagon and car;
They came up in groups and two at a time,
The gals all so lovely and beaus in their prime.

They wore fancy ginghams and fine calicos,
And gay pantaloons with the ruffles and bows;
And shirts of gray chambray with overalls blue
All starched and sharp-looking from shoulder to shoe.

The lanterns were lit up and hung on the wall
To brighten the hoedown for dancers and all.
The floor was made ready and everything neat,
With hay bales a-plenty arrayed for the seat.

Musicians were honored at these gay affairs—
Reserved for them specially were cane-bottomed chairs;
A pitcher of cider was standing near by
Lest fiddler and caller might get a bit dry.

The evening got off in a wondrous big way
As fiddle and banjo were tuned up to A,
Their drags and their plinks for perfection did strive,
And when struck the first tune, every foot came alive!

The caller sang out in a clear monotone,
And sets all in squares, every lad with his own,
They circled to left with a hold of the hand,
Then allemande left and a right and left grand.

Each couple in step, and a rhythm of feet
All moving in unison, full with the beat—
A once-and-a-half and a smooth dosados
The promenade home, and the swing high and low.

So on went the dance in the sheerest delight
With jolly square dancers up late in the night;
But came in due time to the faces aglow
The wave of the hand for the signal to go.

They left as they came, on the trails everywhere;
Their shouting and laughter on still mountain air
Re-echoed in distance and faded away—
A dance to remember in life's later day!

SCRATCHIN' OUT A LIVIN'

Goin' 'bout my reg'lar bus'ness
  Meanin' nary soul no harm—
Just a-scratchin' out a livin'
  On a rocky hillside farm.

Sort o' has me licked 'n' beaten
  'Fore I even get a start,
'Cause there's dirt enough just barely
  For to keep the rocks apart.

Hardpan and that cloddy gumbo
  Three rails high up on the fence,
But've got to keep a-goin'
  Even if it don't make sense.

Hogs a-rootin' up the pasture
  Where there's mostly poor joe grass,
And the corn patch went to growin'
  'Simmon sprouts and sassyfras.

Cowbrute's jumpin' all the fences
  And the corncrib's fallen down;
Mules keep kickin' o'er the traces
  Ever' time I go to town.

Harness comin' all to pieces—
  Never was much to desire;
An' I'll swear I'd done been finished
  If it wan't for balin' wire.

Then my britches hain't much neither,
  So will say whate'er befalls
That the next calf goes to market
  Better fetch new overhalls!

No one's got it ary rougher,
  I would bet a leg or arm,
Than one scratchin' out a livin'
  On a rocky hillside farm!

THE FARMERS' CO-OP

One of my early crusades was for bettering the plight of the farmer. My concern was that in too many instances the rewards for his labor are sorely inadequate, and at best he ekes out only a bare existence. Improved methods of farming increased production per manhour, but this did little when the products still had to sell below cost of production.

The farmers' marginal means of operation has been like an insidious cancer, eating away at their resources—slowly but surely undermining their base of existence. It is self-evident that farming consistently at a loss can predicate only indebtedness and eventual foreclosures. As a consequence many of our old pioneers and their descendents have in time lost their homesteads, the moneyed interests moved in, while the dispossessed and the displaced swelled the numbers on welfare in our overcrowded city slums and elsewhere.

Despite the fact that in my generation we saw ours pass from a nation of agriculture to one of industry, the truth still remains that in the world's economy there are essentially only four basic sources of wealth—farming, forestry, mining and fishing. Upon these must rest the entire structure—the primary and the secondary endeavors of mankind. The primary is bringing forth the basic elements of wealth; the secondary is processing, transporting, storing and merchandising these elements. When the secondary exacts more than its rightful share it gradually but surely thrusts its way to the center of the economic stage and the primary must move into the background and to the sidelines. Always in the wake of any transition of this magnitude there are those who take the brunt of the shock, and many fall victims by the wayside.

So we see the farmers' cooperative was born of desperation; it is sustained and nurtured by sheer determination to hold back in a measure the tide of secondary forces which have ever encroached on agriculture. For some it holds hope for survival in a world of many adversities. Above it all, it sets its goal at assurance of cost of production with a reasonable profit—and this can best be won at the market place, and only through concerted effort. Thus, the cooperative movement is more than a carry-over of the pioneer spirit of neighbor-help-neighbor; it is a vitally essential business, too long in coming and too late for many in the struggle.

THE FARMERS' CO-OP

While agriculture's many facets
  Have always fed both man and beast
'Tis sad, the hand that yields the harvest
  Should glean, of all, the very least!
As in the ways of jungle creatures
  The wolf first stalks and kills the prey;
Then lions and tigers crash the scene
  And deftly steal the prize away.

The farmer with his pride and honor
  Engaged with livestock, trees and plow,
Pursues his endless days of labor
  To live somehow by sweat of brow.
His fields give forth in great abundance
  Despite the threats the seasons mete,
Then when he comes at last to market
  Encounters there his sad defeat.

To hold his own against the forces
  That would take his fruits away
He finds that he must wield a hand
  Where price is made each trading day.
So he and fellow plowmen parry
  In a hard-won co-op race
To beat the money changers' game
  And plug the leaks at market place.

THE TIN LIZZY

While Fred Moseley was a good coach for the basketball team and the other athletic activities at Salem High, he was also a capable teacher in the academic departments of our school. As is the case in most small town high schools with a limited budget, the athletic director is often required to do double duty by taking on a class or two in history, social studies, English, or other, depending on his qualifications in these fields of learning.

One of Mr. Moseley's nonathletic assignments at Salem High was English IV. There were times when I fancied he undertook this task more out of duty than of preference, for his first love indisputably was the gymnasium, and more specifically, the basketball team which made impressionable records year after year under his able coaching.

There were times, too, when I fancied "Coach" showed a bit of favoritism in English Four to those of the class who were stars on the A team. This could not have been true, however, for some on the team (perhaps after a bad night on the court) were subjected to what seemed rather sharp criticism on shortcomings in their English efforts. Moreover, I did not have a free period for even his phys ed, and yet felt that he always accorded me all that was due—and perhaps more. At any rate, Mr. Moseley always impressed me as a man of strong, personable character, firm in his requirements, but underneath it all warm and understanding, and this seemed to rouse the best in us as we struggled with Beowulf, Chaucer, Shakespeare and other renowned contributors to our literary heritage.

I think Mr. Moseley enjoyed our English class more as the term wore on and as he became better acquainted with us on an individual basis, for he somehow shared personally in our accomplishments and our failures. Obviously he desired that we come alive and emulate the literary greats of the past, but yet was amenable to accepting considerably less—pleased nonetheless that we made a noticeable effort. The accompanying short story resulted from what some might have termed an "impossible" assignment, but which surely served to brush away a few cobwebs in our stolid craniums. More than for its own merits, the story is included herein to afford opportunity to laud in memoriam a fine man, a dedicated coach, a commendable teacher.

THE TIN LIZZY

"Rattle, rattle, squeak, squeakity, squeak!" These sounds came from Jed Hanson's garage and unmistakably indicated that Jed was engaged in a very vigorous attempt to start the used Model T Ford car he had bought the evening before. For nearly an hour Jed had been there, but thus far the engine had refused to snort even the first bit of encouragement. Again and again the sound was heard—rattle, rattle, squeak, squeak! And at regular intervals there burst forth loud verbal explosions which very definitely expressed Jed's indignation at the unco-operative old automobile and the world in general. As time went on the cranking became more and more vigorous, and the swearing increased in proportion. Suddenly there came a bang, and then a crash, followed by the sound of shattering glass. Almost immediately the garage doors burst open and Jed emerged with long and determined strides, his ruddy, grease-smeared face wet with perspiration, and his lips firmly pressed and white with anger.

With all the strong-headedness characteristic of him when in a fit of temper, Jed made straight for the house, and took the back porch steps in a single stride. Clearly he was not in a mood for trifling with anything or anyone; and even Rex, the household dog who was peacefully asleep on the door mat, did not escape the fury of the irate Hanson. His flying foot not only sent the unfortunate animal limping and howling pitifully around the corner of the house, but also startled the family cat so that she spat fiercely and scrambled to safety over the yard fence.

Inside the house, Hanson lost no time in reaching the telephone. He gave the crank a vicious jerk and clapped the receiver to his ear. "Give me Jones's Garage!" he barked into the transmitter, then shifted from one foot to the other while he waited for the operator to make the connection.

"Hello! Guy Jones speaking," came a pleasant voice from the other end.

"Hello! Say, Jones, this is Hanson!" blurted the caller. "That tin lizzy you talked me into buying is nothing but a pile of junk, and you knew it when you delivered it! I spent the whole dad-gum morning cranking the blamed thing, and I want you to get it off the place right away!" With this he threw the receiver back on its hook and wheeled away from the telephone.

In due time a light panel truck bearing the words "Jones Motor Company" stopped in front of the house, and from it stepped Guy Jones, who had come personally to investigate Jed Hanson's difficulty, and especially to defend the integrity of the Jones Garage.

"A fine way you have of taking advantage of the public!" were Jed's greeting words; and without giving Mr. Jones an opportunity to defend himself, he went on assailing the man with a barrage of masterful invective. However, this was not the first time that Jed Hanson had demonstrated his temper to a citizen of Stitesville, so Jones stood quietly until Jed had at length given vent to all that he could momentarily think of.

"Now, now, come down to earth, Jed," ventured the garage man in his usual mild manner now that Hanson's verbal storm had subsided somewhat. "It may be only a minor adjustment that is necessary. Let's see the car." And straightway the two proceeded to the garage.

"Hmmmm! You certainly wrecked the windshield," muttered Jones half to Jed, half to himself, as he surveyed the so-called "pile of junk" before him.

"Yes," retorted Hanson with renewed anger and a menacing glance, "and I am also capable of wrecking a skunk of a car dealer who would dump such a crate off on an unsuspecting buyer!"

Guy Jones pretended not to hear Jed's last remark, but busied himself measuring the contents of the gasoline tank, testing the choke, and looking in general over the various mechanisms which may have been causing the difficulty. He carefully set the spark lever, the throttle, and then turning to Jed said in a very casual tone of voice, "Now let's have the switch key and we will see if she will start."

"The switch key?" queried Hanson, a change of expression beginning to spread over his face. "The switch key!" A trembling forefinger brushed across his lip. "The switch key! Oh, yes; why it's—it's in the house on the bureau where I put it last night when you. . . ."

"You mean you've been doing all this cranking without turning on the ignition switch?" demanded Jones with a sharp squint of the eye.

"Well, er, that is—well, I reckon so!" stammered Jed, twisting uncomfortably, looking mostly at the ground as he went on muttering something more that was neither intelligible nor evidently of much importance.

"I was afraid of that," put in Mr. Jones, now definitely master of the situation. He shook his head in obvious disbelief as a half-smile of mingled amusement and disgust screwed up one side of his face. "You'll learn if you drive a car very much, Mr. Hanson, that the switch key is a very important little gadget."

Jed, now fully aware that he had made a foolish blunder, wilted like a leaf in hot water. A sheepish look drove the fire from his eye; his face turned from red to white and then to red again; and he hung his head apologetically. After what seemed a long and awkward pause he turned toward the house. Presently he returned with the key which he laid gingerly in Jones's outstretched palm.

Quietly the garage man inserted the key and turned on the ignition. The engine started with the first jerk of the crank. "There, you see the 'pile of junk' runs very nicely," he said with no attempt to disguise an overtone of sarcasm. With this he turned and departed, chuckling to himself as he went down the walk, leaving the abject Jed Hanson to the misery his own hasty actions had brought him.

EDUCATION

Oft on a summer evening as darkness settled over the hills, my buddy and I lay on a grassy hillside contemplating the vastness of the star-studded universe out and beyond . . . and just talking. I suppose we were trying to put our lives together, so to speak, for we were seniors-to-be in high school and searching for meaning and purpose in this great bewildering world about us. These were times when it seemed that the future ways of life's pursuits offered infinite possibilities. Despite an understandable sense of confusion, there was a strange excitement in the thought that we would figure somehow in those far-reaching undertakings that waited out there in the wings of the world's vast arena. But, alas! one short lifetime could make a mark in but one or so of these callings, and the rest with all their exciting promise and appeal would have to go by virtually untouched!

After high school, fate conspired with the beckoning outside world, and the ways for Glen and me widened beyond the horizons of the Ozarks. We took separate courses as time unravelled our respective balls of yarn, and I am sure that both of us were duly challenged, and often, by the many hurdles that confronted us on our way. It was well along in college days, however, that the unsearchable vastness of learning finally became real to me. At last it was clear that even a comparatively simple facet of man's many endeavors could entail a lifetime of intensive study—and still he could never fully master all there is to know about even that one facet! Man, proud man! He might as well know that he can never become fully educated. At best, it is all relative—in kind, depth, and to a degree!

A little knowledge, it is said, is a dangerous thing; but the true danger lies in that a little knowledge can indeed blind us to reality—to what lies beyond. Continued effort at learning is doubtless the mother of man's most resounding humility. Each bit of knowledge gained is but a key that opens another door in the world of mysteries, and this goes on and on ad infinitum.

It was from one such youthful contemplative moods that came the accompanying poem. At best, it can render only a weak expression of what I found the world of learning to be.

 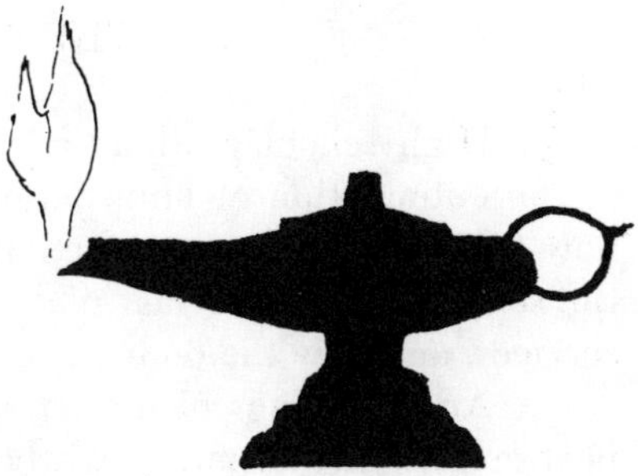

EDUCATION

How like the fleeting, broad horizon
  Is this thing called education—
We gain the knoll we had our eyes on,
  Then there looms another station!

The quest begins in days of laces,
  Leads thru grade school, high, and college;
To dizzy heights and hazy places
  We pursue the god of knowledge.

We make the most of time allotted,
  Aim at nothing less than winning,
And when we think at last we've got it,
  We can see a new beginning.

Yes, Wisdom's volume is eternal—
  All in time reach that opinion;
And though we fail, alas to learn all,
  We have seen its vast dominion!

THE CLASS OF '34

High school graduation! What memorable occasion is this event at the culmination of long periods of effort in the classrooms. These all now highlighted by recent activities still so vivid: getting our class rings, the senior picnic, the class play, hobo day, class night, the baccalaureate services, and now the ominous finality of it all—graduation!

Amid feelings of apprehension regarding what lay ahead in life's next episode, we experienced the sober leave-takings as we turned in our caps and gowns—the mingled feelings of joy and sadness that pervaded the scene; the fond embraces and the many tearful good-byes, punctuated by solemn vows to get together real often and to keep in touch always!

This poem is included, not because of any special literary excellence it may have, but because, as the dubbed poet of Salem's class of '34, I proudly put heart and soul into writing it. I felt it captured a bit of the sentimentality of our class of sixty-some young men and women who proudly took their diplomas and felt for a few fleeting moments at least that the world was surely at their feet.

Doubtless graduation from high school will always represent one of the first major milestones in the lives of young people. For me, however, it was doubly that—it was a pinnacle of achievement with more than average significance, for high school itself came within an ace of completely passing me by. Therefore, gratefully, and with a degree of humility, I would dedicate this writing to the many fine persons who contributed so much to make it possible—to both, those who still share with us in the memories of that happy event, and in memoriam to those who have since passed on.

Among these, first I would place my mother whose admonitions were ever for higher learning; then I would name such talented and dedicated teachers as Glenn C. Smith, Helene Bircher, Alice Dent, Fred Moseley, Ezra Craddock, Mildred Hughes, and others. Too, I would include Senator D. L. Bales, William Hirth, and W. P. Elmer, men whose legislative efforts brought free high school to Missouri's rural young people; and finally, but not least, State Superintendent of Schools Charles W. Lee, and County Superintendent Albert Click. All were instrumental, each in his own way, in making high school possible and pleasant for me and for many others through the years.

THE CLASS OF '34

We thank you for your cheering
  This happy Senior band,
For our hearts are thrilled by hearing
  Your loud, applauding hand.
We have so long been yearning
  For this eventful day
When we've climbed the hill of learning
  And have our word to say.

A dozen years have drifted
  Upon the stream of time
Since first our eyes were lifted
  To the hill we were to climb.
It proved to be a mountain
  As we plodded long and hard
To reach at last the fountain
  And gain a just reward.

Now, from this high position,
  We pause to gaze below,
And see the road Ambition
  We trod so long ago.
We recall our noble rally
  Where the trails to Future part;
There we left behind the valley
  Where all the students start.

We see again the schoolroom
  With timid faces full—
Oh, how we craved the woodland
  When tasks grew hard and dull!
But trudging through the wildwood
  With compass, book, and rule,
We learned in early childhood
  The purpose of the school.

We passed each grade a-flying
  As higher on we rose;
And found that honest trying
  Would overcome our woes.
And for our crafty planning
  Of mischief which was done
We took a healthful tanning
  To pay the price of fun.

Then High School loomed before us
  As up the trail we came—
How those higher did ignore us
  And our hopes to conquer fame!
That we were dumb we're yielding,
  For we were Freshmen all;
We roamed all o'er the building
  And were lost in every hall.

But when the next year ended
  The other students there
Had all of us befriended
  Our knowledge so to share.
And it's no blinding mystery
  Why we soon held the floors,
For in all of Salem's history
  Were no wiser Sophomores.

Our Junior year we treasure—
  How dear each golden day!
That year of work and pleasure
  Will long in memory stay.
'Tis true, our load grew heavy
  Ere the last semester waned—
But all have paid that levy
  Who Wisdom's crown have gained.

Then came the final season—
  The happiest year of all,
When we as learned Seniors
  Controlled the study hall.
Thus we reached at last the summit
  That had beckoned all the way;
And we now so gaily trumpet
  Our achievement of today.

But ere we part to scatter
  Upon the wayward winds,
We want to square a matter
  And thank our teacher friends.
They showed a patient kindness
  As they led the way before,
They turned to light our blindness,
  And eased the load we bore.

And to our kind old parents
  We sing a grateful song,
For they suffered much forbearance
  In helping us along.
They made the time go faster
  Since that day of long ago
When we set our hearts to master
  The things we did not know.

Yes, school at times grew dreary,
  And lessons oft were long;
And we tired of theme and query
  When our answers all were wrong.
But we are happy mortals
  Who know with joys supreme
That our days within these portals
  Will ever live in dream.

Now, to the ones who weaken
  And linger in the vale
We'll make our lives a beacon
  To guide them up the trail.
We'll teach unselfish giving
  While we dwell above the sod,
And so dedicate our living
  To goodness and to God.

MY CHURCH

My church shall be a place so fair
With hosts of friendly people there.
  The structure shall be good to see
  And every part a symbol be.
The outside, faith shall symbolize
The inside, warmth of summer skies;
  Its pillars tall for strength shall stand,
  The pulpit, one great helping hand;
A haven sure, each rugged wall,
The windows, light and truth for all;
  Uplift, the steps and hope, the door,
  With service true, the roof and floor;
The spire shall stand for Lord above,
And its foundation shall be love.

WHEN THE SCHOOL YEAR IS O'ER

In a one-room country school, closing day and final disbanding is much like breaking home ties. Togetherness of teacher and pupils through the school term constitutes a relationship that is meaningful, memorable and beautiful. Working together in "time of books," playing games on the playground at time of recess, huddling around the wood-burning heater in winter to dry out water-logged shoes and wet garments, sharing in morning exercises the time-honored classics: *Evangeline, The Legend of Sleepy Hollow, The Great Stone Face,* and many others—all serve to bond a delightful relationship.

The closing-day exercises bring in the parents, who begin making their appearance in midmorning and who "wouldn't miss the last day of school for a pretty!" Only token classes are recited—usually exhibitionary in nature and purpose to show off the pupils' accomplishments and to cater to the pride of parents. At noontime a bounteous basket dinner is featured with the participating housewives' best culinary accomplishments spread on long improvised outdoor tables. Here everyone strives to outdo and to out-eat one another. The teacher "just must sample" an incredible number of goodies—Aunt Emmy's spiced meat balls, Susie Smith's molasses cake, Elviry's famous gooseberry pie, and many others. Much congeniality and good humor add to the pleasure of the meal.

The afternoon program includes recitations, songs and dialogs by the pupils, these interspersed with live country music. Curtains drawn on smooth wire permit changing scenes on stage and provide dressing areas at either side. A finale is the teacher's presentation of certificates and candy treats to the pupils, as well as passing stick candy among the spectators that often fill the schoolroom to overflowing.

Since the school building in rural areas doubles for a "meetin' house" on the Lord's day, the conscientious teacher (also responsible for custodial duties) returns following closing exercises to clean up the litter and set things in order for Sunday morning. Any sensitive qualities the teacher may possess will come to the surface on such visits, for as the poem portrays, everything serves as a reminder of happy relations with a fine group of youngsters.

This poem was written at close of my first term of teaching, and the school was South Crossroads.

WHEN THE SCHOOL YEAR IS O'ER

How lone is the schoolhouse when the school year is o'er
And the teacher returns to sweep it once more!
Alone and heartbroken, forsaken it stands,
There grieving for absent caressing brown hands.

The playground around it, so pattered and bare,
Re-echoes no footsteps, no voices, the air;
And all of the carvings on white oaks sublime
Are left there to weather and wrestle with time.

Within, all is silent—a whispering tomb—
With no happy faces to brighten the room;
And battered seats yawning in drowsy, sad rows
Are wondering why childhood that fickle way goes.

The finger-worn textbooks laid neatly away
Are awaiting new readers some other school day.
And mute and dejected, the solemn old bell
Is destined to slumber in Arachne's fair cell.

Yes, silence is victor in Wisdom's old mill,
Yet traces of schooldays are evident still—
For here are some drawings, an inkwell o'erturned,
And there is a poem a young scholar learned.

Thus courses forever a year to the past
For those on life's platform, for all in the cast—
A year of achievement we would trust it to be,
A year to remember for them and for me!

EMPTY LITTLE SHOES

This poem in its initial publication was dedicated to Loydie Nelson Harper, the adopted small son of Mr. and Mrs. W. E. Harper, with whom I roomed and boarded while teaching the one-room school in their Missouri Ozarks community.

One winter night after Loydie had been tucked in and the elder Harpers, too, had retired, I was busy with my school papers—an inescapable task of nearly every teacher's day. Pausing momentarily in my work, I permitted my eyes to stray about the room when suddenly Loydie's battered and scuffed little shoes came into focus, one upright and the other lying on the floor there beside the box heater. They were indeed a scene of utter dejection—if one may use the term when speaking of inanimate things like shoes—each so much a part in the rounds of the day's activities and now so carelessly cast aside and forgotten; for no one leaves behind him more completely the cares, the joys and the material things of a busy world than does a child when the sandman finally overtakes him!

In the course of a few moments a panorama of all the ins and outs of childhood play seemed to drift across the scene, and all the events of this little boy's day were contained in them. Somehow these scenes seemed to fall into place effortlessly and shaped themselves into the poem "Empty Little Shoes," which I captured by a few notes hurriedly scrawled on a scrap of paper.

Although Loydie has since grown into young manhood and the subject "little partners" have long ago returned to the dust of the earth, these little shoes have nevertheless stayed with us in the poem, little and battered and scuffed as they were that winter night; and moreover, they bid to remain so for the Harpers, for me, and for others for many, many years to come.

EMPTY LITTLE SHOES

Empty little shoes abandoned
  Where the sandman caught him tight—
Comrades through the day so faithful
  Left forsaken for the night;
And two roving little gypsies
  That so nimbly took them 'round
Now are tucked beneath the feathers
  And in restful slumber bound.

Empty little shoes a-tattling
  Of adventures near and far,
Tales of mighty deeds emitting
  From each telltale cuff and scar—
How they roamed a trackless region
  Hidden treasure to retrieve,
How they bore a fearless pirate
  On the ships of make-believe!

Empty little shoes forgotten
  Now that closed a strenuous day;
Partners, ready, true and tireless
  In a rough-and-tumble play!
Loyal little shoes ill-fated,
  For when service rends them wide
Then the future years will find them
  In oblivion cast aside.

Though your tongues go uncomplaining,
  Well your destiny I know;
O wee shoes, you're like us mortals,
  And as old as man your woe—
For so often we in sadness
  At the close of Duty's day
Find our efforts unacknowledged
  And are left beside the way!

I'M JUST A BILL

Next to the self-satisfied person who has mastered the realms of sophistication is one content with comparatively little in the way of life's many offerings. Both share the virtues of their respective "cups of tea," and perhaps neither would exchange with the other. Each in his own way regards a set of values peculiar to his own liking. The "aristocrat" of a mountain clan may find few and simple things among the amenities of his existence, but at the same time may feel that attaining more is really not worth his time and effort.

Strangely enough each of our heroes has a place of importance in the order of things, and each takes his lot along with such rewards and penalties as may be inherent in his chosen position. An admirable factor is that each feels blest in his own sphere and is up to singing its praises to the world and all mankind.

This poem, initially entitled "The Hillbilly," was written from the viewpoint of a "bill from up the hill," one singularly proud to be what he is. The poem appeared first in the *Missouri Farmer* but subsequently was featured in a number of other publications. In due time the words caught the approbation and imagination of my musically-inclined friend, William E. Harper. He forthwith set the words to music and later we had this new creation professionally arranged. The Dent County M.F.A. Band featured it in the evening programs put on in many rural schoolhouses in the far-flung farming communities in the Missouri Ozarks. Everywhere it was heard its catchy tune and subtle humor were favorably received, and it still is a novel number to many who empathize with the ways and customs of rural Americana.

I'M JUST A BILL

Big city folks are full o' jokes
'Bout hill folks' backward way;
We've no bright lights an' fancy sights
An' things like that they say.
They call us hicks from out 'na sticks,
An' it makes me stomp my feet;
For this I know an' tell 'em so:
Our hill folks cain't be beat!

The burnin' eyes o' city guys
Cain't see for soot an' smoke;
An' most 'nam there jus' gasp for air
An' by gosh purt' nigh choke!
It's true, I know, we've got no show
An' we don't play ball at night,
But, by the way, I'm here to say
Our folks are livin' right!

To creakin' mills an' likker stills
Go beaten trails, you know,
For we 'uns heed the call o' need
An' know jus' where to go.
Our country stores with 'spattered floors
Are a gladsome sight to see;
An' I'll declare, the nail kegs there
Are purt' nigh part o' me!

I well recall when I was small
An' roamed them mountain trails,
I et pawpaws an' bitter haws
An' wild grapes by the pails,
I've eat poke greens an' weev'ly beans
An' those skippers in the ham—
I'm just a bill from up 'na hill
An' pow'rful glad I am!

Frank Fuis, Jr.

I'M JUST A BILL

Music by W. E. Harper
Arr. by Sylvester L. Cross

makes me stomp my feet; For this I know an' tell 'em so: Our
don't play ball at night, But, by the way, I'm here to say Our
glad - some sight to see; An' I'll de - clare, the nail kegs there Are
Chorus
hill folks cain't be beat!------
folks are liv - in' right!------ Oh, th' world may jeer for all I keer With a
purt' nigh part o' me!------
sneer, a hoot an' slam; For I'm a bill from up 'na hills, An' am
1
2
pow'r - ful glad I am. Oh, th' pow'r-ful glad I am.

THE CHESTNUT GROVE

It was near traditional in rural America to gather nuts in the crisp, sunny days of autumn. Many varieties flourished in our hills—black walnuts, butternuts, hickory, hazel, chestnuts, and others. Young people often made a big thing of it as they took gunny sacks and went nut-gathering on these leisure days—and in their way these outings filled a social need. Getting to these gifts of the forests had to be appropriately timed, too, for the wild woodland creatures, as well as the domestic hog population that roamed the free ranges, all competed for these native, generally abundant crops.

A good harvest of nuts promised jolly evenings ahead, for when the wintry winds howled outside and the snow piled deep over hill and dale, a favorite pastime was cracking nuts around the cheery fireside. Here the discarded nutshells popped and crackled as the flames flared up a bit brighter with each new handful cast amid the glowing logs.

The native American chestnut, before a widespread blight destroyed it, was a special treat for us, for they were not as commonly found in our area as were some of the other varieties of nuts—they being mostly prevalent in the Appalachian Mountain ranges. At Thanksgivings time these chestnuts were a particularly important ingredient in the dressing that rounded out the festive goose or turkey.

This poem depicts a scene that livened a goodly number of the late autumn afternoons near the West Ozark school where I was teacher. In sight of the one-room schoolhouse stood a clump of chestnut trees on a part of the E. W. Vogel farm where the Roscoe Warden family lived. After the first heavy frosts the burrs with rich brown goodies dropped into the tall grass and undergrowth along a fence row there.

During school hours we observed the rule not to leave the school ground for any reason short of a pressing necessity, and then only with permission. After dismissal of the last class, however, the chestnut grove was fair game for pupils and teacher, and all made a beeline there to gather a share of the day's accumulation.

While this activity was comparatively shortlived with respect to highlights of the months before and afterward, it nevertheless was one that stood out for me and for many of the youngsters in those delightful school days at West Ozark.

THE CHESTNUT GROVE

In sight and sound of school and playground
Chestnut trees stood by the road.
Here, after frost in sunny autumn,
Branches dropped their burry load.

Delighted pupils and the teacher,
School dismissed at close of day,
Would race to find the tasty treasure
That in grass and bushes lay.

Gay shouting youngsters, joy o'erflowing,
Flashing eyes, alert and keen,
And lunch kits, books and coats abandoned,
Made a long-remembered scene!

Romance was present, budding, tender—
Boy gave girl his hard-won prize
And saw his grateful school-day sweetheart
Beam with lovelight in her eyes.

Then, searching done and pockets bulging,
All went on their homeward way,
Each looking to a gay tomorrow
And another chestnut day.

INFLUENZA BLUES

Most young men with a flair for writing have at one time or another harbored dreams of writing a successful song and making the big time. The enticing advertisements in some of the journals that early came to hand fired many a would-be song writer with more than a passing case of enthusiasm. "Send us your song poems," they said; "we will set your lyrics to music—your songs may make the hit parade!"

Fame and fortune, it is true, have fallen that easily into the laps of a few—but few indeed they have been. What the advertisers never tell their readers is that a pitifully small percentage of these hopefuls ever realize a mere pittance for their effort in the songwriting field. And the few who do make it often do so through means other than writing a lyric that is particularly better than the legions of those that fail. But there is always the speculation that our writings are perhaps the ones that will make it, and one can never know unless one tries! Certainly, one success can give rise to a thousand failures, for as P. T. Barnum aptly said of suckers, "There's one born every minute."

Despite all this, however, I was one of those who was never convinced that though others failed that I would likewise fail, and so I tried again and again (remitting, of course, the required fee with the lyrics), and hoped and dreamed. This poem was one such effort that seemed to me, at least, to have some potential. Even now, I wouldn't discount the importance of unsuccessful ventures. Failure often teaches better lessons than does success. In any event I would not have missed the many hours of speculation these illusions afforded me. They added spice to an otherwise unflavored routine of life on the farm, and thus filled a void here and there with something of special interest.

INFLUENZA BLUES

There are blues for every feeling
  From the saddest to the gay;
Blues with melodies appealing,
  Blues to drive the blues away.
Yes, there're doleful blues a-plenty
  Sung this wide old world around,
But bluer far than any
  Are the blues that got me down.

Chorus:
Oh, I've got the Influenza Blues,
And I'm seeing everything by twos;
Just a groanin', shakin', and my bones all achin'
From my whirlin' head down to my shoes.
Now I'd give this dizzy world to know
What would ease me from this dreadful woe,
For I lie a mopin', 'bout to die a-dopin'
With a dozen kinds of pills or so.
You may stake your all to win or lose,
But at last you'll surely pay your dues
With a coughin', sneezin' and an awful wheezin'
When you get the Influenza Blues.

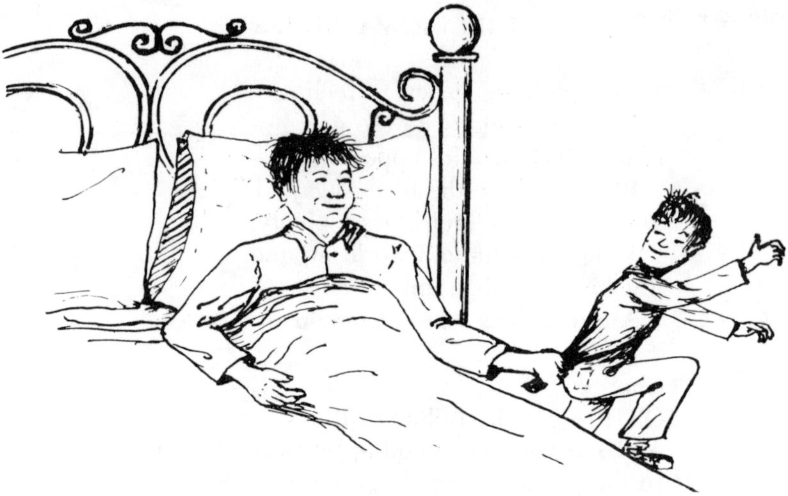

THE SUNSHINE EVERYWHERE

A child, robust and healthy, often does not know what to make of it when an adult is suddenly out of circulation because of an ailment, and so is not up and about, romping, playing, or jesting with him. And it surely does change the complexion of one's day where there is illness, when that customary smile or cheery word is not forthcoming from the ailing one.

One such youngster was Loydie Harper, who for several days looked into my sickroom, obviously wondering why I just didn't hop right out of bed and resume my customary way of frolicking with him. However, desiring a thing doesn't always bring it about, and here is where wishing and wanting must give way to patience and understanding—those builders of fortitude which undergird and sustain us through the long periods of waiting.

Events during a brief illness of mine suggested the accompanying poem, which appeared soon afterward in a number of midwestern publications. It is a comforting thought that sunshine, literally and figuratively speaking, is ever near us, and that usually we possess the necessary resources to let it break through if we so desire. Undoubtedly, when we do make the effort all those concerned are the better for it. We, too, find that there is a wealth of therapeutic value in assuming a positive attitude—regarding our plight with the proper frame of mind.

THE SUNSHINE EVERYWHERE

He was playing near my bedside
  Where in illness I lay bound,
And his childish, gleeful laughter
  Somehow gathered sunshine 'round.
Leaving all his toy things scattered,
  He would tease with playful hand—
For a child he was, so happy,
  And too young to understand.

He could fathom not my ailing,
  Nor the driving pain I knew,
But his watchful eyes were eager
  For a smile so long o'erdue;
So I caught his open jacket
  As he slyly near me stood,
And I found my playful gesture
  Did us both a world of good!

Thus as we go traveling onward
  O'er the trying ways of life,
We encounter many lashings
  And the blows of worldly strife;
But Good Fortune made it easy
  To remove the lashes' sting
If we let the sunshine 'round us
  Bring us joy in everything.

JESUS IS MY FRIEND

This hymn is a product of collaboration with an esteemed friend in my past, the late William E. Harper. The title and basic thoughts expressed in the first stanza are in the main his contribution, and to him must go that portion of what glory may be inherent in this effort.

Himself an accomplished musician, Bill delighted in trying his hand now and then at writing and composing. On occasion he would come up with something we felt had a good deal of merit. At any rate, during the two years I boarded with Bill, his congenial wife Millie, and son Loyd, we had fun in our many ventures, including efforts in the field of music.

In Sunday school services at West Ozark, the country school I taught at the time, Bill took a very active and commendable part, serving in time in the capacities of superintendent, teacher of the adult class, accompanist at the piano, and song leader for the assembly hymn singing.

Never endowed with much of the world's material things, the Harpers nonetheless always seemed given to the spiritual requirements of daily living—grateful always for small favors and content with the gifts of Providence, whatever the portion. Moreover, despite their share of trials and tribulations, their love, good humor, and enthusiastic outlook on life constituted a generous abundance for the Harpers, and happiness blessed their household in goodly measure. The foregoing characteristics, together with Bill's love for music and his talent with most instruments, kept the Harper home a focal point for gatherings, and ensured a standing invitation to all social events in their West Ozark community.

What prompted Bill to want to write this hymn dominated his life and his relationship with his fellow men. While he has long since gone to join his "Friend," no one to my knowledge can say he failed to live the principles his Subject prescribed for all mankind. In this vein we may reflect on Bill, along with our joys for having known him, and repeat our pet saying: "Greater love had no man—and not many women!"

In subsequent years through mutual and professional interests in Oak Ridge, Tennessee, Yale E. Payne set our words to music, and he and S. G. Fouts published this composition in their hymnal *The Living Fountain,* a book which remains a gem among my prized possessions.

Jesus Is My Friend

Frank Fuis, Jr. in "The Living Fountain" Yale E. Payne

C-H-R-I-S-T-M-A-S

Finding appropriate material for putting together an entertainment program for special occasions often taxed the ingenuity of us one-room country school teachers. Besides having to fit the theme of the occasion, selection of this material also had to take into account the ages and number of pupils on roll, with the object that each pupil from the smallest to the largest had an appropriate part in the program.

Entertainment programs made certain inroads in regular "book-larnin'" time, for rehearsals and memory work usually took a week or longer, part or full time. However, most teachers agree that the students' participation in public exercises is an important facet in the educational process. Many of the roles in grown-up life afterwards require our appearing before a crowd and making more or less lengthy statements regarding issues about which we are concerned. For this reason we regard with thanks our early training in facing an assemblage, even though we may have trembled, and our knees knocked together in various forms of stage fright. Those early parts we spoke before our parents, friends, and neighbors helped build a degree of poise and self-confidence in facing the public. The teacher's conscientious selection of the parts we had here helped greatly, for accordingly, the presentation was either easy or difficult, smooth or rugged, and we participated willingly or otherwise. Moreover, an accomplished child maketh a proud parent. As the timidity gradually vanished and self-assurance brought successively greater ovations from the onlookers, responsible participation in these programs swelled the pride of not only Johnnie and Susie in the dialogue, but of mama and papa in the audience as well.

This presentation was specifically written for one such Christmas program to give the beginners a part to speak when nothing else was available. Each pupil held a large cardboard letter in the word "Christmas" and proudly spoke his or her lines. Then, at the ensuing applause, they took an appreciative bow before the curtain was drawn.

There were numerous occasions when dialogues and plays had to be written, rewritten, or altered to suit the requirements of the school, the taste of the community and the pleasure of the teacher. Even so, those programs usually turned out to be quite rewarding efforts.

C-H-R-I-S-T-M-A-S

C is for Christ, the infant who lay
  Long ago in a stable on a coarse bed of hay.

H is for holy, a gift from above
  To brighten our Christmas with warmth and with love.

R is for reindeer on Santa's red sleigh
  They bring us much joy on this glad holiday.

I is for ice that clings to the eaves—
  Like lollypop candies that gay Santa leaves.

S is for snow that comes every year
  To whiten our Christmas with beauty and cheer.

T is for toys piled up by our tree—
  Let's give some to children less favored than we.

M is for merry as our Christmas shall be
  Love and good will can set your heart free.

A is for alleluias with trumpet's sweet blast
  To commemorate Christ and the saints of the past.

S is for the star that shone in the East—
  Its light through the ages has never once ceased.

BAREFOOT TRAILS

Although the grass and trees greened early in the spring of 1941, for most engineering students at the University of Missouri it might as well have not been spring at all. Driven by heavy academic schedules, the confinement of daily classrooms and laboratories, burning the proverbial "midnight oil" to the wee hours of morning, and getting in reports just under the deadline, there never was time enough for hiking out in Nature's awakening fields and forests, or relaxing in the warming sun of the great out-of-doors.

Life itself is essentially a trade-off in which we constantly give up something we have in return for something we think we desire more, and oftentimes man's contracted obligations turn out to be the very warden of his self-imposed incarceration. On campus, engineering students were at times known for their antisocial tendencies, however unintentional they were; and the fair sex frequently shunned the slide-rule-packing youth because of his well-known lack of time for regular dating. Despite all this, however, the promise of future rewards somehow made the sacrifices seem worthwhile at the time, and thus many of us endured it and survived.

But to say that college days were one glorious picnic would be quite an overstatement. Life in many ways stood still, as it were, waiting for that long-sought day of liberation—graduation! Meanwhile, the student indulged occasionally in fleeting moments of reverie—revisiting in thought the cherished haunts of his more idle days when life was relatively simple and schedules less demanding. This poem came into being at such a time of reflection, and appeared soon afterward in several midwestern publications.

Liberation or no, there have been many times since college days when the lines in this poem still rang true; when they expressed again and again the sentiment of my feelings. And if a confession is in order, those feelings persist even to the present day!

BAREFOOT TRAILS

I long for fields and the open sky
   Where crops are lush and a creek runs by,
Where Nature smiles in a thousand ways
   On childhood fair in barefoot days.

I long for trails in the wildwood shade
   Where plays the cottontail unafraid,
And leaps the squirrel from tree to tree,
   Content at heart, and blithe and free.

I long to rest by a placid pool
   Where moss is downy, damp and cool,
And watch through whispering leaves on high
   White bits of fleece go drifting by.

Oh, I must yield to this urgent call
   To steal away to the rubble wall,
The vine-grown haunts and the fence of rails,
   And roam once more those barefoot trails!

THE ENGINEER

This essay was written to fill my initiatory requirement for acceptance into the Tau Beta Pi engineering honorary society, and was published as first-prize winner in the *Shamrock* at the University of Missouri. With the honor came an engineers' handbook which thrilled me at time of presentation, and served long and well in my work, even to this day.

Understandably, the essay reveals much of the enthusiasm typical of every young engineering student with visions of remaking the world. With more than something akin to loyalty to the profession, we must concede here that the engineering and scientific communities can indeed bring about earth-shaking accomplishments—some good and some otherwise; the good always when working in fully-considered compliance with the steadfast laws of nature and human values, and a veritable self-destruction when pursuits are heedless in this regard.

Growing up in the wide expanse of the Ozark's unspoiled regions, my intimate contacts with nature served to impart to me a concerned understanding and an abiding appreciation of the intricate simplicities that ever surround us. Here was opportunity to learn how things in field and forest function and the wonderful way each relates to the others. Even the machines on the farm—those "newfangled" contrivances that thrill every imaginative person—proved to obey unchanging basics in natural laws. And so indeed the transition from farm boy to engineer was surprisingly unruffled and painless.

Nonetheless, the intervening years served to confirm the fact that in her pristine order Nature is sensibly yet delicately balanced to a fine state of perfection; that wonderful though the marvels of technology may be, most of man's feats of accomplishment do not come for free. A major exploit may in fact create more problems than it solves. And here is where impatience and greed must be reckoned with, lest the fine order of our creation be irreparably unbalanced!

Now, as in days of a starry-eyed dreamer, I must reiterate that engineering in its many facets is indispensable to the life styles it helped bring about and which we have come to enjoy; that this profession has worlds of wonders still to reveal, and that the engineer himself serves best when he, as a helper in creation, directs his efforts only to tasks that are prudent, unselfish and meaningful.

THE ENGINEER

Our world is virtually a house of countless wonders—and the engineer is the keeper of the keys! From year to year he unlocks new doors in Nature's labyrinth and opens the way to new corridors of achievement. Once he opens them he leaves the portals wide, and generations ever afterward avail themselves of the many treasures thus placed at their disposal. Each new discovery, each new accomplishment is in truth a treasure, for each represents a steppingstone to a better and more comfortable existence.

Obviously, the civilization we know today is the product of many centuries of constant and persistent effort. In this respect it is interesting to note that the early stages were gained largely through means of trial and error. Progress, moreover, was made very slowly down through the centuries of ancient and medieval times. In fact, it was not until engineering became firmly established in the realm of human endeavor that civilization made its greatest strides forward.

Without disparaging the work of men in other fields, it can be said that the various specialized departments of engineering have probably contributed more to the modern age and to the welfare of mankind than has any other one profession. Hardly a field exists into which the engineer has not ventured and from which he has not brought forth something worthwhile. Every part of the earth has become his laboratory; every land his workshop; and every element his tool.

Contrary to the old adage of grammar school texts, bridges *are* crossed before they are reached. They are crossed and recrossed by the engineer long before the first excavation is made or the first beam placed. Being a man of vision, the engineer sees in detail every bridge of the future; mentally he not only builds the piers and lays the spans, but also tests each section analytically and mathematically for strength and durability before a single step is made in actual construction. Bridges of steel and bridges of human progress are alike in this respect. In either case it is primarily the engineer who pioneers the way for the oncoming traffic, and it is he who makes easy and pleasant the never-ending trailways of Man.

Thanks to the creative imagination and the tireless persistence of our engineers, the world today is a wonderland almost impossible to appreciate. The passing years have long since brought into reality the one-time wild imaginations of men like Jules Verne, and many of our present-day achievements have surpassed even the wildest dreams of our predecessors. Ingenious machinery has with its iron shoulders lifted the burden for all civilized races; new developments in food, clothing and shelter have brought a delightful variation to every home and family; and the atmosphere of our times is traversed not only by powerful air-liners but also by waves of inaudible voice and song, and invisible pictures flashing in every direction with the tremendous speed of light!

Strange as it may seem, however, science is as yet in its infancy, and the future is unquestionably rich with possibilities for outstanding contributions to the progress of our civilization. In this respect the student who chooses engineering for his life's work bids fair to become a benefactor of his fellow men. Moreover, his choosing an engineer's career at once elevates him above the common herd, for his choice in itself marks him as one who would not take the easiest way through college and through his useful years after graduation. By nature he is a crusader who seeks out tasks which challenge his ability; instinctively he investigates a moving machine part in order to determine the reason for its behavior; he delights in problems which tax his ingenuity; he burns "midnight oil" of his own will; and he cheerfully denies himself many hours of leisure on the campus. In the classroom he absorbs facts and fundamentals which later become tools in his life's equipment, and his every achievement, be it great or small, is a building block for a greater civilization of tomorrow.

Verily, the engineer is often forgotten because of the glamor of his own accomplishments, but that is as he would have it. His analytical mind, his thorough training, and the precision of his work place him among the honored men of all time. The engineer is one who consults frankly and freely with his fellows—weighs their opinions and respects their judgment; he pursues his work without ado, and makes his contributions unselfishly. Truly, his is not merely an occupation, but rather a service to which he has dedicated his life, his name, and his professional honor.

WALTZING SHADOWS

This composition represents another of my efforts to break into the songwriting field. While this, too, did not get off the ground, it did bring me the personal comments and the cherished autograph of the world-famous Paul Whiteman.

Needless to say, it took a good many such efforts and consequent repeated rejections to cool my ardor, and to squelch my hopes of crashing the fabulous and jealously-guarded dominion of songwriting. Since those days of fantasy I have learned that success in this field is manipulated pretty much by connections with the "inside," and that even with this advantage much promotion is required for one to become even moderately favored.

It is no wonder, when as a boy I first showed a flair for writing poetry and songs, that my father predicted with a good deal of fatherly concern that in this field I would starve to death in an attic. This prediction would doubtless have been doubly ominous had I endeavored to make a literary tendency more than a mere hobby. However, perhaps because of my elder's dire prediction my writings have remained very much in the background of my life's activities. Nonetheless, they have proved to be an intensely fascinating pastime through the years. And attic or no, a degree of the sensitivity that must be part of every writer has enriched my life and work in many ways, and for this I am very grateful.

WALTZING SHADOWS

How like a bit of heaven
  Is an evening, dear, with you,
Here beside a cozy fireside
  In our firelit rendezvous.

Happy moments to remember
  Ever, ever and a day;
Each is like a glowing ember—
  Slow, so slow, to fade away!

Chorus:

Dreamy waltzing shadows
  On the firelit wall I see;
Happy dancing shadows,
  Shadows, dear, of you and me.
With you for my own,
My partner alone,
I could dance my whole life through
  And step to the strain
  Of truelove's refrain
As our waltzing shadows do.

H-A-Z-E-L

Sooner or later there drifts into the life of every man that girl who suddenly looms above all others, dominating most of his waking moments by day and his dreams by night. The sweet and tender ways of the girl that strikes that responsive chord—the things she does, the things she says, the ring of her laughter, the mannerisms all her own—make her that special person, a delight to be near, to love and to cherish.

Throughout my adolescence and years of young manhood I regarded girls—mostly from a distance—as a masterful part of our creation, this based principally on respect and adoration of a devoted mother and an understanding sister. Despite an occasional clash with maternal authority, and the normal brother-sister differences, I grew up with a feeling that by far the greatest good for the interests of our society is conceived and influenced, even if behind the scene, by the female of our species. Naturally, in the course of years I developed that vulnerability to the prospects of matrimony, and sort of cultivated a discriminating eye while remaining heart-whole and relatively uninvolved. During this time I made the acquaintance of many very fine young women, but somehow held a fairly even keel—until Hazel in her indescribable way tottered even my desire to hold a keel at all! The sun seemed to follow her about and a warmth and sweetness pervaded the scene where she happened to be. Little wonder that bachelorhood soon lost any charm it might have held heretofore, and so Hazel became a delightful part of my life.

The accompanying lines were penned along with many more in the period of our courtship and engagement—the latter a time during which Hazel waited the long years for me to finish college.

H-A-Z-E-L

H is for happiness
   That you brought unto me,
A is for always
   Together we would be,
Z is for zealous
   As my feelings impart,
E is for ever
   You'll dwell in my heart,
L is for love
   So tender, so fine,

So in total this makes you
   That sweetheart of mine!

T-E-N-N-E-S-S-E-E

Reading the daily geography lessons with those vivid pictures of places around the world has always been conducive to arousing daydreams in the heads of imaginative boys and girls. More than others, this old school text is essentially a window on a wide and fascinating world. The ring of faraway places like Timbuktu, Kamchatka, Sudan, Tasmania, Hawaii, Fiji, and others has always incited my curiosity on what these places are really like.

Even places closer to our own Ozark Mountains seemed to beckon in that late afternoon "time of books," giving rise to a strange sort of restlessness to a school-bound, fanciful youngster. Those pictures of a steaming locomotive pulling a long train through Cumberland Gap, views of the wild geography of the far-flung Rockies with snow-capped peaks, the romance of Harper's Ferry, the breath-taking beauty of the Blue Ridge Mountains, the great expanses of the Spanish Southwest—all registered their respective impressions, indelible and almost storybookish as never-never lands far away.

Many of the pioneer families that settled the Ozarks came from some of these faraway places—mostly Kentucky, Tennessee, Virginia, and other states along the Appalachian Mountain ranges. Their ancestry always held a fascination for me, and hearing old-timers talk about their past only served to stir my curiosity more. At one time back then I even had the fleeting ambition to spend some part of my lifetime in the Appalachia, perhaps teaching school and hopefully recapturing some of the romantic past with these good people and their descendants. This I felt would better enable me to understand the ways and philosophies of our own Missouri people.

Little did I know at the time that in the cards Fate was to deal me I would be spending most of my professional years in the Appalachian region, not as a school teacher, but as a mechanical engineer in heretofore undreamed-of exciting atomic and space age programs; living, driving and playing beside the still waters of the many scenic lakes impounded by the Tennessee Valley Authority in the wide sprawling valley between the ranges of the Smoky and Cumberland Mountains; that indeed my children all would be born here, would grow up, marry and make me a grandfather—all in the beautiful hills of East Tennessee!

T-E-N-N-E-S-S-E-E

T is for time and traditions
    that have blest this fair state;
E is for early in history
    that she first became great.
N is for noted and noble
    as her pioneers were;
N is for Nashville, the capital,
    of her cities so fair.
E is for eyesome endowments
    in her mountains and plains
S is for sixteenth in statehood
    in our Nation's fair gains.
S is for statesmen and service
    that have proved a mainstay;
E is for effort and eminence
    that lead forward each day;
E is for eons and ever
    we would keep her this way.

Unite all these letters
    in a vertical row,
Set them in the order
    as presented, and lo!
A state's name is spelled out
    that's delightful to know!

AMERICA, O LAND SO FAIR

Initially published in the anthology *The Spirit of the Free*, by the Haven Press, this poem was written during our Nation's engagement in World War II. It echoes the sentiment of patriotic men and women grateful for a land where people are not subjects of an autocratic overlord or dictator. For too long and in too many countries around the world people were subjugated, used and abused by kings and tyrants so oft intoxicated with their own power that nothing else mattered.

In America, however, the authors of our liberty were mindful of sad events prominent in history. They were aware of repeated conflicts through the centuries where the serfs with never a voice in shaping their destinies went to war at the whim of their lords. Wisely, therefore, they wrote into the basic law of our land that the will to go to war shall be the decision of the people who are to bear the arms of battle—this through their own kind elected and sitting at the helm of government. Indeed, this was a giant step toward freedom for those who never before enjoyed this privilege.

It goes without saying that the words which guaranteed free men these basic rights were wisely conceived and ably written in one of the greatest documents of all time—our beloved Constitution. Now, since history has a disturbing way of repeating itself, it behooves every one living under the Stars and Stripes to maintain a constant vigil to keep undefiled the principles so ably prescribed and presented us by our forebears lest we lose the greatest heritage in history of the ages. In preserving the freedom we cherish, it is imperative that every good American watch all forces without and within our land. Blindness and implicit trust regarding affairs in government have many times in the past cost people in other countries their sovereignty. For this reason we should never permit complacency and apathy to take the place of concerned alertness and vigilance. Patriotism shall never take second place to patronage and politics per se; human values shall never be prostituted for ill-won material gains; and the right of franchise shall never be neglected or compromised.

America! Let us keep her strong to perpetuate her as a land of free and informed people; unreproachable in ways of integrity; great in virtues of humility; yet proud in matters of honor and respect, here and around the world!

AMERICA, O LAND SO FAIR!

America, O land so fair,
No man but would your glories share,
  No heart but greets with quickened beats
  Your colors fair upon our streets
And sings your praises everywhere!

For all the world you bear the light
To shame the time's ill-gotten might,
  And while guns roar on distant shore
  We rally to your cause the more
And proud are we to own the right.

America, it's good to know
A land where cherished blessings flow,
  Where homes are free for you and me
  Enveloped in security
That naught shall dare to overthrow!

ACROSS THE BLUE PACIFIC

World War II brought out a slew of songs—as have all wars before. Some examples were: "Praise the Lord and Pass the Ammunition," "Don't Sit Under the Apple Tree With Anyone Else But Me," "White Cliffs of Dover," "Coming In on a Wing and a Prayer," and so on. It will never be known how many other lyrics and songs were written that also expressed wartime sentiment dear to the hearts of the American people, but that failed to catch the eye of the publishers. Not an exception among the World War II writings, the accompanying lyric came into being. Hopefully it is not overly presumptuous here to say that but for wedding the words with a catchy tune and a little luck, this might have been another wartime number to be listed with those above.

In the days of war tensions, partly for reason to pass the time and partly to contribute to the supply of essential materials needed by the men overseas, many of our deeply concerned young women spent their otherwise unattached days and nights working in defense plants across the land. Always they dreaded the news that might be forthcoming from the wake of each of our missions over enemy territory. And as too many remember, the news at times was heartrending, to say the least.

By no means were all our young men serving on starry wings, however, and by no means were they all over the Pacific, as the lyric here puts it. Nevertheless, the words express an anxiety that was ever present with many of our young women everywhere who waited out the years, the days, the hours while the men in their lives were away flying missions over treacherous territory, or were engaged in other duties equally noble and perilous. As expressed by the lyric, each mission could well have been the last—and many were! With each such flyer unquestionably was the heart and literally the "everything" of that girl at home. Also there were the love, concern and prayers of many others, and doubtless these helped to encourage and sustain both in those precarious days and nights that never seemed to end.

ACROSS THE BLUE PACIFIC

At home alone today
There's only part of me;
The rest is serving far away
The cause for victory.

Chorus:

Across the blue Pacific,
Somewhere on a starry wing
With a hero, brave, terrific,
Is my heart, my everything.
Across the blue Pacific
Soaring, diving, scoring,
O'er the islands and the sea;
Swinging, praying, winging,
On a mission for the free.
Across the blue Pacific,
Somewhere with Old Glory free
And a noble one in khaki
Is the living heart of me!

THE OLD GRIST MILL

Some years ago one of America's calendars displayed the beauty of a picturesque old grist mill. This picture had nationwide distribution and thus many enjoyed the rustic qualities of this relic of the past. Those of us who live near the Norris reservoir were rightly proud of this bit of impressive calendar art, for we daily enjoy a close relationship with this selfsame national landmark—the old Rice grist mill.

Relocated in the early thirties from its original site farther up the valley, then an area soon to be flooded by waters impounded by Norris Dam, the mill attracts and fascinates twentieth-century passers-by from near and far. With the preservation of the mill, a nostalgic link is here perpetuated with early days of Tennessee.

Nestling on Clear Creek branch in the verdant and hauntingly beautiful valley below the dam, this old landmark stands withdrawn and unpretentious in the shadow of lanky poplars and huge sycamores. Although it is visible from U.S. 441, the unwary passer-by might easily overlook it as it is all but secluded by natural growths in the area and the rising slopes of mountains, lofty yet round-shouldered by unrecorded ages of Nature's sunshine and rain.

The water from Clear Creek, a sequestered mountain stream, tumbles over the massive wooden wheel and makes it go its creaky rounds, then rejoins the footbridged stream to the Clinch River, which runs sparkling in the sun to merge with waters of the big Tennessee River some miles above Kingston.

The building itself stands gray and weathered from the many seasons it has resisted the elements since its initial construction in the eighteenth century. However, its state of preservation is remarkable in that nowhere has it lost its impressive appearance and the original fort-like sturdiness. Of course, it was necessary to make repairs from time to time, particularly to its moving parts, and doubtless its millstones have been replaced a number of times in the long years of service it rendered Tennessee folks down through the years.

THE OLD GRIST MILL

To every curious passer-by
It speaks with voice of ages gone,
And while the centuries live and die
Its splashing wheel keeps rolling on.

Though dispossessed of early site,
Still near the brink of Clinch it stands
To tie this day with former times,
Display the skills of other hands.

From up in Clear Creek's wooded vale
The crystal mountain waters flow
And course the sluiceway down the dale
To make the mighty mill wheel go.

Its creaky, rustic wooden gears,
While long in service wore quite thin,
Defying wear and tear of years,
Outlived the fondest dreams of men.

Its massive millstone, as of old,
Still turns its merry way around,
Receives the grain of white and gold
To yield a product finely ground.

So grateful we of current days
To have this landmark with us still,
To cherish ancient works and ways
That wrought for us this old grist mill!

MORNINGS

Each morning brings a start once more
  From failures of the day before;
A gift to all who'd doers be
  And want each day some progress see.

No mortal ever need despair,
  No bygone deeds his life impair,
For mornings come with things to do
  That lift our hearts and build anew.

We need to know each day we live
  Those fortunes that our mornings give;
To start afresh, to wipe away
  Those buffs we suffered yesterday.

When comes the close of morning's day
  We may in truth our deeds survey,
Then look with joy and heart that sings
  To what tomorrow's morning brings!

BUILDING A CHURCH

There comes a time in the lives of most men when the call to erect a new church building is in order, and this must be categorized as something special. It then becomes the honored privilege for the builders to participate in an undertaking not only with their fellows but also for and with their Lord, for it is written: "Except the Lord build the house, they labour in vain that build it. . . ."[1]

Since all men have God-given talents, it is only fitting that these be used in one way or another, and at every opportunity in life, to advance the cause of Christian brotherhood. Certainly providing a sanctuary for worship is helping in the inducement for men of faith to gather in the name of the Lord[2] for worship and perpetuation of good works in a world fraught with strife, turmoil and complexities. Moreover, it helps men to carry out for themselves and their followers an assignment that Jesus imputed to all men: ". . . ye shall be witnesses unto me . . . unto the uttermost part of the earth."[3]

Besides helping do hand excavation for a basement under a St. Charles (Missouri) Methodist Church, the erection of a new church building has loomed twice for me. The first, the Norris (Tennessee) Religious Fellowship Church, was largely a project in which the parishioners did most of the various facets of building, contracting only the few difficult things that men without proper equipment could not handle —for example, setting up and securing the huge arches.

The second such project, the Norris United Methodist Church (see illustration) involved us more in basic planning and follow-up: selecting the type of building, location and orientation on the lot, submitting preliminary sketches, studying the architect's proposals, following details of construction, and of course in helping with the financial end of the matter. Most of the actual construction for this building was let to contractors who performed the actual work.

Building a church, whether in the sweat of brow, or in helping to plan and following the project, is a religious diversity which has the commendable effect of bringing men together for a monumental task, one with the result of contributing something to leave the world a mite better than we found it—and that is a justification in itself!

---

[1]Psalm 127:1; [2]Matthew 18:20; [3]Acts 1:8.

BUILDING A CHURCH

Hope and purpose predicate
  Placement of each plank and board;
Undergirding love prevails
  In this labor for the Lord.
Every timber, every beam
  Consecrated, hallowed, blest,
Each a tribute long to stand
  For a faith that dared the test.

Diligence in sweat of brow,
  Brick by brick and stone by stone;
Humbly sharing, each for all,
  Builders with one thought alone.
Structure of all structures here
  Emerging slowly bay by bay;
Brain and brawn with joy and pride
  Raise the sections day by day.

Most of us are builders, though,
  Some of structures, some of men;
Time will judge and rate this work
  In accord with what it's been.
Greater gifts are never made
  Than of talent's willing hand
In pursuits that build in love
  Monuments to God and man.

As the arches rise above,
  As the steeple points on high,
Man is shown the lofty way
  Where his greatest fortunes lie.
And we builders, full aware,
  Know that though we build it well,
Church is folk in worship come—
  Here we fashion but a shell!

TOMORROW

Tomorrow was the day
  He vowed he would begin;
For one must be adroit
  The game of life to win.

Tomorrow he would start
  To make himself a name;
Tomorrow was his day
  But . . . tomorrow never came!

PITTER, PATTER, LITTLE FEET

The busy little feet of son Gary and daughter Anita Kay inspired this poem, and to them it was dedicated in its first appearance in print. Like busy little feet in homes everywhere, they were motivated by a seemingly inexhaustible source of energy that never ceased to elicit our amazement. But those versed in the behavioral patterns of children reassure us that this period of excessive activity is an essential and important part of child development, and this helps them grow into the fine young men and women all parents so much desire.

While tiny feet are pretty much on their own as regards going here, there and everywhere, there is ever present that paternal responsibility to see that they do not carry their curious, unwary owners into hazardous places, and even into tragedy as so often happens. These little people necessarily depend so much on their elders that young couples are often seriously challenged in their new role in parenthood. From ministering to baby's first daily needs through development of habits, attitudes, relationships, and countless other things, the parents' work is never finished. Parents, however, are not paragons of perfection, and they by no means are infallible. Their many deeds in love's labor are not altogether performed without mistakes, for unfortunately no one ever takes specific lessons in how to be a parent! Unwittingly they even cause some unpreferred characteristics to develop in their children. One such example is when parents cause lefthandedness in their children by how they place the infant's crib and how they orient the tiny one in it—the hand most convenient will first and consistently reach for and grasp the rattle, bottle, or teething ring!

So, one way or another they grow up. Then eventually comes the day when the tiny feet, having grown into an adulthood of their own, carry away the fine person that developed from the erstwhile toddler. But despite all this, those feet never really walk out of the hearts of those who loved and cherished them through their growing years—and neither does the long-ingrained feeling of responsibility and concern vanish when they go!

PITTER, PATTER, LITTLE FEET

Pitter, patter, little feet,
In and out the door all day;
With a happy rhythmic beat
They go the rounds of childhood play!

Pitter, patter, to and fro,
Busy feet so light and free—
Everywhere they seem to go,
And not a step but has to be!

Pitter, patter, here and yon,
Little feet, play on today
Lest tomorrow finds you gone
Where duty grants no time for play.

Pitter, patter, down the street—
Heartbeats follow where they go.
Bless them, Lord, and guide those feet
From all life's harm and grief and woe!

REWARDS OF SUFFERING

To a child pain seems so unnecessary, and even to many adults pain makes no real sense. Certainly the varying discomforts it brings can indeed take the joy out of almost anyone's day. In times past some people believed that pain is punishment for past moral or spiritual transgressions. While this may have some foundation in effect, few can reconcile a concept of punishment and pain in our enlightened day.

Despite its detested misery, however, we know that pain has a very real and important purpose, for it serves us in several ways, and all of them for the good. A persistence of pain, for example, is always an urgent reminder that something is wrong; when early pangs come they may be a benevolent warning to us at a time when corrective measures may still be made for whatever is amiss. Moreover, we accept pain as a most effective institution in safeguarding us from disastrous impairments which would early incapacitate us, as when we inadvertently come in contact with fire, hot surfaces, sharp objects, and so on. Here the instant warning it gives us is an indispensable asset in giving us opportunity for immediate correction.

Further, pain is an effective teacher. With it as an experience the effects of imprudent action are remembered much longer than volumes of verbal warnings. Only a cut finger, the stone bruise, the stubbed toe, or similar encounters with harsh realities of daily happenings can teach a child that pain may be a penalty of sorts for failing to exercise due caution.

Finally, although perhaps more a side effect, pain and suffering are indispensable factors which tend to make mankind more understanding, compassionate and humane. Pain, whether physical or mental, has softened and refined many an otherwise rough character. A traumatic experience tends to stop one in his wayward tracks, often with a jolting suddenness, and make him aware of important facets of his existence that would otherwise have never come to his attention.

We cannot hide the rough spots in life from a child—nor should we want to. Better to help him understand that they do exist and to teach him to avoid as many as possible. For, in the final analysis, like it or not, we must concede that pain is, always has been, and always will be, a purposeful part of our complex creation.

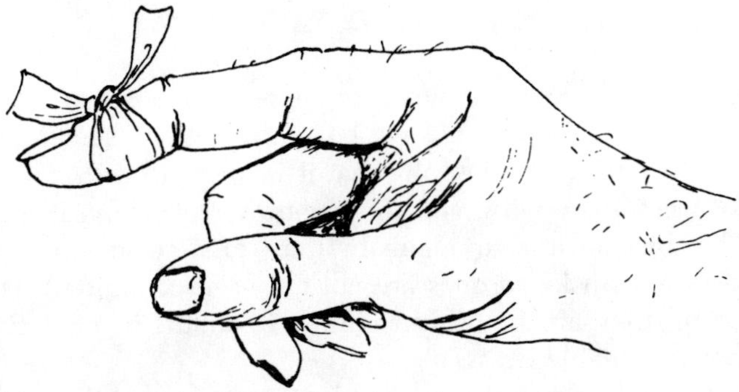

REWARDS OF SUFFERING

"What good is pain?" inquired the tot
  With quavering voice and tears aflow.
" 'Tis part of man's time-given lot
  And not too much for us to know.
But in my years," her mother said,
  "I've seen so much of strife and pain,
And while I much have heard and read,
  There's legion still I can't explain!

"One thing is sure, as all soon know
  There's purpose here in everything—
The guarding thorns on roses grow
  And depths of snow lush grasses bring.
The hurts that come in early years
  Leave wisdom when the pain is gone,
And doubtless spare us many tears
  From graver dangers later on.

"Thus suffering brings its strange reward
  In ways we scarcely understand;
The ordeals that we oft find hard
  May thrust to us a kindly hand—
For we would hardly love the sun
  If never storm clouds were to roll,
And surely sufferings, every one,
  Are touchstones that refine the soul!"

HAVE I PLAYED FAIR TODAY

This poem I would dedicate to those with a sense of misplaced values. Doubtless there will always be with us that element of people which subscribes to the philosophy that it is quite all right to take whatever one can get away with, and this regardless of whom it hurts in the process. This, of course, is an anomaly in a Christian society, for persons disloyal to their own loved ones are not only self-committed liars before God and man, they are foolishly trading off dollars in potential joy for pennies in questionable dross.

Somehow these people feel that happiness is something which falls into their laps as a magnanimous gift from benevolent gods somewhere on high, and they think it comes for free. Too late, alas, these hapless creatures learn that happiness is born of selflessness, and is nurtured by love, compassion and service. Few indeed ever learn that true happiness has to be earned and deserved, and that as a by-product it must always be interwoven with the happiness of others.

So the selfish spend their lives searching, but always wanting; chasing rainbows but never finding that pot of gold. While no one is above reproach in all his daily deeds, all nevertheless should know what is good—to borrow from Micah: . . . to do justly, to love mercy and to walk humbly with your God. And knowing, we can do much for the cause of happiness by striving our best to carry out the three stated tenets of Micah's.

The practice of selfish deeds leaves in its wake heartbreak, tears, disillusion, and death. One consolation is that in most cases there comes a day of reckoning for the perpetrator of the world's evils. Helping to solve the world's problems or personally being part of the problem is pretty much each individual's choice. However, when one shirks his share of responsibility, it means that his portion falls upon the shoulders of others, and so the shirker comes out a freeloader on society.

Forbidden fruits are always costly because they are bought with coins of self-respect, trust and integrity. Those who partake of them must count the cost, for no one ever escapes that. The cost can be paid for immediately at time of the transaction, at intervals on the installment plan, or may be deferred for a lump sum settlement in later life. But it is always safe to say that forbidden fruit is never free!

HAVE I PLAYED FAIR TODAY

Have I played fair today
  With those who trust in me,
Or did I go some lowly way
  I would not have them see?
Did I seek ways to shield
  Temptation's realm of vice,
And in a moment's weakness yield
  To something not so nice?

Because I was away
  Where mine would never know,
Did evil lead my steps astray
  Where fruits forbidden grow?
And when I come at eve
  To trusting love's embrace
Do I have reason to deceive
  Or feign an honest face?

Yes, strength to do the right
  Is valor's foremost guard,
For every deed is in the sight
  Of Him who grants reward;
And, oh, the peace of mind
  At close of this good day
To search an honest heart and find
  That I've played fair today!

ON PARTING

The vicissitudes of life are fraught with a more or less constant leave-taking of friends and loved ones, for people are ever coming and going through the portals of our day. Disappointment, sadness, and the need for readjustment all come in the wake of the departures of those with whom we have lived, loved, worked and played. Having become accustomed to the ways and character of our fellows, we sense a degree of stability in their presence, and naturally feel a loss when changes in the status quo have to take place.

In the process of associating day in and day out through the years with those around us, warm friendships and close ties tend to develop. However, nothing stays constant for any great length of time. Accordingly, we find ourselves seeing go what often seems a very part of us. Some of the virtues and traits of the leaving individual—the qualities and contributions upon which we had learned to depend, understandably unbalance our state of equilibrium when they go.

It is said that no man is an island unto himself, and we can understand this, for we know that by nature people are gregarious. This must have been the intention of the Master; otherwise he might have stopped with Adam in the business of creation. He gave us hands to clasp those of our neighbors—not to thrust them away. He gave us hearts big enough to encompass a goodly circle of those about us, to include them and to share with them in the fortunes and failings we encounter from day to day. We, with the presence, the love, and the encouragement of our fellows can weather losses and reverses more easily than when we go it alone; with them we can bridge seemingly impossible chasms and do this with grace, self-composure, and even with some to spare!

Some by their deeds, their ways and their nature, tend to impart to us the importance of human association. Each nonetheless makes his own contribution to those around him, and they to him. Even our adversaries make their contributions to us however unwelcome they may seem at the time they are given. Whether consciously or not, we eventually add all these contributions, the good and the bad, the pleasant and those otherwise, into the sum total of our being, and to a large degree we are what we are because of those about us.

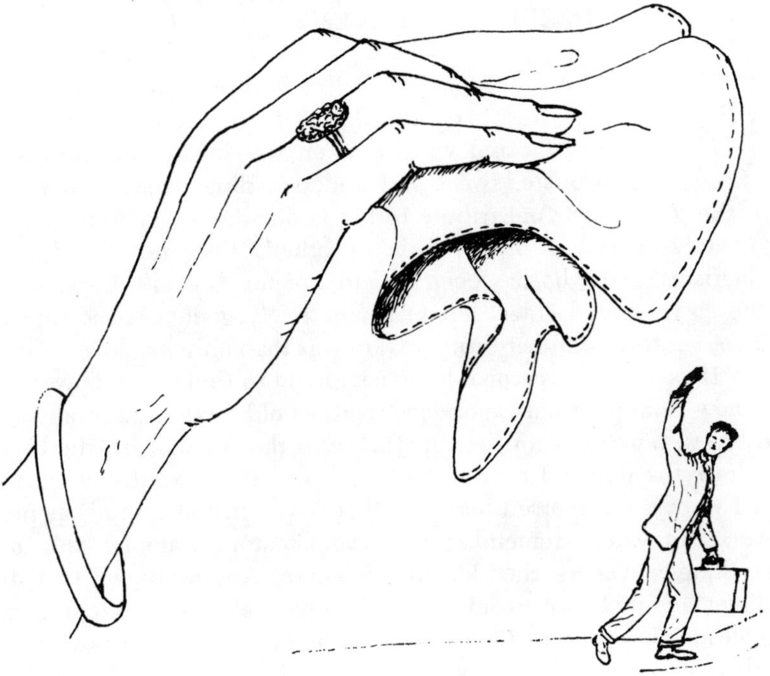

ON PARTING

Comes the time when we must part,
  Each to go a separate way,
We cannot help but own the thought
  That all must losc this parting day;
For life is not a one-way thing
  But a store of give-and-take,
And how we use this interchange
  Will in the balance make or break.

Each person is a living well
  From which sustaining values flow.
These nurture passing fellow men
  In ways we often never know.
So let us shed a timely tear
  For the loss we feel today,
And trust that God will mend the rift
  To keep us strong along the way.

HAZEL, OR HEAVEN'S BOUQUET

This poem was written for, and dedicated to the memory of my wife Hazel, whom we lost in childbirth, together with son Dennis Charles.

Nothing that I could write now or ever could fully do justice to the fine, compassionate, sweet and understanding person she was. Perhaps the greatest virtual tribute to her is our daughter, Anita Kay, who fortunately inherited many of her mother's fine traits, features and mannerisms, and who has been a source of much comfort and joy to us in the ensuing void Hazel left in her untimely going. At the time Anita was not yet three and her brother Gary was then only six.

If people can reasonably be compared to things in a flower garden we know from personal experience there would be the run of all varieties and types, ranging from the superlative to the commonest, the bright to the drab, the graceful to the plain—and, yes, there would be even occasional weeds interspersed here and there. Also in the case of people, like flowers, we would remember that the Creator fashioned only *one* of everything—never another like it anywhere! And were we to gather a bouquet of such we would instinctively seek out the choicest, the brightest, the loveliest, the most nearly perfect for our purpose, with the result that such a selection would be a delight to every beholder, a joy in any scene.

Among the most comforting words spoken to me in the tragic hours of our loss were those of my nearest and dearest friend, the late Carl Green. He expressed it in this way: The Lord surely had greater need of Hazel and Dennis in another place in His infinite scheme of things, and so He took them away.

While the significance of all this and death itself necessarily evades the full understanding of mortal man, we somehow feel secure in the thought that some day all the answers to our present mysteries will be revealed to us. Meanwhile, the Lord's need to which Carl alluded might well have been a bouquet in heaven; and being that He created only one each of our two, no others could in any way have filled their places.

HAZEL, OR HEAVEN'S BOUQUET

She embraced the sunshine in her smile,
  The gentle breezes in her ways,
And in her voice the merry notes
  That swell the songbirds' roundelays.
The twinkling stars were in her eyes,
  Where dwelt a bit of heaven's blue,
And rays of love and tenderness
  Were ever softly shining through.

She, a flower the Master plucked away
  While yet in springtime of her years,
And took with her a bud so fair
  To grace the realm of other spheres.
Throughout this world the rarest blooms
  Are seldom ever found with ease—
So heaven's finest sweet bouquets
  Are surely made of such as these!

THE WEIGHT OF TEARS

While most of us are quite ready to admit that death is part of the process of life, few indeed are really ever prepared to accept the presence of the grim reaper in our midst. The passing of a loved one, even one who has attained a ripe old age after a well-rounded life, brings us face to face with that dreaded sense of irreparable loss. More so when parting with a person still in early life; here the loss can be utterly devastating.

Until we know more about the mystery of death we shall harbor reservations regarding any virtues it may hold. Relatively few of us are imbued with a faith sufficient to venture an exchange of the known for the unknown. On the subject one old-timer said: "Heaven may be nice, but I am better acquainted here!" Largely because we are creatures of habit we become accustomed to a world alive with the presence of those about us, and so are never willing to reorder our lives to encompass the giving up one near and dear to us. The envisioned road ahead following a bereavement looms drab and forbidding, and we are crushed.

Death in its method, grim and certain,
  Never fails to be unkind—
A portion to the victim,
  More to those it leaves behind!

In words of condolence the late Dr. Martin Hart expressed a personal observation which can have signficance only to the initiated, and I have pondered this truth many times afterward. In substance he said that when death brings our sphere to a stop, we through our tears of hopelessness and despair are pained even more to note that the apparently unfeeling world moves along as before; that while things for us are suddenly so different, for most others nothing has really changed!

Those well-meaning individuals who come with compassion and words of consolation can help smooth the immediate way to a degree, and we are appreciative even in the numbness of those hours, but as those who "too the crepe of death have worn" can testify, it is time, and time alone, that can mitigate the pangs of sorrow and permit eventually some sort of viable rehabilitation for the mourner.

THE WEIGHT OF TEARS

When sorrow comes, as sorrow will,
  My heart goes out to those who mourn,
For none can weigh their tears as he
  Who too the crepe of death has worn.

Despite the breach in our life's way,
  The world keeps rolling right along;
So much, in fact, one cannot guess
  How much has really gone so wrong.

While grateful we for thoughtful deeds,
  For clasps of warmth from each in turn,
For gestures ever kindly made,
  For whispered words of deep concern,

Yet little can those near us know,
  And even less the public share
The anguish that is born of grief,
  The strain from throes of gross despair.

Without discounting those who come
  Consoling bent with heart in hand,
The greatest help comes nonetheless
  From those who know and understand.

BACK TO SHORE

This poem was inspired by one of the sermons of Rev. Ron Ingram, then pastor of the Norris (Tennessee) United Methodist Church. Most of Ron's sermons rate above average in my estimation, for they contain enough substance to impress one at time of delivery, and also to linger a goodly time afterward.

Occasionally the subject of a sermon strikes a particularly responsive chord in the heart and mind of the listener, usually when the subject relates personally to an experience past or current. In such instances the benefits in reassurance and encouragement may reach immeasurable proportions, and thus afford those on the brink of faltering a way to gain a new "grip on the willows."

Back to Shore in Ron's sermon (as in the poem) makes the point that with the right attitude, and a bit of resourcefulness, almost any harrowing experience can somehow be weathered. The spirit of mortals should be so indomitable as never to dignify the wiles of Fate by sinking passively with the ship; better always to seek the alternatives, for there are usually escape avenues left open for one to pursue when a crisis befalls him. Here, as always, Hope which ever encompasses the human spirit is our salvation in time of need, and so it serves as a guiding light for seeking out means to "take us back to shore."

No implication was made in the sermon nor in the poem that losses sustained are ever recovered when one survives a storm on life's sea, but what is true is that in the wake of the storm there invariably remains *something* to salvage for a new beginning—and for the potential of many sunny shores in days ahead notwithstanding.

BACK TO SHORE

When Paul a Roman prisoner was
  And shipwrecked on a stormy sea,
We're told the floundering men survived
  On floating bits of ship debris.

Upon the sea of life we, too,
  Are tossed about from day to day,
And when disaster wrecks our ship
  It leaves us each a castaway.

The fate that sets our course from there
  May still a trace of kindness show
By casting fragments of the wreck
  To shape somehow a way to go.

Then out of grief and dark despair
  May come a lease on life once more—
If we make use of what is left
  To take us safely back to shore.

IN MEMORIAM

Remembering is part of a healthy readjustment when we lose a loved one. Although the course we take may change completely from thence forward, we must never blot out the past, for it is a vital part of the present and the future. Even when a drastic change is not effected, a more or less serious adaptation is predicated nonetheless. Since we by nature tend to mold ourselves into fixed patterns, we become accustomed not only to ways that best suit our preference, but also to persons and things in our sphere of activity. Being human, we naturally resist changes which upset our mode of life and operation, and an abrupt change can be a traumatic experience in a very real sense.

Most of us, chiefly because of our love, responsibilities, obligations and commitments to others in our circle, must continue on despite the loss itself and the changes it necessarily wrought. Therefore, with or without heart, we are forced to carry on and do the best we can in this undertaking. Some do commendably well in this regard while others need personal help and much encouragement. Those who try to carry it alone are sure to be inviting serious problems in time under the strain brought on by keeping it all inside. Sharing our problems with others, and the passing of time are two indispensable factors in helping to keep our ship on course. Both can prove invaluable, but time alone is the greatest balm for easing the pains entailed in the transition—and lest we forget, time is always on our side!

Releasing that which tends to "stack up" is a safety measure for rational persons. Hiding our feelings and going into seclusion are both imprudent from the standpoint of preserving our well-being and discharging our responsibilities to others.

In Memoriam here, as are all other similar writings and published articles, is a heartfelt gesture indicating both remembering and sharing.

IN MEMORIAM

'Twas a year today you went away
　It broke our hearts to see you go;
'Twas all so wrong, the days so long,
　And every hour we've missed you so.

Along life's miles your pleasant smiles
　Had brought the rays of sunshine 'round.
How we rejoiced to hear your voice—
　So good to know its happy sound!

We're told the years will dry our tears
　Somehow the pain, too, will depart,
But this we'll stake: no time can take
　The love you left in every heart!

WE BLAZE A TRAIL

Heredity and environment both are credited with contributing to our traits and character, and in fact to the sum total of our being. A favorite subject for debate in my adolescent years sought to resolve which of the two is really the greater contributor to shaping the enigmatic Homo sapiens of our time. Like religion and politics, this was a matter never decided, but we somehow managed to go on living and developing our respective characters. To me, however, it always seemed logical to say that heredity gives us more or less the physical basis of our being, while environment principally dictates what we do with these basic assets.

Up to a point in our development we progress only as imitators. Some of us in fact never develop beyond this stage! As imitators we invariably seek to emulate a grownup near and dear to us—an admired friend or some popular figure in our community. But every person is profoundly affected, good or bad, by the society in which he lives and the associates who are more or less everyday contacts.

Man's action, precepts, attitude and many other inclinations are well established before his years of accountability, and once the pattern is set, it is very difficult to change him. Those who learn later that their's is not the preferred or accepted conduct often undergo great mental and emotional stresses in striving to reshape their ways.

In light of the foregoing, it follows that we, too, are being imitated, whether we are aware of it or not. Human behavior being what it is, we even in our unawareness are virtually helping to shape the lives of an undetermined number of our fellow beings. Depending on our own character, our conscience and our scruples, we are helping to build either good or bad, strong or weak, pleasant or unpleasant men and women. And since we can never be sure of the magnitude of our own influence, we are behooved, yes, even morally and ethically charged, to go the "straight and narrow" to the best of our abilities—lest we lead someone astray!

WE BLAZE A TRAIL

We blaze a trail for others
  By deeds we do each day,
And lest we go the narrow
  We lead someone astray.

Our tasks may all be lowly,
  Our stations quite unknown,
Yet some will make our actions
  A pattern for their own.

We make a way for youngsters
  Who ape our every deed;
And oft know not they follow,
  Nor even that we lead.

The words we speak so freely
  Though good or bad or so
Are all quite fit to utter
  By those who do not know.

Our tots should see those standards
  That shape their way to go;
Then if at length they stumble,
  We feel less cause for woe.

Our lives then should be spotless—
  A beacon on the way—
So men may trust and follow
  The trail we blaze today!

HEADLIGHTS INTO THE SNOWSTORM

Despite the hazards of winter driving, there comes with every snowstorm that awesome and complete transformation of the world about us. The drab, the gray, the ugly, all become scenes of grandeur by the magic touch of the soft white snow, and scenes of natural beauty are further embellished to a virtual wonderland!

For the youngsters and those given to winter sports, snow spells fun with a capital *F*. On the other hand, snow can be a disagreeable and untimely entity for those who must pursue an ongoing outdoor activity for a responsible necessity. At times under such circumstances we are caught off guard when we are ambushed, as it were, by an unannounced snowstorm. When this happens during a winter's night drive we suddenly become aware that this may change every plan and purpose. Concern grows about reaching the sought destination as the going gets progressively difficult, the landmarks become deceptive, the road ahead more obscured, and traction less and less positive. Many a traveler is compelled to compromise his most urgent schedules and take instead a fate-imposed holiday in the silent fascinating status of a snowbound world!

Everyone who has breasted the myriads of descending snow crystals in a winter night's drive has marveled at the sweeping paths taken by the flakes as they come out of the vast darkness ahead and above—a darkness deepened by the contrast of bright flakes in the light. Forward motion heightens the illusion that the snow is driven in direct opposition toward us in a manner not unlike to sheer defiance. The headlights show each flake, large, purposeful, determined and beautiful, pausing there seemingly for a trice and then plunging up and over in the wake of air movement set up by our vehicle moving in the night.

Driving through a snowstorm of grave intensity and undisclosed duration brings those mixed feelings of excitement and concern—and the former wanes in proportion as the latter grows. Always there prevails with impatient man, however, that element of determination to try for the originally-planned destination, and even in the face of calculated risk the drive continues with a dogged perseverance—an undefined faith that all will come out well, snow or not.

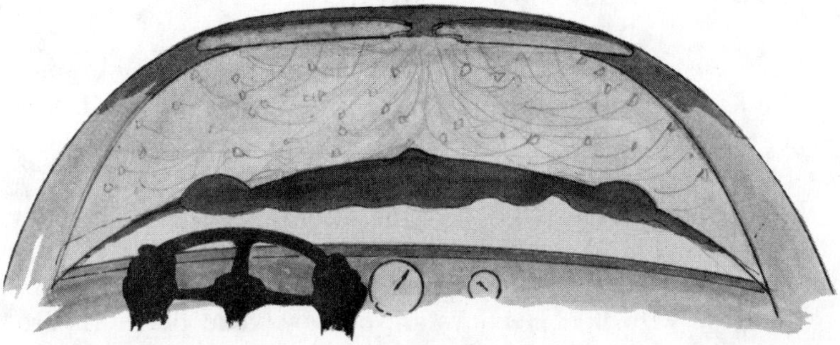

HEADLIGHTS INTO THE SNOWSTORM

Starbursts of crystals from the darkness
emanating from unseen chutes high before me,
dipping, darting, driving,
in wild descent from heaven's icy reaches;
sweeping, swirling, charging,
shooting up and over; diverging to right and left,
streaming past the windows,
the while muffling, hushing all the sounds of travel.

Splendor in blasts of silent fury
from out the shredded blackness
in relentless onslaught challenging all determined progress,
impacting hood and fenders in ceaseless barrage,
exploding on the windshield in sprays
of cryogenic embers, then falling spent, defeated,
to blend into the clinging ermine mantle
building softly, steadily on the cowling.

Then when the last mile is accomplished
and through a busy veil of descending
flakes in gray silhouette, loom and beckon at last
the warm and friendly lights of home!

MY REDHEAD

When we observe a little girl at play most of us see exemplified here all the beauty, femininity and charm of tiny womanhood. Her sweet innocence, trust, and warmth of affection make it readily understandable how she can so completely steal one's heart away.

When the little miss happens to be our own, we delight even more in her presence. We feel somehow that having her as she is must be a divine reward for some magnanimous deed in our past. As she grows, we grow with her. Her joys are our joys, and her hurts are our hurts even as much as they are hers. In the course of time we become aware that this fledgling of frills, ribbons and lace will eventually fly out of our nest, and that someone else will become predominant in her life. So when she goes, our hearts go with her, together with the hope and deep concern that the man who takes her for his own fully appreciates her and will henceforth and forevermore truly love, honor and cherish her.

Occasionally in a serious moment we may realize that the girl we married, too, was once a little girl who grew up with bright hopes and dreams of a life of ecstasy with her Prince Charming some day—that man who vows before God and man to honor and keep her even unto death. Thus we are brought face to face with the oft-forgotten realization that we are *that* Prince Charming in her life! And here we can do a bit of soul-searching, for whether we are aware of it or not, we are challenged daily on how well we perform in loving, honoring and cherishing this fair one who was once somebody's little girl. It would indeed be interesting to know how many could give themselves a top rating on this score!

The poem *My Redhead* is dedicated to my wife, Ethel, whose childhood pictures had much to do to inspire it—this together with the joy she has remained through the years to her parents, to her children, and to me.

MY REDHEAD

In her playing alone
  And with other little girls
The golden gleams of ensnared sunbeams
  Scintillated from her auburn curls.
And in those happy playtime rings
Her thoughts were then on childhood things—
Books and games, her doll—and not at all
  On where her future led.
In those years ago she could not know,
Nor would I have thought it so,
  That in some time ahead
At last for me she was to be
  My redhead!

Her delightful childhood days
  Were never mine to know,
Nor all the prayerful hopes and cares
  Of those who loved her so.
Yet in a way I entered there—
The unknown figure in their prayer.
For a worthy man who'd understand
  They to the Master pled.
Then the years in turn raised their concern,
But withal I could not learn
  Was theirs a joy, or dread,
When came the day to take away
  My redhead.

Since she well has shown
  That it's my life she'd help to live,
This girl, erstwhile somebody's child,
  Deserves what reassurance I can give.
I never want to take away
Her sunshine for a single day
Nor thwart her smile this second mile
  And prove she was misled.
For she at best, with time the test,
Will lose the roses in her crest,
  And white replace the red.
But come what will, she's ever still
  My redhead!

I'M GLAD I'M ME

"I'm glad I'm me," chirped tiny Barbara,
  Curls tumbling 'round her head,
And then embracing mom and daddy,
  She snuggled in her bed.

"I'm glad I'm me," thought two proud parents
  For this fine gift to them.
With gladness theirs, and cups o'erflowing
  They breathed their thanks to Him.

"I'm glad I'm me" speaks to the listener
  Of joys and peace inside;
A grateful heart for worlds of goodness—
  A mortal satisfied!

"I'm glad I'm me" is one confession
  That bears a tribute true—
"I'm glad I'm me" is also saying:
  "Because this gives me you!"

I TRUST THE LORD

A Sunday school class project can have significant and lasting results, much to the enrichment of all the participants. One such project which endured through the years was an effort made by the eighth grade class at the Norris (Tennessee) Religious Fellowship church to establish a foreign pen pal for each class member. The developments were interesting and exciting as we shared our writings and responses from time to time at those Sunday morning meetings. Pictures, too, were exchanged among the correspondents, some with comments on dress, styles and customs native to the respective countries. At least one member of the class is still continuing this correspondence with a pen pal in Australia. Daughter Barbara and her pal, Rose, exchanged events in their lives through the intervening years—grade school days, their years in high school, life on the college campus, graduation, employment, marriage, children and so on. What a delight this has been to these participants! And who knows but that there may come the opportunity one day for these correspondents to meet each other in person?

Another class project was the accompanying effort, the writing of a religious hymn. The lyric represents the input of the entire class and the music was written and arranged by Mrs. Lee Evans, our church organist (this at behest of the class music committee). Perhaps Mrs. Evans's co-operation with our class project was in part prompted by the fact that her twin daughters, Mary and Marcia, were members of our class at the time.

Regardless of what merit this musical composition might have now, or had then, it was nevertheless presented a number of times, and even at the Sunday morning services under the Rev. Ray Marcus Miller, pastor of the church.

Considerable water has gone over the dam since our days at Norris eighth grade Sunday school classes, but these youngsters and their teacher can still recount many happy events in those active years of our Sunday morning ministry. There is little doubt that these humble efforts added a measure of fulfillment to our mutual spiritual development.

I TRUST THE LORD

Norris, Tennessee Relig. Fellowship
Eighth Grade Sunday School Class

Lee Evans

FLEETING MAGNANIMITY

Our many churches, civic organizations, and philanthropists are to be commended for the many fine deeds of mercy they perform. Among their many worthy missions is the work of ministering to the unfortunates, and this is so gigantic a task that it will never be finished. Since the efforts in this field too often take on the appearance of exercises in futility, those who undertake responsibility in this area of concern must have stout hearts, unwavering determination, unlimited perseverance, and the patience of Job.

Many men and women consistently dedicate their lives to the cause of the needy, and many indeed have made notable contributions here. Those who did this in the past, like our benevolent contemporaries, sought no recognition for their efforts; neither sought they fame nor fortune. Despite this, all made history to some degree and their names are ever on the lips of those who follow in this work. When it comes to leaving footprints in the sands of time, what more commendable imprints are there than where one stoops to lift another?

Each evening may find more new problems descending upon the shoulders of the worker than he was able to dispatch during the day, but with the proper attitude the worker continues undiscouraged; for to him each deed, however tiny, is a move in the right direction. This is the type character which readily distinguishes the "men from the boys," to phrase it in terms of an old expression.

Because of the immensity of the problem, with so many areas constantly crying for help, we may be inclined to count our every effort a lost cause, as obviously did the character in the accompanying poem. But we know there is no honor in giving up in this regard, and certainly it is not demanded of any one of us to correct *all* wrongs, nor even to complete a single task; but to see where the needs are, and to minister unto them to the best of our abilities. Were it not so, our Lord would not have said: "For even as ye do it unto one of the least of these, ye do it unto me."[1]

[1]Matthew 25:40.

FLEETING MAGNANIMITY

He sprang upright, his eyes ablaze,
  And his arm swept o'er the land around.
"Had I the world, and my own way
  There'd only peace and love abound.
    Had I the wealth of a millionaire
    With goods and gold, and all to spare
No needy soul would live today,
  Nor a hungry, homeless child be found!

"Had I the strength of a million giants,"
  And he thrust his palm to the open sky—
"I'd lift the load of my fellow man
  So ne'er we'd hear a weary cry.
    No aching back with burdens bent,
    No wasted years with labor spent;
I'd lead the weak with a patient hand
  And falter not till the day I die!

"Had I the power . . ." and his voice trailed off—
  So much to do—too much to say,
A world with problems so befraught,
  O'erwhelming odds that bring dismay;
    And all his gifts so futile, small,
    He best not venture forth at all!
He slowly slumped to his shady spot
  And soon in passive slumber lay.

LIFE'S UNKNOWN GIFTS

Life is in itself a process of venturing into the unknown. Confrontations with events that come to pass day after day present undetermined situations to us, each with unpredictable consequences. This is true chiefly because we are individuals and each unique in his own way. Any one of these events may affect us greatly, not at all, or to some degree in between. One such event may pass virtually unnoticed by one person and yet drastically alter the life of another.

Were we given the wisdom instinctively to cope adequately and abundantly with the myriad situations we encounter along the way, we would always make the right decisions and life would be better than we know it now. Since we cannot be infinitely wise, however, we must take what comes, as it comes, and deal individually with each to the best of our own ability. But we can to some extent soften the impact of the rougher events likely to befall us by foreknowledge of them, this with a bit of briefing by one with experience on how best to proceed under the circumstances.

We try as best we can to ward off the blows that may endanger our progeny by imparting to them some of the lessons we learned through the years. We find our practice in doing this (often discounted as preaching) has a double value, one that offers something to both the receiver and the giver. The receiver may benefit from the learned ways of experience and thus circumvent the need to learn each lesson first-hand and anew, while the giver benefits from the satisfaction of responsibly relating to the unwary, and also a reward in the knowledge of being needed, wanted and respected in matters of vital importance. In this, youth will not be wasted on the young and experience on the old so long as a plateau of communication exists between the two. A free interchange can enrich both immeasurably.

Tiny hand posed by granddaughter Amy.

LIFE'S UNKNOWN GIFTS

"Please take my hand," spoke childhood gay
To white-haired wisdom's trusted ear,
"And tell me of life's devious way
You've seen unfolded year by year.
Life's path to me is strange and new
And 'round each turn great mysteries dwell;
Those scenes ahead, pray let me view
So when they come I'll know them well!"

A silent pause with thought beset
Enveloped fully age and youth;
Like travelers two on highroad met,
Each sought for light and hope and truth.
So tense, alert and eager one,
The other wistful, solemn, slow;
One fearful of life's tasks begun
The other sad to see them go.

"Here is my hand," then spoke the sage,
"For I so want and need you, too,
To lift the veil of drab old age
So I may share life's thrills anew.
My path is now so well behind
That all the new is somehow old
And mysteries that you daily find
Can never more to me unfold!"

So in a wrinkled eager clasp
Went childhood's tender, trusting hand;
Thus each from each could better grasp
How God the ways of life has planned—
That joys of seeking surely fade
When wisdom can no more bestow,
And oft life's richest gifts are made
In ways we never, never know.

IT WOULDN'T BE A BOY

No enthusiasm exceeds that of a growing boy once he undertakes a project—particularly when it is a project he dreamed up himself or with his buddies. Building forts and similar structures has been the pastime for many youngsters for generations, and this will continue as long as there are boys around. But of immediate importance is the fact that a busy boy is not only a good boy, but a happy one!

In my family, sons Gary, Jeff and Brian were the fort builders. I was the lucky philanthropist who supplied some of the construction materials and many of the tools—and experienced my share of "rusty saws and broken six-foot rules."

And fort building, too, is *character* building. Besides developing hand skills and the practical use of numbers in making measurements, there is the element of developing imagination in a wide variety of ways. So in the last analysis, any loss or damage sustained in tools and materials is grossly insignificant when compared to the many fine returns afforded by these boyhood projects. In my own case a number of latent capabilities were doubtless awakened by use of things in and about my father's shop. Through the years I have been grateful for having had the privilege, granted or assumed, to use the family tools and materials for my early projects. The least I could do in return was pass this privilege on to the succeeding generation of fort builders, together with my blessings and very best wishes!

IT WOULDN'T BE A BOY

It wouldn't be a boy
if he didn't build a fort,
Taking from your lumber scrap
the choicest long and short;
Using nails of every size
in pocketfuls galore
By driving one and bending three
then skipping back for more.

It wouldn't be a boy
if he didn't take your tools,
Leaving dull and rusty saws
and broken six-foot rules;
Carting off in hurried trips
most items from the rack,
Then when he's through, forgetting plumb
that he should bring them back.

It wouldn't be a boy
if he didn't win your heart
With enthusiasm from
his wide-eyed world apart—
Makes you mighty thankful for
a happy boy at play
And surely, dirty face and all,
you'd have him just that way!

THE DISCIPLES

Many of us use a memory crutch to help recall certain bits of information that have no logical continuity of their own. Experts in memory development programs are advocates of a system they call association. Remembering things by this method is easier by far, and will stay with us longer, than if we use only rote or abstract processes.

Every boy and girl who has had music lessons will never forget "Go Down And Eat Breakfast First" as the crutch indispensable for remembering the succession of sharp keys, and similarly, "Fat Boys Eat Apple Dumplings Greedily" for the flat keys. There are many others in music, and indeed in practically all fields, that simplify what might otherwise be difficult tasks. The first letters of the words in most such crutches give sufficient prompting to permit ready recall of the desired information.

In my own school days I resorted to crutches of my own fabrication to aid in readily mastering information such as the list of free states, slave states, historical facts, dates, and so on. Too, the more humurous and ridiculous the crutch sentences were, the more easily they were remembered.

Making up crutches still proved helpful, interesting and essential in my later years as teacher in grade school or worker in Sunday school classes. Finding that few persons could name the twelve disciples—either having never learned them or, because of no organized system, having since forgotten them—I offered a simple crutch for mastering this useful bit of Biblical knowledge, and an entire class could pass the test in a single session! With a suggested mental picture of being with the disciples at table breaking bread together, the statement went thusly: "Peter Accepted Juice. John Passed Bread To Me, Juice, Too. Some Juice!" Besides the names correctly used in the sentences, first letters of the filler words supplied the keys for remembering the others. In this way a tedious memory task turned out to be a fun thing.

Remembering that a little rhyme can serve a similar purpose: "Thirty days have September . . . ," I penned the accompanying little poem which also gives the names of the twelve disciples. This may never gain the popularity that did the poem for days in the months, but it may nevertheless prove useful to some determined students of our Christian heritage.

THE DISCIPLES

The names of twelve disciples
  Are easily learned, we see:
There's Peter, brother Andrew,
  And James the son of Zebedee;
His brother John, then Philip
  And Nat Bartholomew;
Dear Doubting Thomas, then Matthew
  That publican, the hated Jew.
Next James and trusty Thaddacus
  And Simon the Canaanite,
And lastly, Judas Iscariot,
  Dishonored traitor in the night!

A TOAST TO GERTIE

As the sometimes-dubbed "poet laureate" of the plant in which I have long worked in the engineering division with fine fellow-professionals and associates, it often devolved upon me to contribute a poem to the occasion of honoring a departing member of our group.

The turnover in employees of large corporations is often great, and there are many reasons for this. Some leave because of circumstances beyond their control, some to seek work more to their liking, some to continue their education, or to get married, and others in quest of greener pastures. Any such leave-taking imposes a change in the area where the departing one had made his or her contribution, and few indeed leave after lengthy company service without leaving a void in both the workday and the lives of those who stay and carry on.

Changes in the personnel circles, as elsewhere, may come with bruises or with balm, but in either event they tend to broaden us. The change can bruise us for a time when an associate terminates employment, and yet we invariably take the viewpoint that changes are not all bad, for sometimes they remove an offensive situation or bring new and exciting persons into our midst, and so it is doubtful that anyone would ever want to close the book on a world with changes.

Whether bright or baleful, the leave-takings we experienced through the years have centered around the great and the small, the dynamics and the duds. But it has always been a commendable custom to pause on these occasions for a few minutes over cake and coffee, and exchange words of appreciation and good will. Here is usually presented some token gift to accord the leaving one an expression of esteem—and this is where a personal poem may be included—framed sometimes and signed as a thoughtful parting gesture. These interludes in the day's work are mostly sparked with humor, and good-natured jibes are freely bandied back and forth. The poem, too, deals largely with the lighter episodes in the leave-taker's past—many of which result in a good deal of hilarity.

A Toast to Gertie is a sample representation of scores of such poems I have penned in nearly forty years in engineering. Gertie, by the way, with the violin one of her accomplishments, was a lovable secretary who left to seek her fortune in faraway Alaska.

A TOAST TO GERTIE

Here's to the gal with smiling eyes,
The object of our sad good-byes;
We'll squeeze her tight before she goes
To the land of auk and Eskimos.
We'll miss her grace and flowing charm,
We'll see her off with tidings warm
Then await her fate whene'er she writes
Or sends it code by northern lights.
This gal, we hope, takes lots of wraps,
For living's rough on the polar caps;
And all of Rockwood's warm advice
Is drink your scotch without the ice!

We all have yearned to chuck it all
And yield at last to adventure's call,
But Gertie's files and rubber stamps
Have given way to blubber lamps;
She'll trade that Ford and the old homestead
For late model dogs and a dashing sled.
And we hope her gun is primed for bear
That'll snoop around her igloo there!
May life be gay and lots of fun
In that land of seals and midnight sun;
May wine and music, joy and song
Make short those nights now six months long!

To Gertie fair we give our share
Of all Alaska's fortune rare;
And if she fiddles in a swank saloon
May grizzly miners rave and swoon.
Then may the notes of her fiddle strings
Fetch her a man with diamond rings,
Big black cigars and clothes so fine,
And lots of shares in a nugget mine!
Then when at last she makes it back,
She'll come in furs and a Cadillac,
Flashing tiaras in her lovely locks—
For we wish our best to Gertrude Fox!

JOE AND SCHMOE

This story, much in the vein of a fairy tale, was written for the eighth grade Sunday school class which I taught for a good many years at the Norris Religious Fellowship Church. It was presented successively to the class of new faces at the first meeting each fall, and helped to get us off to a good start.

Most persons are always ready for a fairy tale because this kind of narrative makes for easy listening, and permits one to escape briefly the world of hard realism ever about us. The presentation was a bit unusual, too, in that the story was introduced as one the class would never, never forget; and that kind of statement gets a lot of attention indeed. The point, of course—and this was brought out at the close of the session—was that each member present, like Joe and Schmoe, the characters in the story, is destined to make an important journey—in this case the journey of life itself. And while each is yet in the security of his father's castle he makes preparations, wisely or not, for this journey ahead. (Even at this very hour, we were reminded, an element of this preparation is going on.)

Just as a scout packs his duffle bag for a forthcoming hike, we select from the store of things about us those items we feel will serve us well on our important journey—leaving out those we consider of little consequence. Naturally this process predicates an abiding presence of wit and wisdom, and entails more than a passing gift of discernment, discrimination and long-range planning. The tragedy in our personal episode comes when we find too late that important essentials eluded our early recognition, and we consequently go forth ill-prepared. When the going gets rough we must make do with what we brought, and if that falls short of requirements, we have little choice but to leave our plight in the unpredictable hands of destiny.

A word to the wise is sufficient, they say, but unless someone assumes the responsibility to speak that timely word to the uninitiated, he may never hear it. Once away from the castle, it may be forever too late to recoup the failures of the past, and then going from thence forward may be unnecessarily rough for the rest of the journey!

JOE AND SCHMOE

Once upon a time in a faraway country there lived a king who was beset with a grave and distressing problem. King Alphus had ruled wisely for many years and because of his kindly and conscientious ways, the people in his kingdom honored and revered him as the most beloved ruler of all time.

However, since many years had passed under his reign, it was inevitable that soon his advancing age would render his continuing as king a matter of imprudence. Time was practically at hand when King Alphus would have to abdicate his throne in favor of a younger man. Under usual circumstances for a king with two sons, the succession is a rather uninvolved procedure—the throne simply passes to the eldest son and therefore there is nothing much to it.

Now King Alphus had two sons who were approaching adulthood, but herein lay the source of the king's grave and distressing problem. You see, the sons were born twins, and therefore both were rightfully and equally entitled to inherit the crown.

In his effort to deal in utmost fairness with his two sons, as he had always done with his subjects, King Alphus worried early and late over this problem. Many a long night he tossed and turned in sleeplessness as he wrestled for a solution. At length he was obliged to call in the wisest men in his court to counsel with him, and after numerous sessions a solution to the problem was proposed at last.

The plan that was adopted was worked out in great detail, and everyone felt it was about as impartial and fair a plan for the two princes as could be conceived. In brief, the plan called for a predetermined date on which a knight would plant two golden swords, bearing respectively the names of the two sons, on the peak of a high mountain located in a remote area in the kingdom. The two young men then would be given ample preparation time after which they would be required to travel on foot the entire way there and back to retrieve the swords. The prince who returned first with his sword, indicating superior competency, would win the crown.

Joe and Schmoe, the two young princes, were told of the plan. They listened intently and received the plan with a good deal of anticipation. Indeed, it promised to be a fitting enough challenge for a young king-to-be. Besides, on numerous occasions in past years they had frequented certain parts of this wild, rugged mountainous region in hunt of bobcats, antelope and wild boar.

For the first time in many months King Alphus enjoyed a blessed peace of mind. He was so greatly relieved now that at long last a fair solution, and one acceptable by his sons, had been forthcoming. He felt that not only would his people be assured a king from his own dynasty, but that by putting the two contenders for the crown to a meaningful test, his subjects would be given the more capable leader in the winner.

On the eve of the journey Joe and Schmoe were given whatever latitude they felt necessary to make preparations for the morrow. The entire palace was excited and a-bustle over the mission the two princes were about to undertake. Joe and Schmoe each had his own reaction to the task mapped out for him. Joe was generally noted for being a "worry-wart," but he valiantly defended his way of taking his method of preparation seriously—even when Schmoe chided him with packing in everything in his father's castle. Schmoe, on the other hand, was of a self-confident nature; he felt somehow that easy does everything. As a matter of fact, Schmoe could not bring himself to get any real packing started, the while Joe continued to put one thing after another into his duffle bag. There were his warm blanket, extra socks, his moose-skin pallet, flints for starting fires, quantities of dried fruits, meats, beans and bacon, as well as spices and condiments to make them all more palatable. Also he laid out in readiness his sword, hunting knife, sling shot, canteen, and his heavy hiking boots. Not until he felt that he had thought of everything useful for the journey did Joe retire. Schmoe in his positive state of mind felt that much of his requirements could be trusted to Fate. There were many ways, he reasoned, to supply his needs as time demanded them, and so he refused to worry about the journey. Accordingly, he made a few more parting quips at his brother Joe, and retired early for a good night's sleep.

The next morning at the stroke of six both young princes were up and about. Moreover, the entire court was astir, and multitudes were on hand to see the young men off. Joe fairly staggered under his load of provisions and supplies, and his heavy boots slowed his early progress tremendously. Schmoe, on the other hand, blithely skipped along in his light sandals and, unencumbered by any burdens, he got away to a leading start. At the last minute he had slipped some apples and nuts into his pocket, took a harp off the wall, and so he strummed a tune as he went. A troubled look flitted momentarily across his face as he reflected on the plodding ways of his burdened, overly-cautious brother Joe, for really the boys were quite fond of each other.

Most of the early part of the journey led along the well-beaten trails in a broad fertile valley. The going here was comparatively smooth and comfortable. Needless to say, Schmoe easily outdistanced his brother Joe and in fact, by the time the sun sank beyond the distant mountains, Joe had long since lost sight of his fleet-footed brother. As the way led into the foothills of the far-flung mountain range the going became progressively rough. Soon the traces of all visible trails disappeared, and from here on it meant picking one's way across a virtual wilderness. Once he reached this confrontation, Schmoe began to have certain misgivings—first as the sharp rocks began to cut through the thin soles of his sandals, later as the chill of the higher elevations bit through his light-weight jacket, and then as the berries and sparse vegetation began to fade out altogether along the way, he became aware of hunger pangs.

Joe struggled methodically along, making mile after mile only by dint of his innate determination and his well-planned preparations. When he reached the desolate region, and as darkness was enveloping him, he sought out a narrow cove-like formation in an overhanging cliff. Here he felt he would have natural protection from hostile beasts by the friendly walls on virtually three sides of him. In the opening in front of his cove he built a roaring fire with his trusty flint, and this would give him the protection he needed from this side. The fire served, too, in warming his beans, bacon and some of his other provisions, as well as roasting some chestnuts he had gathered along the way. After he had satisfied his hunger he busied himself in gathering leaves and soft evergreen branches for making a comfortable bed. With his pallet and warm blanket he soon had prepared a bed literally fit for a king. All the while he could hear the roar of the mountain lions and the savage howling of the wolves echoing across the hills and valleys, and often he caught the piercing gleam of eerie eyes staring out of the darkness some distance beyond his protective fire.

Day after day, night after night, Joe pitted his wits against the wilds, the predators, and the elements. After a fortnight he plodded wearily but triumphantly into the royal courtyard. A tumultuous acclaim greeted him as he produced from his now well-depleted duffle bag the golden sword bearing his name. This he proudly held high as the courtiers promptly held the coronation ceremony and acclaimed their new king.

After the hullabaloo and bustle subsided, Joe became more and more concerned over the fate of his brother Schmoe. He inquired of first one then of another on reports on his brother's whereabouts. All he saw was a negative shaking of heads, a searching exchange of unrevealing looks and a dispairing shrugging of shoulders. Thereupon the new young king ordered an immediate searching party to retrace the way to the remote mountain top, but even though the search continued for many days the efforts were without avail. Whatever fate befell his happy-go-lucky brother Schmoe was never learned, and to this day poor Schmoe has never been heard from again.

FORTUNES OF POVERTY

Riches teaches riches, and like a tigress preys,
While poverty treats of kindness in many subtle ways,
Yet both are like a snare to those in their domain—
The one will not release, the other strives in vain.

Riches, hard and heartless, with only drive for more;
Its gifts a baiting pittance from a vast and guarded store.
It plays a ruthless pattern in a solitary league
While gorging on misfortune, on bloodshed and intrigue.

Poverty, unhurried, heeding those who cry in need,
Teaches human values, all values true indeed!
So, nothing gives of nothing, but love envelopes all
And in a firmness that can scarcely see a fall.

Poverty has the blessings no other station knows,
For walking step in step, it with the Master goes;
With such rewards as may, few perils can there be,
And peace of mind is sure for all of poverty!

ARE YOU KIDDIN'

When I penned this lyric I could imagine hearing Bing Crosby, Perry Como, or Johnny Mathis crooning the words, and the airways virtually alive with something of my creation. Although the tune to which the words might have been set never really firmed itself in my mind, it too seemed to come through smooth and melodious in the easy, inimitable styles so characteristic of these renowned singers.

Early I began entertaining hopes that one day some accomplished composer would drift into my life and together our collaborative efforts would give the world a goodly number of hit songs—perhaps a poor man's version of Rodgers and Hammerstein—then with a widely known crooner on our team, how could we fail?

As always, those early notions were largely wishful thinking, spiced perhaps with a smattering of misplaced vanity. Nevertheless, they persisted for a number of years and then eventually gave way to more pertinent and matter-of-fact concerns brought on by the passage of time and the more pressing responsibilities of day-to-day living.

Despite all this, I still have not firmly barred the door against anyone with a head full of tunes and a sense of harmony seeking a partner who might supply the lyrics in the joint venture of creating songs to charm our workaday world.

ARE YOU KIDDIN'

When you look at me that way
As though you wanted me to stay,
Tell me, are you kiddin'?
Though your lips say I must go,
Yet your eyes keep saying "no"—
Makes me think you're only kiddin'
And you really want me so.
Sometimes you sigh as if you cared,
And then you act as though you didn't.
Tell me, dearest, what is wrong;
Darling, are you kiddin'?
Are there feelings deeply hidden,
Tender words somehow forbidden
That you long have yearned to say?
How my bounding heart unbidden
Turns around and goes to skiddin'
When you cling to me that way!
So tell me, are you kiddin'?

HOW MANY TEARS

The church is a bright and happy place, a veritable oasis in the literal wilderness of any busy and hectic community. There is something here for everyone, for it is a place of spiritual hope and assurance for both the firm and the faltering. Through its friendly doors pass people of every walk of life. In this variety there are the rich and the poor, the social and the reserved, the young and the old, the blithe and the burdened, those with smiles of radiant sunshine and those sober of countenance, those adorned in their Sunday best and those (reminiscent of sackcloth and ashes of old) staid in the reassurance that raiment makes no difference. All are children of the one great Father they come to worship, and under Him all are brothers and sisters in a far-reaching kingdom of love and concern.

Present in the pews then are persons with varying and distinctive needs and purpose. Some are here as a matter of habit, and others by pressing compulsions. Moreover, some are here to give and some to receive, some to serve and some to be served, some who see works of the church an opportunity and some who see it an ordeal. But all make up an exciting and complex congregation, and each has an express place in it!

Thus every comer sees the church in his own way, regarding it in the light of his own requirements in that hour. In this perhaps the greatest personal good comes to those who enter heavy laden and who seek a place for getting new perspective on the woes of humankind. Then depending on the effectiveness of the minister's message and the general attitude of fellow worshippers, they leave much as they came, or they go forth elated with a song in their hearts, and perhaps even inspired to serve as benefactors of their more unfortunate fellow creatures.

In any event, moments in the Lord's house afford us the opportunity for soul-searching—enabling us to come to grips with vexing situations, both ours and those of others. The poem here came to mind once as the varying needs of individuals in the congregation impressed me particularly, and it seemed most obvious that we all need the comfort and assurance that an abiding faith in a higher order can give; that all can be better for the challenge of exploring the unsearchable reaches of a magnanimous and understanding Creator.

HOW MANY TEARS

How many tears were shed by you
  O'er the hurt on the tiny knee,
O bright-eyed toddler in the pew
  Beside your mother across from me?
What was the thing you went to do,
  And did this injury have to be?

How many tears were shed, and when,
  By the man in the corner there,
The one who wears a carefree grin
  And seems to live without e'er a care?
How we would have him help us in
  The work we all as brothers share!

How many tears were shed in past
  By the lonely miss near by;
What is it makes her seem downcast,
  And hides her sun in a clouded sky?
Deeds of our love can't be surpassed
  That'd bring her joy if we but try!

How many tears has Jesus shed
  O'er the obstinate ways we see;
How many times hung He his head,
  And all because of the likes of me?
When will I heed the words He said
  And grow to what I ought to be?

So many tears there yet will flow
  Ere from trials our world is free;
We trust that love in time will show
  Those better courses that by decree
Smooth out the hurts we have to know
  And banish those that needless be!

FLUFFY

Fluffy was an adorable feline of well above average intelligence for her species—even when she was but a tiny fluff ball crying frantically outside our kitchen door. Her soft white coat with rich black splotches named and characterized her. The markings of her face were cast in a delightful symmetry that helped win the admiration of all who shared her presence, her friendly manner and magnetic personality.

Almost as if by preordination she came to us—with an unquestioned air of belonging to us alone, and wanting it so. She never exhibited the slightest doubt that our relationship was anything but mutual, so reassuring was her self-confidence and that conveyed understanding of our complete acceptance of her. Neither we, nor apparently she, felt that we were ever strangers, for with her she brought a warm unexplained feeling that our family and she were definitely meant for each other. And so it was all the days we were together!

She came, grew up, and tarried awhile in a household that grew with her. She gave so much so enthusiastically that we shall never know who contributed most in our relationship. Indeed, we felt that she overpaid her way with all those who gave to her, for what she gave back was something that cannot be bought anywhere at any price. In this we must count her playful antics and innocent clowning for hours on end, her smile and silent meow when spoken to, the exuberant purring when taken in arms, and those vigorous figure-eight love-strokes around our legs when we came together.

Then, while we had only seen and enjoyed a comparatively small part of her great bounty of gifts and goodness there to give, from a street tragedy she departed suddenly her life and her world of exciting and wondrous adventures. Despite the loss we still wanted her near us and so, shrouded in her favorite blanket, we interred her remains in the same soil she once adopted and gladdened with her dynamic being. Even the intervening years since that interment, though full and eventful they were, have never dimmed the tender memories of that vital feline presence in our household—and a lasting gratitude that she came our way.

FLUFFY

At dawn one chilly autumn morn
  Her frantic cries announced her there,
A fluffy handful, black and white,
  With full intent our home to share.

We could not know that fateful day
  In taking her from out the cold
For kindly efforts that we made
  She'd pay us back a thousandfold!

Somehow she knew that things worthwhile
  Are best attained with proper starts,
So forthwith she before we knew
  Beguiled her way into our hearts.

This gentle kitten grew and grew
  And beauty blessed her all the way;
'Twas sheer delight for young and old
  To watch her antics while at play.

Two years, alas, is all we had–
  The Good has never long to stay;
For as she crossed a thoroughfare
  Her precious life was snuffed away.

A cast-off kitten, hungry, cold,
  That came to give so much each day–
Our thanks to him, the heartless one
  Who knew not what he cast away!

LIONISM

Next to one's church I would rate a good civic organization—one with a dedication to humanitarian beneficence. Every community is a better place in which to live if it has one or more good groups of active, well-intentioned persons to provide the desirable extras here and there.

The benefits from affiliation with such organizations are twofold in effect: First, by direct association they afford the participants a mutual and meaningful opportunity for fellowship, friendship and fun. Secondly, the projects successfully completed contribute to the delight of those for whose use and purpose the projects were initiated.

High on my list of special organizations is Lions International, with legions of local clubs, and membership well exceeding the million mark. Moreover, it constitutes a brotherhood in practically all the free countries around the world, crossing easily and beautifully the geographic barriers and also those of race, color, nationality and creed.

Lions are on the scene actively serving unfortunates in such selfless efforts as sight conservation, health programs, sponsoring boys and girls activities, and many others. Their very presence in any town constitutes that image for good—a virtual memory-maker for growing youngsters who because of Lions will remember their town with a special fondness.

Under Lions International, with the motto "We Serve," men of good will are extending a helping hand around the earth to help lift their fellowmen wherever found to be in adversity, misfortune or distress. Schools and hospitals have been built in remote areas through these efforts; food and clothing are freely distributed where these needs exist; new ways of agriculture and discoveries in science and industry are proudly shared with the needy everywhere. Exchanging eye tissue for corneal transplants for bringing sight to the blind is even more meaningful and positive because of international affiliation. Small wonder it is said of Lions: "No man stands so tall as when he stoops to help a less fortunate brother!"

This poem appeared in *The Lion,* an around-the-world publication, and is now framed and hung in many Lions meeting places. It was inspired by firsthand association with fellow Lions in the club at Norris, Tennessee, where my more than twenty years of perfect attendance stands as its own testimonial.

LIONISM

Taking time to help another,
  Sharing part of every day,
Seeing men, each one a brother,
  Helping take his cares away.

Going to a troubled neighbor,
  Bringing courage with a smile,
Shirking neither love nor labor,
  Walking, yes, the second mile.

Understanding our young people,
  Making theirs an easier way;
Caring for the old and feeble,
  Bringing joy to close their day.

Serving proudly, keeping humble,
  Giving hope to all mankind;
Leading those who grope and stumble
  Bringing eyes to heal the blind.

Listening for the call of duty,
  Staying till each task is done,
Adding to the world of beauty
  In good fellowship and fun.

All these things and many others
  Cast their light on human scenes—
Living love for all our brothers,
  That's what Lionism means!

GRANDPARENTHOOD

Shakespeare is credited with having said that everyone is an actor and all the world is a stage. In a manner of speaking this is a statement so profound that few could dispute it. True it is indeed that each person fills many roles in the span of a lifetime. Some of the roles he acquires by choice, determination, decision and effort, while others devolve upon him as a function of time, circumstances and events—many well beyond his control.

Early we are infants, tots, children, brother, sister, male, female—all in a world that ever changes the parts we play. Most of these early roles are neither ours by choice nor effort, but they are nevertheless ours to fill. In due time we take on one activity after another, these in the ways of students, professionals, laborers, leaders, and many other such vocations and endeavors that distinguish us in specific roles from day to day, week to week, year to year.

Life's scene changes more or less abruptly when by choice or circumstance we take on a marital role; then again by choice or by circumstance follows the role of parenthood with its chapters of various associated characterizations. Simultaneously we play many parts on the stage of life—jolly uncles, favorite aunts, fat or skinny cousins, dedicated civic workers, do-gooders helping make the world better, or deadbeats adding to the burdens of society, and so on ad infinitum.

Then usually along at about middle age or soon afterward comes a new role for many of us—and this in a scene for which Fate alone selects the players. This is the crowning role of grandparenthood. With it comes the opportunity to relive many scenes now half forgotten from the time our own children were in these years. Now, however, with more experience, with wisdom gleaned from the years, and with less anxiety, we find we enjoy the grandchildren in a more relaxed and leisurely way, and certainly always with greater indulgence.

Some attribute this state of equanimity to the precept that years do mellow persons. If true, perhaps that is what makes grandparents so special—an attribute that firsthand I was never privileged to know, for mine all lived in lands across the sea. In this regard I am sure that I lost immeasurably for never having known them, but hope in turn to make up for the loss by playing the role of grandparent in the best way I can.

Pictured are grandchildren Amy, Bridget, William and Shannon.

GRANDPARENTHOOD

Events in turn that come to pass
  Are each a milestone in our years;
We welcome some with open arms,
  Yet some we dread and meet with fears.

So few indeed can we avoid,
  Though be they lowly or sublime,
And all bid fair to change our pace
  Within the daily march of time.

Each big event brings something new
  And something also takes away;
'Tis so decreed that we all make
  Adjustments ever day by day.

But in the case of one I know
  The bad is offset by the good;
When we consider precious ones
  That bring on our grandparenthood!

THE NONAGENARIAN

When we count our blessings, one in the main that should head the list is Providence's gift of a good mother, and even more so when she has been part of ones life for a great many eventful years. The subject nonagenarian, Anna Zimmermann Fuis, had long been an inspiration to us, and to her memory I dedicate these lines.

Born in the Swiss village of Vitznau in 1881 to parents of pure Swiss ancestry back to the legendary William Tell, she was second of the eventual six children, and must have been accorded her rightful share of importance. The mention of bells ringing harks back to the old custom that prevailed in many small European "burgs"—properly heralding the arrival of a newborn by prolonged ringing of the village bells.

Her father, she recalled, used to take the cog railroad train up the steep slopes in the foothills of the Rigi to a hostelry where he was employed as a chef. Life must have been exciting in the midst of the picturesque Swiss Alps and the time-honored Vier Waldstetter Sea, which afforded the travelers of her day direct water transportation among the Swiss towns and villages that clung to the lower slopes of the mountains and fringed the shores of the inland seas.

Apprenticed to a master seamstress in Paris, this Swiss miss early learned the fine art of dressmaking. Later she set sail from Le Havre for the shores of America to seek her fortune here. So she was destined never to see her native homeland or her family ever again, for her marriage and her family pre-empted any notion she might have had of eventually returning to the Alps of her childhood. However, Felix, the younger brother, later came to America, only subsequently to lose his life in a lumber mill accident in the state of Washington. At the age of ninety-two, mother had survived the last of her family.

Living her last thirty-five years in widowhood, she busied herself in keeping her own home, gardening, seeing her grandchildren grow up, and even in enjoying three great grandchildren in her four-generation family.

The poem was written while we still had mother with us, and at a time we dared to hope she would pass the century mark. But in this as in all earthly events 'tis not our will but that of the One who decides all things!

THE NONAGENARIAN

Swiss village bells were doubtless heard
  Full ninety years ago today–
A blessed, bright event occurred
  As mother first saw light of day.
The village folk these tidings voiced
  With glad events that morning brings,
And angels must have all rejoiced
  To bless her with the finer things.

A tiny girl with eyes of brown
  That brought the sun to one chalet
Soon won the hearts of her fair town
  And gladdened those who came her way.
The years in her initial sphere
  Gave her an azure inland sea
And crowned each early childhood year
  With Alps in all their majesty.

When blossomed into youth, we find
  Adventure's call and fate's reply
Had lovely jungfrau leave behind
  Her charming land of sea and sky.
First to the nation on the west,
  Then resolutely o'er the sea—
'Round half this planet led her quest,
  A girl so fair, so fancy free.

At midpoint in her newfound land
  Romance ensnared her youthful heart.
In time we joined this lady grand
  To claim of her a cherished part.
In lesser mountains here unveiled
  Time's episodes for scores of years;
Some dreams came true while others failed
  As weathered she her joys and tears.

And now the trail of years behind
  Attest a life of goodness spent;
To love of God and gestures kind
  Her admonitions all were bent.
For ninety years we're grateful, glad;
  For tender ways and tenets strong—
The Lord a purpose surely had
  To let us keep her for so long!

CIRCUMSTANCE HERO

The paper hero beats his drum
  So men his dubious halo see,
With ne'er a hint as plaudits come
  That his a windfall honor be.

He, neither good nor bad but so,
  Pursues a pattern year on year;
And reaps no prize, as laurels go,
  But, too, escapes the critic's spear.

And yet no mortal could surmise
  The key that undergirds his day
Is that no taker met his price—
  No real temptation came his way!

A real man's man is far the best
  Who proves true blue as tempered steel—
Though ever challenged, stands the test,
  Still holds his ship on even keel.

THE ATOMIC CITY

In the archives of our nation's history for centuries to come our descendents will read of phenomenal events in the twentieth century that changed the course of mankind in many ways. Ever since scientists discovered the basic structure of the elements of our creation, man contemplated the possible consequences of splitting the atom, and many dire predictions had been postulated. The first such accomplishment was virtually earth-shaking indeed, and the echoes of this event will resound throughout man's allotted eons in this universe.

The Manhattan Project in the early 1940's undertook the task of separating and collecting radioactive isotopes of uranium, and utilizing the vast resources of released energy of split atoms in a weapon to bring an end to the bloody war in the Pacific. In secrecy the project was pursued with its many workers not only unaware of what they were doing individually, but each guarded his own facet of the work with remarkable fidelity. A classical example: When asked what he was making at the mysterious plant in the hills of East Tennessee, a worker replied simply and dutifully: "About two dollars and fifty cents an hour!" Another noted answer was: "We make garters to hold up liquid stockings."[1]

The mystery cleared up for everyone when news came that an atomic bomb brought the war with Japan to a sudden termination, and that an unconditional surrender was under way. For her participation in the nuclear program the city of Oak Ridge became widely known as the Atomic City.

My work in the engineering division in the Oak Ridge Y-12 Plant for some thirty years has been most interesting and challenging. Association and collaboration with fellow engineers and scientists in a great many of the accomplishments related to atomic. naval, space, and other fields has been a rich and rewarding experience. Nothing being perfect, however, I felt that a noteworthy flaw in it all was the exclusion of our families from the environs of our work. Consequently no member of my family has seen my office, and perhaps because of this exclusion and the necessary secrecy of our work, none of my progeny seemed impressed enough to want to follow in the field of engineering.

---

[1]Because of wartime shortages many ladies painted their legs to simulate the various shades of silk hose.

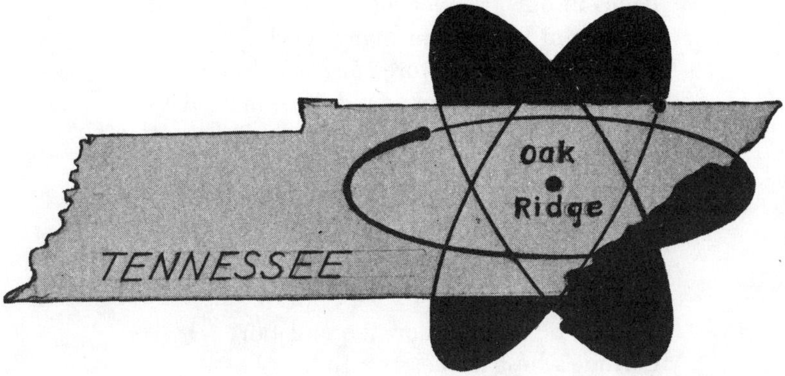

THE ATOMIC CITY

Born of war with mission peace
  Beneath the eagle and the shield,
Mushroomed as a growth of night
  She rose from woods and stubble field;
Responding first to freedom's must
And christened well in mud and dust,
So blandly named yet worldly famed,
  The fair atomic city.

Manned by folk of every race
  Who came from near and states afar
For a labor hushed and new
  To force a sudden end to war.
She smiled through tears that history's day
Then took her crown a modest way—
By Fate's decree it had to be
  The shy atomic city!

Pages in our archives all
   Acclaim her role in many ways,
And as time had favored her
   'Twas destined she would have more days—
For when dispatched a weighty task
'Tis only meet again to ask
That more she'd take in victory's wake
   The staid atomic city.

Through ensuing years we've seen
   The Master give her due and fair
Fortune's best in measure full,
   While she gave back her honored share.
In joy and pain she waxed and grew
To give of love and hope anew,
To show the way from day to day,
   This bright atomic city.

As new frontiers come and go
   She answers science's beck and call,
Spreads her hand to sea and space
   And gives her wondrous gain to all—
Her famous box for lunar rocks,
Her keys to Nature's guarded locks—
She's always there with much to spare,
   Our great atomic city!

Part IV

Ramblings and Reminiscences

BESIDE THE STILL WATERS

The accompanying poem initially came to mind for the title poem of this compilation, and for a time I even considered the alternate line in the Twenty-Third Psalm for a possible title. Although my younger years in the Ozarks were not so much associated with still waters as they were with green pastures, I somehow abandoned both as a book title, but as a final preference I still retained the poem title as it is here. Reasons for this latter decision were that I felt it would be more fitting as a dedication to the memory of Hazel and son Dennis, and also that most of the days of my adult years were lived in the proximity of the blue waters impounded by dams in the verdant Tennessee River valley. Daily, in commuting to and from work, our way led along one or more of these beautiful TVA lakes. So it was principally here that my years of work and play, joys and sorrows, advent of children and grandchildren, came and went. Despite even my irreparable losses, there still remains that blessing of having shared in those happy years that were, as well as those that followed with Ethel and our interesting and delightful progeny.

Too many of us too often have a tendency to expect only roses along the way when we know full well that there have to be occasional encounters with the thorns here and there. And in all this we need the serenity to put both in their proper perspective—to count our blessings and be grateful for the God-given favors, great and small. Could we but learn in early years never to expect too much of the best, then we would double our chances for happiness. We then would not be utterly devastated by the adversities that come, for we could take them in stride, but also we would be pleasantly surprised when there falls to our lot more of the good than we had bargained for or expected.

As we learn to see and recognize our blessings we show signs of spiritual maturity; as we cultivate gratitude for them we advance toward perfection; and as we share them with others we follow in the way the Master would have us go.

The illustration is a reproduction of the author's painting of beautiful Melton Hill Lake near Oak Ridge, Tennessee, with the Louisville & Nashville railroad bridge in the distance.

BESIDE THE STILL WATERS

Beside the still waters
  Along my life's way
The Lord has thrice blest me
  And gladdened my day.

For my every measure
  He gave me tenfold;
Has made me far richer
  Than he who has gold.

Now all that He asks me:
  Good steward to be,
And to share it with others
  As He shared it with me!

A BOY AGAIN

Who has not delighted in those rain-washed April mornings as each return of springtime presents them afresh to us? There is that undefined feeling of exhilaration these rare mornings always bring us when our hearts are tuned to receive them! Nothing man-made can begin to touch the charm and perfection of such an April day in its early hours, and few indeed can fully appreciate this recurring gift to our kind.

It is unfortunate that modern conditions of employment are such that they require so many of us to forego the joys of natural beauty in our daily surroundings. At best we enjoy but a brief glimpse of an April morn as we commute to our respective places of work. Then we may enter our windowless walls and close the door for the entire day on the grandeur of the world outside. Here we pursue unnatural tasks predicated in turn by requirements also artificially contrived. We do this in an artificial environment, under artificial lighting, in artificially conditioned air, and on man-made terra firma stacked many levels into the sky.

But foregoing the joys of April days, May days, June days, and all the rest, is the price we pay for the fruits of technological and industrial pursuits—the stepped-up productivity which sustains a world ever teeming with greater numbers of human beings. Without these and other sacrifices there would be no busy highways or droning airways, no atomic power, no Apollo and Viking missions to take man to the moon and elsewhere in space, and no aquanauts probing the mystic depths of the seas. Moreover, we wistfully acknowledge the fact that all our people could hardly exist in the confinement of one Garden of Eden, and so resignedly agree that whatever has come to pass is doubtless something that had to be. Yet we cannot help but ponder the question that while our industrial complex was developed to serve mankind, may it not be true that mankind now serves it instead?

Without wishing to disparage the benefits of the foregoing, I confess that the April mornings I knew as a country boy have never lost their charm. Their pleasant misty skies, enchanting green meadows, dripping forests of mornings, and laughing wayward mountain streams, all have remained treasures, priceless and undiminished, through the long industrial years that have since intervened.

A BOY AGAIN

When day breaks mild
  And spring birds call,
New blades are green
  By the garden wall,
And the morn is fresh
  From an April rain
Then at heart I am
  But a boy again!

When earth looks up
  From a slumber done
To stretch in the rays
  Of a morning sun,
And buds breathe sweet
  In a dewy lane
I go drifting off—
  Just a boy again!

When the water's fine
  At the swimming hole,
And the well-dressed lad
  Wears a fishing pole,
Then the busy world
  Seems dull and vain,
For I'm far away
  And a boy again!

DESTINY

Working with young people is always a rewarding experience. At any rate I have found this to be true in my own activities through the years. This opportunity presented itself to me first when a country school teacher, and later as a perennial Sunday school teacher of elementary school-age children, this not in the least to discount living, working and playing with our own five youngsters, each so much an individual, so uniquely motivated, so keenly bent on pursuits of his or her own choosing.

A deep and lasting belief that the Master has a definite plan for each person was long with me. Were it not so, I feel that He would not have created in humanity each only one of a kind, and this but once and never again! Moreover, I am convinced that this singleness strongly indicates *importance*. If the lowly sparrow figures so much that his fall is significant to its Maker in the vast scheme of things, then it makes sense that man, too, is each a significant being in the same creation.

Inherent in the make-up of each youngster is the drive to participate freely in the fortunes of life. These include in general the desire for pleasant and happy days, the abundance of food and other necessities for his sustenance and comfort, the privilege of engaging in interesting and exciting activities, and most importantly, the love and favor of the persons in his sphere.

By his very nature this drive compels him to seek and pursue those avenues which he believes best promise his finding and securing the above-named fortunes. However, this being a hit-or-miss pursuit, governed by the vagaries of opportunity and the random circumstances of fate, some do find the avenues best for them, and even find them early in life—and succeed phenomenally. Unfortunately others never seem to find them at all. Consequently, there are successes and failures to varying degrees, and necessarily every life is fraught with the determinants "if" and "what might have been."

The thoughts in the poem here have recurred to me on playgrounds and in past associations with children at work and play, together with the awareness that ours is an undeniable responsibility to help them as best we can to find those avenues which they ardently seek and which they must find if life is to serve them in the fullest measure.

DESTINY

The playground is a joyous place
  With happy childhood hard at play.
How sweet the sounds that echo far—
  They tend to take life's cares away!

A tag, a squeal, and laughter rings
  As scores of tiny flying feet
Go circling ever here and yon
  In bold advance or wild retreat.

The girls all bright with mirthful eyes
  And shouting boys so carefree, small,
Take life as is in measure full,
  The joys, the hurts, the buffs and all.

And as they scream and shout with glee
  In endless frolic to and fro,
I would that I could bless them each
  With all the best life can bestow.

But as I watch I know that, too,
  The eyes of Fate are full awake,
His scorebook poised with master sheets
  To chart the course that each will take.

And even now his finger picks
  From unsuspecting, gleeful tots
The ones to go four score and ten
  And those who draw the lesser lots;

The pairs who are to share life's way,
  The destined ones alone to go,
The bodies that shall early break,
  And those that are to bloom and glow;

The ones who'll live for labor lost,
  Or those to carry Fortune's name;
The ones whose deeds will go unsung,
  And those who'll grace the halls of fame.

For some the path will sunlit be,
  For others only clouds and rain,
And some will draw a bit of both,
  The heights of joy and depths of pain.

And while these children take the hours,
  Pursue their playing unaware,
How grateful we who cannot know
  The cross or crown that each will bear!

BIRTHDAYS

When birthdays come, as birthdays will,
They leave us farther on life's hill.
But nice it is this day alone
That's given each for all his own!

A milestone they along the way
So mark the past year's work and play;
And, too, a starting point, 'tis said
To go the stretch that's next ahead.

Our memories of these treasured days
Remain bright spots to last always;
They stand out first as days aglow—
The finest we each year will know.

And as we travel up the green
Our birthdays seem so far between;
We'd wish to speed time's ordered flight
To hasten on our next delight.

But when the summit we have passed
Time surely changes pace at last,
And per the laws our birthdays will
Come faster as we go downhill!

THE PUBLIC SALE

Everybody likes an auction! There is always an atmosphere of excitement as the onlookers and bidders crowd around the auctioneer and the many items arrayed at the scene. A sale bill posted at the village store, at a country crossroad, or in the local paper never fails to bring in a sizable gathering. For us public sales were ever a delight and, like most other sale-goers, we went to make a full day of it.

In former times on day of the sale the womenfolk "cooked up everything in the house," as an old-timer put it, and all in turn were invited in for coffee and a bite to eat. Then followed the hurried washing of dishes, tableware, pots and pans, so they could be brought out and sold. Selling the kitchen stove had to wait until it had cooled off enough to be carried out. Here the auctioneer in good humor reminded the crowd of the stove's culinary capabilities so recently tested, and the bidding was off to a rousing start.

In our Ozarks county the name of Tom Dulworth was practically synonymous with the word *auctioneer*. He as dean of the profession was sought by most folks selling out to cry their sales. We enjoyed the confidence with which he pursued his work, the humor he injected here and there, his customary lead-off shout preceding the flow of his chant, and his tapping the item of the moment with that buggy whip he always carried with him.

Children enjoy sales, too, but rather than in the sale itself, they usually are more interested in climbing into the seats of the farm implements or playing hide-and-seek in the house and outside among the pieces of furniture.

Yes, everybody likes an auction—well, almost everybody. We can't overlook a sometimes sober side of the picture, such as when an auction is held to close out settlement of an old estate. Here it signifies loss of fine old neighbors from the community where we long enjoyed them. The sight of familiar pieces of furniture, trinkets and household items here going under the finality of the auctioneer's hammer leaves one a bit wistful, for it means not only the moving along of material things, but of time and people with it. Thoughts on one such sale inspired the accompanying poem.

Despite everything, folks continue to like public sales, will keep going to them—and may we always have them!

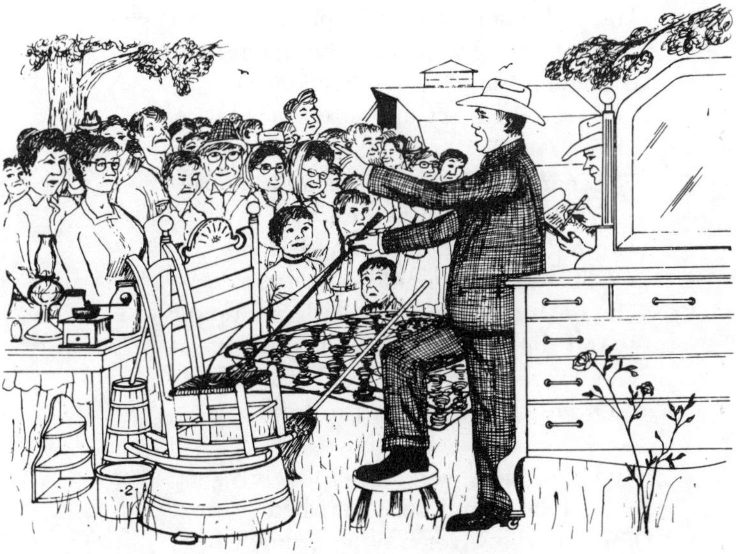

THE PUBLIC SALE

The lawn stood full of time-worn treasures
One delightful morn in May.
Endeared by years of love and service,
All were up for sale that day.
The crowd milled 'round the many items
Cluttered on the new-cut green;
The roses bloomed in gay profusion—
Lost in this unusual scene.

There was her precious bed of tulips
We had learned to step around.
It brought a fleeting twinge of sadness
Now to see them trodden down.
And nothing seemed a trifle sacred;
Things passed freely hand to hand.
From cold indifference it was obvious
Few their worth could understand.

There were the bureau, hutch and dressers,
Mirrors casting back perchance
The knavish youngster's playful grimace,
Or shy maiden's stolen glance.

The bedsteads bare with spring and mattress—
  Long they graced their bedroom floors.
It seemed but short of desecration
  To see them set up out-of-doors!

The many things on chests and tables—
  Frying pans and kettles, too;
The rolling pin, the pots and ladles,
  Chinaware, some old, some new.
The beater that made countless toppings,
  And the well-worn wooden churn;
The coffee mill whose stubborn handle
  Often seemed so hard to turn.

And, too, there were those priceless keepsakes
  That she loved and cherished so;
For one, the silver tray he brought her
  From that trip to Buffalo!
Machinery brought out in the barnyard,
  All arrayed and grouped to sell—
The plows and harrows, forge and anvil—
  All the tools he used so well.

"What am I bid? I hear the seven,
  Now, good man, just make it eight!"
The auctioneer kept up his chanting,
  "Going, gone—and you're too late!"
The bidders pushed and shoved and followed,
  Curious what was next to go;
The clerk stood by with pad and pencil
  So they'd bid and bidder know.

Then when the last load had departed,
  Empty stood the house and sad—
The voices stilled, its contents vanished
  With those many joys it had.
The roses bloomed on much as ever,
  But the scene a different stage,
For here was closed a life-long chapter,
  And time had turned another page!

GRANDSTAND HARRY

He stole his way in at the gate,
  He stood in front of those who paid,
He told the umpire what he was,
  The players how the game is played.

He bummed a smoke, he begged a light,
  And said he smoked a different brand;
Yelled out his tonsils at a run
  Then sat down on a neighbor's hand.

He trotted in, he trotted out–
  He had more chores than a cur has fleas;
He munched his peanuts big as life
  And threw the shells to the passing breeze.

He twirled a bunch of noisy keys
  And whistled at each passing dame–
You know the kind, you've seen the type,
  There's one at least at every game.

We somehow stood it all until
  A home run ball brought forth a cheer;
It flew into our section and–
  'Twas he who copped the souvenir!

THE ONE-ROOM COUNTRY SCHOOL

The one-room country school that molded the minds of so many of our contemporaries great and small is fast becoming a mere fact in recorded history, its ways now generally considered inefficient and outmoded. With its passing, however, goes a proud landmark, not to stress a goodly number of virtues in its comparatively simple methods of learning.

Good educators today, as in the past, know students grasp the principles of new subjects readily when they are first properly introduced. In the old school, hearing subjects recited years ahead constituted this introduction in a very positive way, making young minds easily receptive to one subject after another when at length the time came for these to be personal assignments. Moreover, hearing over and over again these subjects reviewed in past grades served to fix indelibly these basics in mind for all the years to come. So it was that parsing nouns, conjugating verbs, reducing fractions, and many more simply became second nature.

The old one-room school had a unique personality, as it were, simple but unmistakably beautiful and unforgettable. This carried forth both in "time of books" and on the playground where hard-played games taxed the efforts of pupils large and small, and usually all playing together. Games like Wolf over the Ridge, "Annie" Over, Steal Sticks, Red Line, Stink Base, Keep Away, and others were popular games in which all ages could participate with almost equal facility.

It was a proud occasion, too, for youngsters who had recently graduated to revisit the old school, usually sitting importantly in back with the bigger pupils, and later taking due prominence on the playground at time of recess. Huddling in whispering and giggling twos and threes, the older girls often made it a point to be noticed by the handsome visiting lads, even by such ominous warnings as: "Don't you bother us now—we have a handful of rocks!"

All in all, to have been a pupil in the old one-room school is to have been privileged in a proud old American tradition. Despite its currently recognized shortcomings in some ways, and without wanting to sound unprogressive, I for one am glad to have had the pleasant, unforgettable experience, first as a pupil and later as a teacher!

THE ONE-ROOM COUNTRY SCHOOL

Give me the one-room country school
   And the well-used school yard where we played,
The great old oak trees where we lunched
   In the friendly cool of noonday shade.

Give me the ear to hear the bell,
   With opening call to books and song;
The teamwork learned with others there
   And the friendship shared the whole day long.

Give me the hushed but busy room
   Where the kids in all grades studied hard;
The honor rolls and well-kept charts
   Where the ablest pupils daily starred.

Give me the battered, knife-scarred seats
   Where we gained the skills to read and write;
The recitation bench up front
   Where the tall and short came to recite.

Give me the call to take the chalk
   And pass in turn up to the board,
To diagram a sentence there,
   To extract a root, or write a word.

Give me the way of the one-room schools
   With their simple joys at work and play;
So well they made their cherished mark
   That the memories never fade away!

LILACS 'ROUND MY DOOR

Having grown up in a rural environment, I learned to appreciate the God-given little things around me—chiefly because there wasn't much else—and to value very highly the things men are often inclined to take for granted. What, after all, would our world really be like without the warming sun after a cold winter, the reawakening of the earth after months of dormancy, the jubilant warbling of the busy spring birds, the drone of the bees rejoicing in the profusion of blossoms in the orchards and gardens, and the delightful heavenly fragrance that pervades the great out-of-doors everywhere?

I shall always remember fondly a large lilac bush that stood near the kitchen door of my boyhood home back in the Missouri Ozarks. How bare indeed would have been that spot without it there! And as I have reflected many times through the years, I am glad that it was there, for I shall always count it one of the treasures of my childhood!

LILACS 'ROUND MY DOOR

Though winter finally goes away
  And takes her ice and snow,
The season's change is never sure
  While the chilly breezes blow;
But I can more than certain be
  That spring has come once more,
When the breath of morn is scented sweet
  From the lilacs 'round my door!

How good to throw the windows wide
  When sunny days arrive—
To drink in depth of Nature's gifts
  When the world has come alive!
What, when the friendly zephyrs come,
  Can complement them more
Than fragrance, rich and pure and fresh,
  From the lilacs 'round my door?

Though God meant man should take and use
  The best in his domain,
We know of those who hoard but chaff
  And never see the grain.
So many count their wealth in gold
  And yet I wish the more
To live in peace with little things
  And the lilacs 'round my door!

THE WHITE OAK TREE

Most of us remember a tree somewhere along life's way that stands out as the greatest. Perhaps it was the huge majestic old oak that no one could climb; that tree with a high limb where we tied the old rope and swung nearly "as high as the sky," or the tree that did nothing but just stand atop a hill where it had outgrown everything for miles around. All of us enjoy the comfortable shade beneath a great spreading tree. Here is a place where children in turn set up their playhouses, oldsters pause in their day of labor for a breath of fresh air, and animals seek the refreshing breezes that come here to play.

Most of us know more than one such impressionable tree, and regard them for their own unique characteristics. On our farm where a hilltop overlooks Halbrook hollow and the dry branch that meanders through it on its way to Gladden Valley, there stood several huge white oak trees whose beginning well antedated the time of white settlers coming to this part of the Ozarks. One of these seemed to be our favorite, for it impressed itself most favorably on our minds. There's no question but that it witnessed a lot of history in its time; saw tribes come and go in their periods of unrecorded history; saw both ends of a great many life cycles; and through sun and storm, war and peace, weathered the seasons with masterful dignity and perseverance.

When we are in the presence of a great old tree like this we cannot help but feel a reverence in its being. While we cannot communicate directly with this other living creature we can almost sense its life—and perhaps the thought that it knows our presence, too; that it is standing there virtually holding its breath lest it divulge something of the deep mystery it holds within. Of all the wonders about us, a majestic old tree can in no way be rated among the least of them.

THE WHITE OAK TREE

This landmark of our childhood haunts
  Stood proud and tall on Halbrooks hill—
And though I write from memory now
  The tree is said to be there still.
Old-timers shook their hoary heads
  When asked how long the white oak stood;
No span of memory 'round about
  Recalled its days of acornhood.

The red men doubtless saw it first
  When bison herds and deer ran free,
And heedless feet so oft perhaps
  Trod down this tender giant-to-be.
But Fate decreed that it should live
  To grow at last so wide and high,
And seasons like a steady stream
  In endless cycles passed it by.

How tall and steadfast stood it there
  Like cliffs beside a driven sea,
While time like breakers smote its bark
  And challenged hard its right to be!
Each passing year increased its spread
  And left its trunk more deeply scarred;
Its sturdy roots had grown so deep
  That all around they heaved the sward.

In wintry days when ice bore down
  And swirling snow piled white and deep,
The northland's wild and fiendish song
  But lulled it deeper in its sleep.
And on the sweltering afternoon
  Of every breathless summer day
Around its friendly mossy foot
  A pool of lazy shadows lay.

The march of time and passing scenes
  In long parade went past each day;
In buckskin, taw and nylon garb
  Gay fleeting childhood came to play.
Thus men went by, and passing, paused
  Beneath this tree with weal and woe—
It saw their toddling footsteps come
  And teetering sadly saw them go.

How long the white oak graced the scene
  Forever may remain unknown,
And how much holds the future still
  Is wisdom for the gods alone;
But doubtless we will long have gone
And others like us passed away
Before the Reaper cuts it down
  And once more turns it back to clay!

THE LULLABYE OF MOTHER'S

Childhood songs are each a treasure
In my golden treasure hall;
Joy they bring in fullest measure,
And I fondly cherish all.
But one dearer than all others
Is a lilting melody—
'Tis a lullabye of mother's
That she sang of old to me.

How I roamed to dreamland's wildwood
When those strains brought slumber nigh,
And it takes me still to childhood
Just to hear that lullabye!
Time may come and go but never
Will that medody depart,
For its drowsy notes forever
Will be living in my heart.

Every mortal holds so dearly
Things that bring him greatest joy—
Dreams of wealth, of fame, or merely
Memories of a simple toy;
Yet I doubt that much is giving
Quite the pleasure all along
As the happy thought of living
In the memory of a song.

SMOKE NOSTALGIA

Long before air pollution became a subject of environmental concern, occasional smatterings of smoke in open rural areas were accepted as a necessary and natural by-product of man's daily routines. The fragrant scent of wood smoke in the air was a common presence to all mountain folks, not only during the winter months when the chimneys of scattered rural homes each contributed their respective wisps and columns of pale blue smoke to the atmosphere around about, but perhaps more so in the early springtime when cleaning out fence rows, burning over wooded acreages for wild pasture grasses, and burning brush and treetops where the clearing of newground was under way.

Here it must be remembered that the smoke in our area was never the black, smudgy variety belched from huge stacks where coal-burning equipment is operative; nor was there the acrid, offensive effluvium which emanates from burning wastes in sanitary land fills. Quite to the contrary, ours was a remote and sheltered countryside, still unspoiled by the residue of modern industrial complexes. Oddly enough, the scent of smoke at times seemed even to add something strangely desirable to our surroundings as it diffused through the hills and valleys in our Ozarks region. Thus, gently pungent and aromatic, smoke was an element which remains a cherished memory to those who in former years experienced it, for certainly it takes its place with other intermingled happy associations in the scenes of a fondly remembered past.

And while we are on it, perhaps it was in part the associations we harbor that made it all what it is now—associations that encompassed the pleasant scent of distant wood fires, along with happy barefoot days in the hills, a bounty of nature's delightful disclosures from day to day, and all this cast in the frame of youthful exuberance!

Whatever it is, or was, once it's a part of our lives, the presence of a wisp of spicy smoke in the air can prod a lot of happy memories, recapture thoughts a long time tucked away, and stir the imagination of the most lethargic beings anywhere.

SMOKE NOSTALGIA

The smell of wood smoke in the air
  Makes that something in me sing;
Brings many happy memories back
  Of childhood in the spring–

Those lazy wisps that rise and drift
  O'er a rolling rural scene,
Diffused with scents of new-turned sod
  And trees in tender green.

A haze of incense, thin and blue,
  On the breath of early day
From newground clearing on the hill
  Or brush fires far away.

The scent of smoldering hickory
  From the smokehouse wafting by
To blend with blossom fragrance rare
  From apple orchards nigh!

All nature's ways are intertwined,
  Thus enhancing mortal's glee;
So smoke is part of rural spring,
  And memories, part of me!

THE ANCIENT ROAD

Few can walk an old abandoned road without becoming "involved" mentally in its history, and in the ways of the fine folk who once frequented its difficult course. Indeed the telltale marks still visible testify to long, slow processes of wear, erosion and repair—harking back to a period when, because of the lack of adequate equipment, earth-moving was an operation done only when absolutely necessary. So it was that the deep cuts and "carved slopes" came about in due process of daily use and years of relentless weathering.

Among the pioneer's early implements of transportation were his sledges and "boats" fashioned from widely-grown forked trees and floored with rough planking. These were drawn by oxen, horses or mules hooked to the stump end, where was drilled a hole for the pin that secured the dray chains.

Wagons, too, in all stages of refinement plied these trails, including the covered variety, hauling their precious cargos of families with their few belongings to new locations. Here love and laughter mingled with toil and tragedy in the simple ways of our predecessors. Poverty and prosperity moved in the same scenes as they passed along and as the years shaped the course of our young nation. Always present, though, was the promise of better tomorrows, of bright, exciting days ahead—and these ancient roads served somehow to blend the past and present with the future for those who went on to new lives in new places, as well as for those who stayed behind and cast their lot wherever they found themselves.

On these early trails, driven herds of cattle, hogs and sheep went their way to market. Then day by day came loads of hides, pelts and furs, grain, feed, flour and meal. The advent of railroads brought on loads of axe-hewn railroad ties chained to the running gears of weathered wagons bound for the town tie yards, and later came stave bolts and pulp wood for our hungry mills. Finally, adding a bit of color and variety, were the now-muddy, now-dusty mail hacks in that day, and the one-horse buggies of the portly drummer—the news-bearing traveling man in store-bought clothes, plying his trade from merchant to merchant, village to village. All these starred in the panorama, the growing pains in development of a mighty nation. And the roads of yesterday, such as they were, played a tremendous part in the process.

THE ANCIENT ROAD

I walked today an ancient road
  Where time and clime had long held sway,
And every step was sheer delight
  Along that trail of yesterday!

'Twas grown with grass and struggling trees,
  With frequent clumps of tangled vines,
And oft there was a barricade
  Where lay the trunks of fallen pines.

Yet intervening years had spared
  Mute signs of that illustrious day
When iron-rimmed hickory carved the slopes
  And plodding hoofs displaced the clay.

The marks of travel year on year
  Had worn away the soil and shale,
And rock was bared and grooved and scored
  By wagons long gone from the trail.

For fleeting moments time rolled back
  And I imagined sharing, too,
The grandeur of the virgin wilds
  When this old road was live and new.

In fancy I traversed the scene
  With folk who questioned not their fate,
But shaped their plans, the hopes and dreams
  That made our nation strong and great.

No more a road to span the miles—
  Now just a tie with bygone years,
This fading landmark helped me see
  How much our day was bought with tears.

And now the trail, though all but gone,
  Can still do much to ease our load—
For it can so refreshing be
  To walk along an ancient road!

POINT OF VIEW

Ol' Hank was a dandy, always there with advice;
He never could hush up for even a trice.
He wanted the world to hear what he said—
All others just simply had rocks in their head!
Whenever you spoke of things that you did
He always belittled with a much better bid,
For his was the mostest, the fairest, the best,
And always outshone the whole bloomin' rest!

When Hank's oldest gal fell in love with Pierre
Hank fussed and he grumbled over this sad affair.
He knew that as sure as he spoke out his mind
That Sue could do better—he was just not her kind.
But Sue was a ringer, had a head of her own,
Ignored her pop's ravin' till he left her alone.
They went to the preacher, shortcomin's or no
Where pertly she upped and married that joe.

Now Hank with a snort and a shake of the head
Was watchin' each day for a "See what I said!"
He knew 'twouldn't work, would show up real soon.
But Sue was determined to bust dad's balloon—
So Hank was a grandpa soon after a year
And all of his ravin's never made it quite clear
Just how from the worst of crummy inlaws
Could come a grandson, the finest there was!

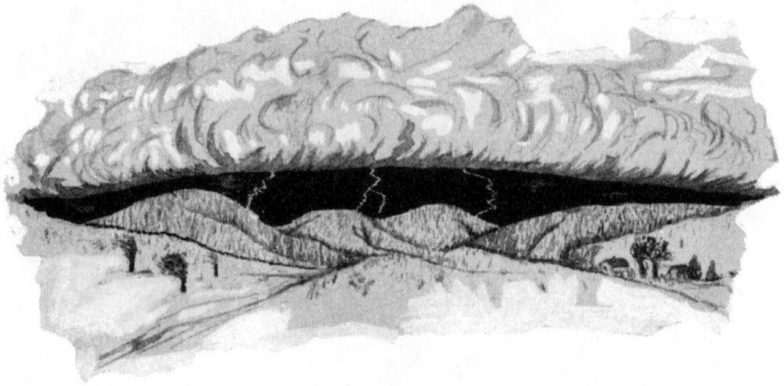

AND THE CREEKS ROSE

Who has not remembered with more or less wistful eye some devastating storm in his past? When the awesome approach of such a storm threatens the very souls of men, it is something that always remains vivid in memory—for neither the advent nor consequence of such a storm is ever pretty.

There are the storms that rage on with a fury, and from all appearances wreak premeditated mayhem in their wake. Often they break forth in dead of night, in which case the damage done is not fully assessed until daylight the next morning. Here on inspection we may find a lightning-splintered tree in the upper meadow, washouts in the fields and road crossings, or the beloved old walnut tree uprooted and down on the pasture fence. There, too, we may find a huge log lodged where a flooding creek left it in a most inconvenient place, sand and gravel beds in the meadow or cornfield, or find that at high-water stage the raging current had stripped out the water gates and taken them irretrievably down to the crest of the mighty Mississippi.

After such a nightmare we must pick up where the devastation left off, often writing off the season's crop or a heretofore valuable piece of bottom land, now cut through or buried in sand by the wily waters. We resignedly undertake a reconstruction which includes rebuilding the water gates to prevent undesired migrating of livestock, our own and that of others, reconstructing a now impassable road, or repairing a damaged fence across the lowground. Then, too, there is the ugly aftermath of brush, treetops, logs and debris thrown up here and there, the scene marred for months to come by leaves, vines and weeds wrapped partly around and clinging to every bruised, battered and leaning bush, tree and shrub that stood in the way of rampaging waters sweeping so ruthlessly down the valley.

AND THE CREEKS ROSE

In late one summer's afternoon
  To show how gods our fortunes hold,
From distant reaches of the west
  An angry front of nimbus rolled.
It came along with much ado,
  With proof how fires the heavens leap;
And all the while there sounded forth
  Foreboding rumblings, long and deep.

The advent of the storm in haste
  Made birds and beasts for shelter go,
As gusts of wild precursive winds
  Bent helpless treetops to and fro.
And then came torrents unrestrained,
  Of much concern to all around;
The gushing onslaught settled long
  In furious pelting roof and ground.

Full on into the night it held,
  The roar of water everywhere;
Too soon the creeks before us rose,
  And with them, too, our deepest care—
For in the valley corn was high
  With promise of a harvest good,
And in the meadows lush and fair
  A field of new-made hayshocks stood.

But flashing skies from hour to hour
  Showed creeks now rising out of bank.
The passing time full sapped our hopes
  As even best of spirits sank.
Then hearts indeed were heavy, sad,
  When under throes of deep dismay
We in the flashing lightning saw
  Our entire hay crop float away!

HOW TALL

Assessing one's own stature as a true Christian can be quite difficult. Too often we cannot be sufficiently objective in appraising our own values. Then, too, the bases on which we attempt to reckon these values are unfortunately beclouded by undefined inner thoughts and feelings.

Our respective roles in the broad spectrum of church activities do not always shed a clear light on the kind of Christian each really is individually, for two workers can labor side by side in identical tasks, yet each pursue his part with motives totally different. In fact, it is possible that one can lose himself so completely in church-related programs and yet never wet his feet in what the church itself is really all about. In these instances such commendable deeds as arranging a Sunday school outing, heading up a building committee, or directing a youth group can be either an honest act of labor for the Lord, or a well-disguised dodge from true Christian involvement—and there are all shades in between.

Most of us tend to do the things we feel are good. All know this is expected of us. But we also know it is better to do good for goodness' sake. Doing otherwise only serves to steady our ships on the sea of public opinion. Therefore, what we do and the extent to which we put our all into our labors of love help determine in the final analysis our true status as Christians—or whether we are merely engaging in a busy program of majoring in minors.

In the church, as elsewhere, we have every kind: the giver and the taker, the concerned and the indifferent, the strong and the weak, and so on. Here few indeed can properly categorize themselves—and much less others. We at times and in certain circumstances fit both categories of the foregoing, and this may be good. For had we only strength we'd never know the warmth of a helping hand; and had we only weakness we'd never experience the compassion of lifting up the fallen.

Were it possible for us to fully measure how tall we stand in a Christian way, I am sure it would afford us the priceless opportunity to live more meaningful, satisfying lives. However, this not being readily and simply accomplished, we at best can say there is always room for soul-searching, and what is perhaps of most importance: that each feel comfortable in the stature he believes he has attained.

HOW TALL

How tall do I as a Christian stand;
How much is mine a willing hand?
  Can I be strong when things go wrong,
And always try to understand?

In work and play do I do my part
Each day to take with a fresh new start?
  How quickly heal the hurts I feel
And how forgiving is my heart?

How tall am I in a Christian way
In how I feel and in things I say?
  Are things I do a witness true
And mine a life to show the way?

And is my height my height alone,
Each inch a man, every inch my own?
  Or do I try to tower high
On stolen tiers of others' stone?

Lord, better short than tall to seem
If height be but a baseless gleam.
  So give me ways throughout my days
That virtues true and souls redeem!

HOUSE OF YESTERDAY

Visiting an old abandoned house is generally fraught with curiosity, interest, and sometimes sentimentality. Whatever it was brought us to the site—berry picking, hunting, or just tramping in the hills—we are inclined to step inside and look around. Curiosity leads us room to room to see what is there, and to speculate on what has been. Expertly we see where the living room (which invariably doubled also for family room, bedroom, and whatever else had to be) with its fireplace hand-fashioned from slabs of native field stone; the kitchen where its telltale flue now is fallen into a pile of broken bricks, stone and mortar; the bedrooms with perchance the remains of a straw tick, its wooden pegs high on the walls which functioned as a clothes closet (without the enclosure, of course), and the crude ladder to the attic space which evidently served as sleeping quarters for some members of the family.

Everywhere one looks, pieces of the past can be put together. Evidence of painstaking efforts to make a prideful, serviceable and comfortable home are seen in metal-covered knotholes in the floor, clay-daubed chinks in the wall openings, flour-pasted paper covering on the walls, hand-planed boards that once made a work table in the kitchen, and so on and on.

If one is inclined to sentimentality, he might imagine life for a few fleeting moments with families of the past who shared mutually and much within these walls—the hearth around which young and old huddled in the blustery days of winter, the side yard where young folk gathered on summer nights for occasional play parties with games like "Drop the Handkerchief," "Last Couple Out," and many of the old singing games; the porch where young lovers blended heart and soul in courtship; and the lean-to where love and concern waited out long hours over a feverish child, where were born the progeny now grown and gone elsewhere, and where kind neighbors paid their last respects in a death watch, sitting in silence around the rough handmade coffin.

A home such as this, although in its last phase of existence, is not only what is left of some family's former abode, it is part of America's past—and, yes, also its *present,* for our todays are built on the foundation of many, many yesterdays!

HOUSE OF YESTERDAY

On a crooked road back in the mountains
  Where now saplings encroach on the way,
At a point overlooking the valley
  Sits a house at the end of its day.

In its gray weathered form of dejection
  It presents an emotional scene,
With its sagging and fallen-down porches
  And the moss on its shingles so green.

All the panes are long gone from the windows
  Where wild brambles grow rank through the sash
And some stones have come down from the chimney—
  Thanks to Time's inexorable lash!

Everywhere are the signs of mud daubers
  Here their crafts are both recent and old,
And the nest of a peewee is plastered
  O'er the mantel so many years cold.

From the newspapered walls in the lean-to
   Ragged remnants hang amber with time.
Many boards are quite thin at the threshold,
   Worn by feet of good folk in their prime.

Broken bits of blue glass in the corner
   Once a lamp with its glimmering ray,
Strewn about an old shoe so twisted
   Where abandoned and mouldering it lay.

In the back grow the weeds in profusion
   Where the fences succumbed to decay;
Here outbuildings are leaning and fallen
   And the cellar has given away.

Tread it softly while walking the premise,
   Lest we startle this home of the past;
It's remembering its love and its laughter,
   And we'd have those fond memories last!

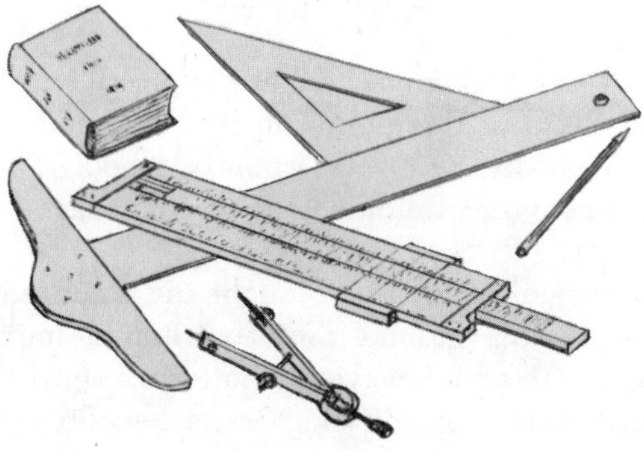

THE ENGINEER

The engineer, proud in humility, student of the laws
of creation,
A virtual gardener in the infinite fields of endeavor—
Directing and pursuing desired products of the elements.
Hand in hand with timeless fundamentals co-operating,
Working with patience and learned understanding,
Ever and constant in compliance with the immutable
mandates of the universe.

With vision his inspiration, service his motive, research,
reason, and mathematics his implements,
The engineer fellows with, and respects, the awesome forces
about him.
Never with a thought to change a single basic, even if he could,
Rather to harness, to cultivate, to augment and apply them.

His garden, a mere plot in the vast estate
of a Master Gardener—the eternal Engineer of it all—
He whose rules are firm, defined for timeless generations,
The exactor of common rigid requirements of all who would
labor in His boundless domain.

The engineer, even as a gardener, creates naught;
Given him is leave only to help, to direct, in a finite
measure a process that motivates and perpetuates
itself;
His license, a mere privilege to enter and labor in the Master's
Wondrous garden in a purposeful service for all mankind.

SCHOOL DAYS

The early years in grade school are impressive years indeed. Few experiences rival those of this period in life, and none stand out more vividly in after years. In the Ozarks country schools I knew and loved new and exciting activities unfolded for us each day—these along with some not so exciting.

While classroom exercises brought us knowledge in varying amounts, it was the playground that contributed importantly to the development of social and behavioral patterns. Unwittingly or otherwise, we in fact derived a goodly number of benefits from this facet of schooldays. The pleasant but invigorating exercise of jumping the rope, for example, doubled also as a foreteller of the very fortunes of the participants: "Rich man, poor man, beggarman, thief; doctor, lawyer, merchant, chief," chanted the helpful playmates rhythmically, swinging the rope, one at each end, for the persevering jumper. Then they pegged the time for the exciting future nuptials; "This year, next year, now, never . . . " and so on, including even the number of children that were to bless the happy marriage-to-be!

Heard also was a favorite ditty for choosing up sides:

"The needle's eye that doth reply,
The thread that runs so true,
Many a beau have I let go
Because I wanted you. . . ."

And here, as everywhere else, London bridge kept "falling down" regularly, as it had for centuries, and delightful as ever was the resounding collapse of it!

Surely the playground proved an ideal place for toughening tender feelings—for children can be affectionate and ruthless at the same time. In our days frankness often conspired with meanness when one pouted on the schoolyard. Many then joined in a chorus that bared the very soul of the pouter with a singsong chant that went: "Tommy's mad and I am glad, and I know what's to please him—a bottle of wine to make him shine and Susie Smith to squeeze him." This either salted further the wounds of the hapless subject or instantly healed his hurt when a grin broke through his tears.

Is it a wonder that school days take on so much importance? Or that they constitute, as the famous lyric put it, "dear old golden rule days" for men and women ever afterwards?

SCHOOL DAYS

School days mark a time in life
  Between the years of six and ten
That defines the worth of books
  And shapes the basic ways of men.

School days well afford us all
  A means of learning work and play,
Vying with the world in teams
  And coping with new tasks each day.

Much of what we grow to be
  We learn through ways of give-and-take;
In the conduct of these days
  We set the stage for future's stake.

All the while the world awaits
  The day, the hour when comes our turn
To rise and take the pilot wheel,
  Our marks for history's page to earn.

THE OLD WOODYARD

Strange it is how places in days of our childhood that held no particular significance then, and yet when remembered years later, seem to come alive with volumes of importance! Actually, the old woodyard was a place where much effort had to be expended in cutting and splitting wood for the kitchen range, and more so in wintry days when the heating stove or the fireplace, or both, also had to be supplied. Any virtues it might have held were certainly taken for granted by those of us who frequented this spot many times daily. However, climbing on the woodpile, stacking the cut sticks into fort walls, hiding behind the ricks in games like hide-and-seek, and cracking walnuts on the chopping block, all contributed a more pleasant side of the picture for us in our growing years.

Many years' accumulation of decaying sawdust, chips and bark (the latter two in bits too small to gather into the chip basket) added fertility to an otherwise hopeless and rocky soil so that rank growths of ragweed, fennel, burdock, lamb's-quarters and hollyhocks threatened to take over the entire plot.

At times the cows gathered at the woodyard, for here usually was the salting place, and often this spot served also as a milking lot. At such times the farm cats would perch atop the woodpile, watching the proceedings intently, hopeful of a taste of fresh milk squirted in their direction by a kindly and understanding milker.

Though it perhaps was lacking in glamor, one cannot deny that the old farm woodyard was a very busy place. Many of the functions of daily living had ties with this unsung part of the farmstead, and the years have only served to enhance such importance as it might have had.

THE OLD WOODYARD

The old home place had many spots
That linger on in memory—
The woodyard near the garden gate
Was one that long delighted me.

It was a pleasant, busy place
Where childhood chores played quite a part,
At first in bringing kindling in,
Then tugging at the old wood cart.

Here was the ring of axe and maul
A most familiar sound each day;
The bucksaw graced the old sawhorse,
And all around the wood chips lay.

Bull nettles grew through wood scrap there,
Dog fennel fringed the chopping blocks,
And morning-glory climbed the fence
Where stood the stately hollyhocks.

'Twas playground, too, for childhood games—
The logs and ricks were forts unique,
The woodpile was a mountain high,
And all were great for hide-and-seek.

In work and play the woodyard taught
Of life in ways we like to tell;
For warmth and joy, and tasty meals
The woodyard taught these lessons well!

THE WITNESS TREE

"What's a witness tree?" asks the modern youngster. And in present-day things it is understandable that a question such as this is well in order. Few indeed in recent times have ever seen one, or knew one to be a witness tree.

The witness tree held more importance in former years than it does today. It was well known to early surveyors, particularly when land parcels were staked out by metes and bounds rather than by the more modern grid method using ranges, sections, and townships. The odd, irregularly-shaped land plats were often defined by bordering creeks, winding ridge tops, cliffs, and other more or less natural landmarks. Since land "corners" were not always easily found after the original wooden stake rotted away, the surveyor recorded its location with respect to a prominent landmark near by, entering such information as: ". . . the corner lies twenty feet south and seventeen feet east of a large water oak tree standing in the sharp bend of Dry Fork branch. . . ." The same information was subsequently a recorded item in all documents pertaining to the description of this specific plot of ground, and also in the huge books in the county office of Recorder of Deeds.

Year after year, there unmindful of its special importance, the tree stood its ground—all its life "witnessing" the location of an important land boundary stake near by. So with the "corner" duly and permanently recorded, locations of lost stakes were readily found despite the total ravages of time and the process of decay. Eventually, however, even the witness tree becomes the victim of time, and then the stake location bids fair to be lost forever. To obviate this happening in past, successive owners drove new stakes from time to time, preferably the more permanent iron rods, at these corners. Also the surveyor often safeguarded the original stake site by placing a ring of stones close around the peg. Many a "lost" corner has been reidentified by this ring of weathered, half-buried rocks around a telltale hole in the ground.

Thus, in its time (and even to the present day) the witness tree played an important role in the place it happened to grow, as well as in the archives of land subdivision. Here in this poem we honor the witness tree and seek to perpetuate its place in the treasured pages of American history.

THE WITNESS TREE

Now gnarled and old and weathered
  Yet charged with much importance still;
Among its peers, throughout the years
  Held special honors on the hill—
Guarding long on valued grounds
The stake from ancient metes and bounds,
  A mission great to proudly fill.

Not strain nor kind, but circumstance
  Determined what none could foresee;
'Twas not its wood, but where it stood
  Ordained its noted role-to-be.
As skilled surveyors on the job
Laid stones around their driven stob,
  Commissioned they this witness tree.

Thus lofty purpose crowned its being
  And doubtless spared its very soul;
No axe nor saw now dared the law
  That held it for a higher goal.
Then sun nor blizzard, calm nor quake
Deterred its vigil o'er the stake
  Which gave it place on title's scroll.

In time it waxed so tall and stately,
  And witnessed much beyond its care;
A landmark true for old and new
  Served generations fine and fair.
No greater legend could we seek,
If had the forest words to speak,
  Than tales this witness tree could share!

HOME REMEDIES

Resourcefulness in all things makes for self-sufficiency. This does not imply that resourcefulness enables one to supply all needs, but it does include the capacity to make-do. When one has a choice between something and something, one might be considered fortunate; but when one must choose between something and nothing, then this calls for the finer kinds of ingenuity.

Nothing cultivates a sense of values as does coming by necessities the hard way. In this regard we must take off our hats to the men and women of a generation or two past, and to the remarkable resourcefulness they possessed. Unspoiled by the many modern conveniences, they banked on the simple, practical and effective means at hand, and did commendably well in their limited way.

Many of the medicines of America's past were the home remedies handed down from one generation to the next. Usually, it was not known what the chemical constituency of these concoctions was, or exactly how they wrought their curative wonders, but they worked most of the time, and that was good enough for all concerned.

Throughout my childhood and adolescent years the doctor was never required to visit us, for our simple ailments responded well to the standard home remedies. In more serious cases in past years neighbors ministered to the needs of one another, and this with no compensation ever thought about. Responding to the call of need was a service proudly and willingly given, and the privilege of being there to help on such occasions was more than ample reward for the effort.

Science and technology came into their own and advanced the state of the art in the world of medicine, and great indeed are the wonders they wrought. In due time the old methods were discounted and relegated to the realm of forgotten things. Now, however, medical science in some instances has been taking a second look at many of the old home remedies, and the worth of some of them has accordingly been re-evaluated. So the poem hereby is a tribute to our old-timers, and the phenomenal job they did with home remedies at a time when there was naught else.

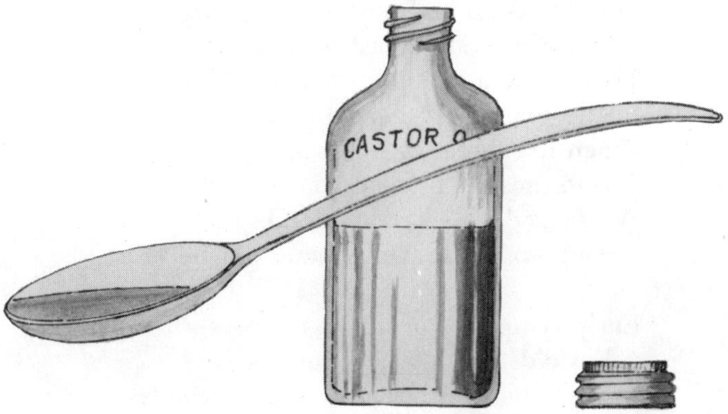

HOME REMEDIES

In these days of antibiotics
And all our many wonder drugs
We still have many trying ailments
And many vile, elusive bugs.
Back when we were growing youngsters
We had a lot of miseries, too,
But with home remedies and grannies,
We always knew just what to do!

When in spring we felt so draggy
A dope that always nipped the bud
Was good old sulfur and molasses
For toning up our sluggish blood.
Then as summer's dread infections
Behooved us all to be on guard,
We kept the finest antiseptic
Made up with kerosene and lard.

From the winter colds and sniffles
We'd all snap back just feeling fine;
We used that dandy decongestant
Of sugar cubes and turpentine.
And when fighting those discomforts
That came with asthma and catarrh
We took a natural home concoction
We made of honey and pine tar.

For that deep and raucous coughing
  Our elders knew just what was best;
They made a rubbing goose-grease poultice
  And placed hot flannel on our chest.
When the threat of influenza
  Had most of us a nervous wreck
We sacked a dab of asafoetida
  And wore it bravely 'round our neck.

Early symptoms of throat rawness
  For oldsters down to tiny fry
Brought on that hot and soothing toddy—
  That draft of good old rock and rye.
Broth of weeds called "Thousand Guilders"
  Relieved straightway our inner cramp;
And for a general purpose tonic
  We ate the lowly mountain ramp.

Sassafras was a conditioner;
  For worms we took dog fennel tea;
Tobacco cuds were fine for soothing
  Bites and stings of wasp or bee.
Epsom salts for constipation
  Ran neck-and-neck with castor oil,
And used for treating diarrhea
  Was flaxseed tea brought to a boil.

Squeezed out juice from roasted onion
  Was recommended for the croup;
For weakness and debilitation
  Came herbs and granny's chicken soup.
Cow's horn drink for yellow jaundice,
  And gensang roots for aching head;
Then catnip tea for restless sleepers
  Assured their settling down in bed.

Poultice made from bark of linden
  An ailing open leg would cure,
While roasted poke root cataplasm
  Would kill most nagging pains for sure.
Stomach trouble with its misery
  Responded well to juice of kraut,
And sheep dung tea when taken proper
  Was sure to break the measles out.

Whiskey was that panacea
  For ills from nausea to snakebite;
For feverish patients near delirium
  It brought on sweating in the night.
Granny's salve for cuts and chafing,
  For aches and pains and bruises, too;
And what she put in for ingredients
  Was something that we never knew.

"Feed a cold and starve a fever,"
  Was spoken oft, with much appeal
While soaking baths of simmering ashes
  Soon made those boils and risings heal.
So that's how we attained adulthood—
  And saved a lot of money, too,
For few newfangled drugs are better
  Than home prescriptions that we knew!

THE OLD COURTHOUSE

The old courthouse always loomed a prominent landmark in Salem, our county seat. It stood out in particular on those exciting, but infrequent, trips to town I was privileged to make when a boy. Sitting importantly beside my dad on the spring seat of the farm wagon and thrilling at the first glimpse of town was enough to make my cup virtually run over. There were sidewalks and kids on roller skates, and bicycles; the aromatic after-smell of an automobile just passed, and tall poles with waves and waves of wires hanging from many cross arms, and the light brackets that suggested extra hours of playtime—long after darkness completely enveloped our farm.

Special sounds, too, added to the delightful environs of life in town—the clop-clop of the horseshoes on the pavement, the screaming planer at Roberts-Judson's lumber yard, the ring of the anvil in Key and Pace's blacksmith shop, the busy putt-putt and accentuating puffs of steam discharging from a pipe in the roof of a huge dusty building we knew as Durham's roller mill, and at the noon hour the good-natured bantering of the men seated family-style around the long table in Manuel Goacher's restaurant.

But there in the midst of it all towered the old courthouse with its high arched windows and huge oaken doors. To a wide-eyed country boy it exemplified the very essence of government in action. The massive desks in offices with high metal ceilings, the smell of cigars, the tremendous ledgers on shelves and on counter tops behind ornamental wrought iron scrollwork, the staccato of typewriters, and the buzz of adding machines—all added to the dignity of the atmosphere there. Truly, the early impressions I received here were enough to last a lifetime.

Now, years afterward, it is still a courthouse, but recently it was recorded in the National archives as a preserved monument to the past. Those of us who grew up with its austere presence in our lives are relieved in the thought that it will not be torn down to make way for a twentieth-century parking lot, but will continue to symbolize and consecrate the past years of the county, together with the lives of many generations of fine people who came and went through its great impressive doors.

THE OLD COURTHOUSE

A monument to a century past,
  To those events which made it great,
And to a county come to be
  A pillar in a mighty state.

A tribute to the courage known
  To sons of stalwart pioneers,
Their labor that begot a start
  And saw it grow through passing years.

A shrine to those who cast their lot
  To serve their fellows great and small,
To those who won and those who lost
In bringing forth the best for all.

A witness to undaunted strides
  In progress long and proudly made,
To efforts fraught with sweat and tears
  And those effective parts they played.

A link from now to long ago
  To public pump and watering place;
With pride it spans the old and new
  From streets of mud to metered space.

A landmark nobly holding high
  Ideals that firm for freedom stand,
And with them, prayers that God may keep
  Our country's future in His hand.

O COUNTRY ROAD

O country road of turns and mysteries,
  Your ways have long intrigued me so;
You lead beyond the far horizons—
  O country road, where do you go?

Your wayside flanked with black-eyed Susans,
  Your shoulders draped with Queen Anne's lace,
While heavy heads of elder blossoms
  Adorn your fence rows place to place.

Serene and silent, through the valleys
  And off to mountains high and steep;
You pass by meadows, woods and farmsteads,
  And all your treasured secrets keep.

Some day I would in sheer abandon
  Set out your devious way to know—
O country road, your length I'd follow
  And ease my mind on where you go!

TRICKS THAT MEMORY PLAYS

Time is not only the architect of old age with its associated confusion and distortions, but for a great many of us Time is also a prevaricator! Anyone who harbors any doubts on this score need only go back to the place where he lived as a child. Here he can see for himself how untrue many of his early recollections prove to be. This is particularly the case when one moved away in childhood and has not had occasion to return until well along in maturity.

Old-timers used to tell us, "Iffen a body drinks water out of a cow's track they allers come back!" Whether because of this or for other reasons, when we do go back after a lapse of many years—and I did this—we cannot help but sense a feeling of excitement. There is nostalgia, too, for invariably the scenes of old are steeped in memories of joy and happy times—days lived amid the love and presence of our parents, brothers, sisters, and friends. Each individual will have memories peculiar to his own past. As for myself, these memories include places where games were played, the spot where a play-farm was marked off by field stones and sticks driven into the ground to simulate fence posts, hillsides where we coasted down what seemed long and steep grades in crudely fashioned contraptions on cultivator wheels, places where the first wild strawberries ripened, the tree where the swing used to be, the place where wild grapes hung thickest, the deep valley where the creek meandered on its rustic way, and so on and on.

Always in revisiting the old haunts it behooves us to be prepared for many surprises. In general, we will find the basic landmarks pretty much as they used to be, but the features and details that we thought we remembered so well will be quite different in many ways. There perhaps is no very good explanation for the disparity we find between the remembered and the fact at hand except to attribute it to the prevarications of Time, and to the tricks that memory plays!

TRICKS THAT MEMORY PLAYS

Returning to the haunts of childhood
  After years of being away,
Impressed I was with realization
  Of the tricks our memories play.
A visit to the old home premise
  Straightway set my mind aright;
Surprises came at every turning,
  Viewed this time in seasoned light.

The slope descending from the barnyard
  Really was not long and steep;
The swimming hole that thrilled us often
  Now seemed neither wide nor deep.
The spring of gushing crystal water
  Where we daily took our pail,
Was now a wasted feeble trickle,
  And much shorter seemed that trail.

The boulder that stood in the meadow
  I remembered, oh so tall
But found that all its vast dimensions
  Really proved not large at all.
And cliffs that brooded o'er the valley
  Once I thought so wide and high,
Reclimbed again with strides now grown-up,
  Seemed just so-so to my eye.

When getting cows from upland pastures
  Was a dreaded daily chore,
The path that seemed to go forever
  Does not seem long any more.
And so it is with mental pictures
  Of the places in our youth,
In spite of memory's fond reflections
  Time so oft distorts the truth!

WON'T YOU SING ME TO SLEEP

Won't you sing me to sleep again, Mother,
As you did in the days long ago,
Back when life in my childhood was rosy
And I knew not a heartache nor woe.
Let us play for the sake of past seasons
That in childhood I'm living once more,
That I'm lisping a prayer in the twilight
Where I knelt here so often of yore.

Aye, the years that so gaily once beckoned
Only brought to me hardships alone;
Now I sigh for the time that has drifted
And the happiest days that I've known.
So, come sing me to sleep again, Mother,
With that lullabye dear to be still,
So that peace of an innocent childhood
May again this old heart of mine fill!

THE BATTLEFIELD

Although the Christian world has had the formula for peace for nearly two thousand years, and notwithstanding centuries of so-called progress in ways of civilization, wars have become progressively more barbaric and more devastating.

All patriotic Americans should stand firm in the defense of our land against forces that threaten us as a free nation, and these may be forces either *external* or *internal*. Admitted now, recent history recorded wars of questionable prudence. The no-win type wars, as in Vietnam, for example, are wars that tend to destroy our national respect abroad, divide our people at home, undermine our Constitution, give impetus to new waves of crime, and pour millions into the coffers of those who traffic in the fortunes of war.

A trigger-happy, money-mad economist blatantly stated that wars, like Vietnam, are good for our economy, that we should have one every year! I have personally heard men openly express hope that war lasts until they retire. Shocking? Utterly reprehensible! People so unprincipled that dollars mean more than the blood of our fine young men! That men should be sacrificed for job security! Danger here lies in our unwittingly electing these characters to high and influential positions in government, for these make a bad combination with greedy interest groups, certain industrialists, money manipulators, and others who have their own selfish reasons for wanting our country involved in war, under whatever pretext. They take their place with the dubious patriot who sees no virtues in his country other than the history of its wars.

Freedom under our flag and our Constitution is too precious to trust it blindly to irresponsible statesmanship. Here, our undying thanks to the many fine statesmen we do have who see the wisdom of maintaining our national strength by keeping our men and material from being overextended to every remote and ridiculous place around the world! Statesmen, they, with higher goals than those nurturing a perennial itch to keep us constantly teetering on the brink of war!

In view of the foregoing perhaps the greatest *peacemaker* of modern times will be that person who can devise and implement a way to take all the material profits out of war!

THE BATTLEFIELD

Where mortals meet in desperation and fear,
And fearing, feel their mortality;
Grappling hard with a heartless fate;
Gambling, odds o'er priceless stakes—
Each giving fast lest he be taking
In a licensed lawlessness
The while endless hours hover o'er.

Where principles that veneer civilian ways
Hold second to the jungle law,
And the curse of involuntary savagery
Subordinates every rule and tenet
Instilled with care in tranquil days,
Spurring hapless souls to nameless sins
That heaven cannot justify.

The screaming shells and thirsty steel,
The din of missiles booming, blasting—
Each scream a dirge, each blast a summons
To sweet eternal peace.

Here many pay in blood the price
For blunders of a trusted few—
Alas, the debt is never paid
In the self-same blood incurred it!
What matters it that brooks are stained
And the sward no longer green;
That carnal roses wither, fall,
Where birds of carrion feed?
For, lo, reward in triumph won
In name of prestige, pomp and power—
Things smoldering deep in cells perverted
Of imagination, fiendish, wild,
Where kindred abstract isms dwell.

Who in time shall vested be
To judge the wrong and gratify
Avenging hearts with rightful due?
Are years unlived forever lost
To those who beaten fall,
Or can some vast atoning power
Somehow their unused worth redeem?
Can loser win as the winner lost
By standards still unknown
So heroes all—the vanquished, too,
Can go again on even score?

Though time cannot heal the scars,
It may at length cast friendly light
Where darkness now holds forth unchallenged.
Then when the smoke clouds drift away,
And echoes of the slaughter cease,
The man who's up and he who's down
May walk abreast on higher plane.

Perchance there'll be no wrinkled brows
Nor furrowed lines by questions wrought,
And eyes may see that never saw
That sphere of love and brotherhood.
Aye, in those ages long yet dormant,
Let strife in all its sordid vestments
Belong to naught but antiquity,
Its meanings all in the mist of ages lost.
Let no blast of bugle mar
The sweet tranquility–
No call to arms, no grim retreats
To stir the blood, betray the hopes
Of warriors lonely, loved and missed;
No rousing notes of reveille sound,
No call of roll when vesper falls,
And no more taps and silent tears
In the peaceful world of hope-to-be!

KEYS TO HAPPINESS

Why is it most of us have to live the greater part of a lifetime before the real gist of oft-heard exhortations regarding happiness begins to come through to us? Is it *familiarity* that turns us off and insulates us from any real understanding or desire to put to practice what they prescribe?

Granted, our early years are so crowded with revelations ever unfolding to us that many important things are simply overwhelmed in the process. Then later on as innovations slack off we find time at last to sift through the hoard that time brought us and which we only half-noticed the first time around. In re-evaluation we rediscover the keys we well could have used many times along the way.

By this time we may find we have been in and out of difficulties a number of times, that somehow we have been muddling our way along in rather sorry fashion. We notice now that when we place *self* in predominance we discourage chances for happiness. Nature herself gives us a headstart in selfishness, because survival and grabbing for every need, real or fancied, are inseparable instincts from birth. And let us be reminded here that nature does not predicate primarily that we *should* be happy. This we must learn on our own if we desire it, and the lessons require serious, conscious and deliberate effort on our part. Moreover, the means by which we achieve a goal in this regard may be by a more or less clean-cut code of ethics—a set of requirements we here term the Keys to Happiness.

It is doubtful there ever was a time in days of our past when happiness was not a desired part of our lot. However, while still holding on to our instinctive greed, it simply does not break through to us that selfishness and happiness are in no wise compatible. No monarch, no person of wealth or power, no self-seeker, though he had all material things at his command, ever found true happiness in these possessions. Happiness is not something we grasp and possess by force or edict; we cannot ignore everybody and everything and, whether or no, claim it for ourselves. Yes, it may take many years of maturing, half a lifetime or more of disappointments, serious and soulful reassessments of attitudes before we acquire the keys, one by one. Although few of us acquire all the Keys, ever, hopefully all can acquire enough of them, and in time, to live rewarding lives of happiness and fulfillment.

KEYS TO HAPPINESS

1. God in your life
2. Love and forgiveness in your heart
3. Respect for self and for others
4. Others above self in areas of concern, service, and sharing
5. Honesty, sincerity, and responsibility in your dealings
6. Keeping busy with heart in your work
7. Gratitude and humility a part of each day
8. Positive attitude in all things
9. Sense of humor for cheerful living
10. Self-examination and prayer

THE BLESSINGS OF RURAL CHILDHOOD

The accompanying essay is included in this compilation at the risk of being repetitious of other similar topics entered in the foregoing pages and sections. There may be a point, however, in stating that these words were written at an early time in my career, and they antedate many of the poems and commentaries that came into being in the ensuing years.

Because of the broad range of events covered in writing about rural childhood it is understandable that a great number of topics are necessarily touched upon which individually lend themselves to writings in their own right, this with the separate treatment each so richly deserves. This is what in a measure took place as the years came and went. In dealing with each in turn I attempted to give it due moment and significance—to treat each as the separate entity it rightfully is. Hopefully the reader finds that each of the foregoing writings, then, stands on its own feet and portrays its own facet of the American scene. With this a consideration, the element of repetition here, if any, would not loom seriously objectionable.

It is important to note that the composite of events in *The Blessings of Rural Childhood* conveys a glimpse at a *total* picture, particularly in a time a generation or so ago. The prominence of this picture as depicted herein has diminished somewhat in the transition of our nation from one largely agricultural to one now industrially centered. With this transition and with the innovations it brought to every sector, some of the former color and charm of rural life as we knew it were obviously impaired or lost. Fortunately, new and different qualities, still of rural character however, were instituted in the change, and they in their own way make up for the loss. And so it is that rural childhood, comparatively speaking, remains to this day a delightful and cherished reality in the America we love!

THE BLESSINGS OF RURAL CHILDHOOD

Doubtless among the richest gifts of Providence to mankind are the blessings of rural childhood—these with their priceless codes for abundantly living the years before us, and their inimitable capacity for enhancing the blithesome memories of the past. Without meaning to disparage childhood in our cities, nor to discount the advantages for social, industrial and economic advancement open to our urban boys and girls, I think the most of us will be inclined to agree that a rural environment somehow develops a special sensitivity to nature in a way nothing else can equal. This, coupled with the countless simple joys of childhood on the farm, contributes much to the fullness of life itself—a fullness which unfortunately the children in the confines of concrete, brick and steel rarely ever have opportunity to know. In light of these facts, I submit that the person who romped in the freedom of the great out-of-doors during his early years is well blest indeed. Whether he is immediately aware of it or not, it is as if a magnanimous hand touched his life and did it so momentously that the effects will surface again and again to encourage, redeem and sustain him in afteryears.

While still in the early paragraphs, I feel it is in order here to say that in no wise would a treatise of this nature portray rural childhood as being only hearts and flowers, or less impatient than childhood elsewhere. This would not be true of life in any locale, and few of us would want a life without a reasonable balance of ups and downs. Most of us who have a sizable portion of our years behind us know at last that even problems can be opportunities in disguise. Such being the case, everyone should be prepared to encompass both the sunshine and the rain, and accordingly take in stride whatever comes. Uncertainties in our own childhood, like the hills, were an everlasting presence in our lives, and while these undoubtedly left their marks in many ways, we like to think they served a purpose not altogether bad.

We are aware that in keeping abreast with the progress of our age, the rural picture is undergoing a constant change, and therefore conditions of the present and of several decades ago constitute quite a contrast in many respects. However, while it is true that new developments have displaced many things known to former generations, we are ever grateful that the beautiful side of rural childhood has not changed materially as yet, for its interests are still as numerous as ever, its joys full as many, and its memories just as lasting.

In recounting the innumerable adventures in the country, one could not hope in one short essay to include all of them, nor could he possibly bring them in a fittingly vivid manner before the reader who himself has never shared firsthand in those God-given privileges. What then, one may ask, are the brightest of bright spots in rural childhood? Here, since two individuals rarely ever regard any one thing in exactly the same way, it is obvious that opinions concerning this question would differ considerably. One can be reasonably sure, however, that most of us of rural vintage would associate our pet adventures with those timeless barefoot days, and regardless of what other events intervened, we must admit that those carefree times constituted a most eventful period in our young lives.

For one thing, we recall trailing gleefully in the furrow at father's heels in the spring plowing and experiencing the sensation of the cool, freshly-turned soil as it crumbled and rolled over our brown, bare feet; later in the season we delighted to follow through the long rows of whispering corn, to feel the interlacing, tender leaves caressing our sun-toughened arms; and then when the day's work was done and the evening shadows lengthened across the valleys, it was always a thrill to scramble to the seat of "honor" on the back of the gentle plow horse and ride pompously to the barnyard, while in childish fancy the hame tops became make-believe pommels and the jingling trace chains the clattering armor of our knightly steed. No less pleasant were the romps in the meadows among the loose swaths, the windrows and the shocks of newmown hay whose fragrance will linger on through the years! And no draft was more refreshing than water from the old oaken water cask resting beneath a nearby walnut tree or in an aromatic clump of sassafras at a shaded end of the field. In the undulating acreage of growing wheat we marveled at the brood of naturally-camouflaged baby quail instinctively "frozen" in perfect immobility while the mother bird limped pathetically away with some feigned impairment, hopefully to entice our pursuit; watching in wonderment the methodical and brilliant way the doodlebug prepared the place for perpetuating her species—laying her eggs in a paralyzed larva which she deposited in a deep hole she had made, carefully tamped the hole full of earth and then, to hide the obvious, rolled a goodly-sized pebble over the site. Then we recall the hours spent wading around the shallows of the frog pond in the pasture, boldly exploring ever-uncharted sections of that vast "sea"; and those dips in the old swimming hole in the creek where the knurled roots of a huge friendly oak served for a diver's platform, and a convenient grapevine carried us well out into the deep.

In the latter part of the summer came the never-to-be-forgotten days of school when the dew-drenched mornings found us traipsing across the fields and along the overgrown woods path to the weathered one-room schoolhouse. With few exceptions, we were conscious of a definite pride as we went, books and new tablet under arm, a bright new pencil clipped very conspicuously high on the overalls bib, pockets bulging with apples, and dangling from an untiring arm a heavily-laden dinner pail emitting tempting smells of fried potato cakes, peach pie and other delicacies. And what fond recollections are associated with the schoolroom itself! Truly fate has dealt unkindly with the man or woman who has never experienced at least a few of those simple, yet pleasant days in a rural school! Still vivid are the scarred old benches where we carved our initials among those of past generations, and the time-worn textbooks whose flyleaves invariably bore, among various memoranda and autograph verses, the coupled names that a schoolday cupid had somehow linked together, and which in many instances the later years had brought into matrimonial reality. Recess time on the playground brought its triumphs and defeats for the forward and the meek alike in such games as Dare Base, Rounders, Steal Sticks, Wolf over the Ridge, Cops and Robbers, and a great many others.

Once home from school it was fun to make a hurried visit to the apple orchard and climb up into a favorite tree to get the choicest yellow-meated Grimes Golden, or that luscious through-and-through pink delight we knew as a Jonathan. Then when amply supplied here we took the eager pup and bounded off for the pasture to bring home the cows for milking time, or set about doing such other chores as fell to our lot.

Rural school days also brought programs on Halloween, Thanksgiving week, Christmas time, or on the closing day of school. In my time these were always red-letter events as we in the peak of childhood's importance elbowed our way among fellow pupils and onlookers in the well-filled schoolhouse, seeing that everything was in readiness for us to speak our "piece" or fill our respective roles in the dialogs. There were always some with us who somehow were not given to readin', writin', and 'rithmetic, and consequently to them school days may have seemed long and even tiresome; however, there's little doubt that the succeeding years brought back many memories, together with the reassurance that those days were among the finest of a lifetime.

As the earlier years drifted by, our teens brought on the sobering days of youth with their ever-increasing responsibilities. Now a changed world opened before us—a world of new duties which unmistakably taught priceless lessons on values of life and things about us; lessons they were which laid a foundation upon which the passing seasons builded an even deeper-rooted love for nature, for higher, better things, and this with enough respect to keep us humble in it all. And while the work in the fields so often left calloused hands and tired muscles, there was satisfaction in knowing that we had part in the monumental work of creation and nonetheless in self-sustenance; seeing the growing crops drink in the sunshine and the rain, and later in garnering in a generous harvest, we sensed being party to an unparalleled achievement which compensated a thousandfold for any bodily fatigue that the season's work may have exacted.

What rural boy did not swell with pride when he discovered that he was "man" enough to work with the older men at threshing or silo-filling time, or when the best team and the mowing machine or the dump rake were entrusted to his eager hand? There always was a pleasant variation in the regular routine, and possibly the climax of all our boyhood thrills was the permission to take the family flivver rattling on a solo drive to the village at mail time—all the while hoping that special girl down the road would perchance notice who was at the wheel! Aside from running an important errand, this always afforded an opportunity to hear the farmers and village loafers there humorously "jawerin'" one another, and to hear a complete analysis of the ills of the "guvmint."

Other events which wove themselves indelibly into our growing years were such as stealing out alone in the morning mist before sunrise, father's double-barreled shotgun on shoulder, to still-hunt at a fence row where the cornfield adjoined the timber and an excessive squirrel population was appropriating an alarming portion of the crop; those trips to a distant neighbor now and then for Sunday dinner which often caught the old farm wagon laden with its cargo of father, mother, and excited youngsters all in Sunday bib and tucker on the road at an early hour; the wide-eyed trips to town when hogs were taken to market or taxes had to be paid; the hilarious surprise parties, cake suppers, or "musicals" on clear moonlit nights when the words of "The Dusty Miller Boy," "Skip to Me, Lou," and others mingled with the merry laughter and shouting of country youths and blossoming maidens, these breaking the stillness of the balmy summer evenings in our hills; the nut-gathering excursions into the wooded wilds in autumn when the tang of frost was in the air and the blue haze of Indian Summer enveloped the colorful woodland; and finally, the winter evenings spent in cracking the nuts before the brightly blazing hearth, while the north wind whistled triumphantly over fields and farmstead and the snow lay deep on a dormant, sleeping world. The joys of the foregoing were always heightened by the contentment of knowing that there was a sufficiency in the granary and haymow, a well-filled cellar and smokehouse, and ample piles of nature's own fuel in the woodyard—all this adding a sense of peace and serenity entirely beyond the capacity of descriptive words.

These are but a few of the many things that early touched our lives—things that make rural childhood excitingly eventful and memorable. Nowhere else can one taste of the manifold blessings which enrich these glorious years of one's lifetime. At no other place can one breath the mingled fragrance of a veritable Eden of bursting blossoms, or hear the happy notes of so many nesting birds in springtime, see the crimson sun sinking drowsily into the bosom of the bluest of western hills, and in the gathering twilight hear the persistent call of the whip-poorwill in the lane beyond the orchard. Where else can one grow up living and working hand-in-hand with members of one's family and with God and nature, learning the intrinsic values of material things, the purposes in life, the love for higher ideals, and the understanding of beauty in simple things? With these values indelibly instilled in the hearts and minds of rural lads and lassies, it is no wonder that so many men and women who have glorified the pages of our history once were barefoot boys and girls proudly privileged with childhood days in the rural parts of America!

PARENS CUM LAUDE

Too often brief and late in coming,
  Or, most distressing! ne'er expressed,
Our praise for parents long deserving
  Should be in truth more firmly stressed.

When all the world for us collapses
  Their love reflects a deep concern,
And lo! their beams of approbation
  When we the crown of effort earn!

Their joys replete, so reassuring,
  With fortune's blessings opportune;
No ups nor downs more ours than parents',
  No hearts on earth so much in tune.

So pause we now as should we often
  To praise the ones we claim our own,
For parents long so understanding,
  Their love the most unselfish known!

Author's mother in her seventies.

THE MASTER ENGINEER

The accompanying dissertation is dedicated particularly to those of faltering faith. It was prepared for presentation to my Sunday school classes, mostly young people who had reached that stage of development when their minds seek logic and understanding of our wonderful and perplexing creation.

The adolescent-through-teen years of our young men and women are critical in their spiritual stability. Influenced by their more materialistic peers, many reach the stage of uncertainty, confusion, and often even doubt when attempting to rationalize the origin and workings of our mysterious universe.

In this no pretense is made that the answers sought are so clear-cut and easy that one presentation on the subject can suffice, but hopefully it will stimulate a flow of wholesome thought. Whether or not one believes that all things about us are the result of *chance occurrence* will still be one's own prerogative. However, inquiring young minds must be treated with the respect they deserve and given the best guidance we know how to give. Most young people want answers that make sense when gaged by the yardstick of their own understanding. Much of the theological approach is beyond their comprehension anyway—and ours—and so we pass with the exhortation that things of this category must be taken by faith. But faith itself may become a dimensionless entity to young students of elementary sciences who have acquired a somewhat undirected sense of the material realism in their laboratories—and we all know what is said of a *little* knowledge!

Being materialistic by training myself, I could understand the skepticism of some of my young friends, and therefore conceived the idea that the best way to discuss our creation with them is from a materialistic view, and to do it in terms of the language of the classroom and the laboratory they so recently acquired. The approach to answering questions from the facts that science has established and proved through the years is after all one that has acceptance and is, moreover, the most reliable source known and understood today. Finally, in order to get the points across, I felt it important that the entire presentation be kept intelligible, illustrated by examples with which all are familiar. Thus, with the material presented in this way, it all remains simple—so simple that it is both understandable and exciting!

THE MASTER ENGINEER

The statement that "one cannot see the forest for the trees" applies well to our wonderful creation, which we know to be so very, very real and yet evades our understanding in so many ways. Because we are born into an environment with many complexities and are ever in its midst from infancy through development and maturity, it is understandable that we should take so much for granted and see little or nothing particularly astounding in our observations as we go on living day by day. We become so familiar with the things we have ever with and about us that even the most wonderful becomes commonplace!

Familiarity is a long-time enemy of comprehension. Because of familiarity, so much escapes our attention that here it behooves us to follow carefully the material in this presentation throughout all its elements so that the gist of it will not elude us. Despite this advance warning, I dare say that some will not follow it closely enough to do it justice.

In the first place, we are busy people—busy with so many activities and our minds preoccupied with many interests. So much so, in fact, that we have little time to pause and listen—and this is regrettable indeed, for in our hectic pace we miss a great deal. Inspired writers of old so well understood this proclivity of man they included in the Scriptures the admonition "be still and know that I am God."[1] It is in being still, banishing preconceived notions (keeping an open mind), and simply in listening that the importance of the Biblical passage becomes real to us.

Religious enthusiasm in the Christian world has risen and fallen successively through the centuries since its inception, at times reaching a pinnacle of fervor and at other times bottoming out so drastically as to threaten its very future. Fortunately, these peaks and valleys did not occur everywhere at the same time and to the same degree, and so the dominion of faith has successfully survived to the present day. By some the advent of science as a widely-accepted field of learning has been held accountable for a decline in religious following in the current century, for there are always those who doggedly hold that science and religion are incompatible. From a relatively recent spiritual declivity we were left the brash notification that *God is dead.* Doubtless this was music to the ears of the infidel and information most welcome to the agnostic. Whatever impact it had is not overly important here because "revelations" of this nature have both negative and positive effects, with the net result of balancing out fairly much a zero in the overall realm of personal opinion.

What is important to us is how seriously we consider our universe and how we attempt to rationalize its creation. Basically, we are left with a limited choice in possible deductions regarding the matter. One concept would have to be that all things are conceived and brought into reality by some Master Intelligence, and this in such a way that every detail great and small dovetails with, mutually sustains, augments and/or implements, other details in the universe—everything with a plan and purpose, an alpha and omega, and this by whatever text or explanation, or even by no explanation at all!

Alternative to the foregoing concept would have to be the contention that all things are mere happenstance, just a coincidental occurrence, that everything is here by chance or accident. Accidents do happen, we know, and are very real in the experience of everyone. From what we know about accidents, however, we have learned that things which occur in this category are usually limited to one or two successive events and that no accidental occurrence comprises any simultaneous series of ongoing predictable functions that interrelate in a harmonious

---

[1]Psalms 46:10.

pattern—and much less in an ordered and stable arrangement that repeats in exactly the same way day after day, year after year, age after age. Such a chance happening would be an incredible accident indeed!

If the points brought up in this presentation seem to prejudice the merits of the accident hypothesis then this is the way it has to be, for to my knowledge no one who subscribes to the accident theory has ever come up with even a sketchy explanation of how such a system could make sense. But for the time being it is our purpose to remain open-minded to both possibilities and to consider the logic of the ensuing points so we shape an opinion with which we can be reasonably comfortable.

We all enjoy watching a magician as he puts on his show. We observe with wide-eyed amazement the drawing of a rabbit from the hat or the vanishing of a bird cage, bird and all, into thin air. Most of us are not so naive as to think this so-called magic is real, but we are engrossed nevertheless with the illusion, and with the consuming speculation on how the magician does it. All the while we know that if we were to unfrock this showman we would find there is a clever trick for his every act, and so rightfully we conclude that in reality there is no magic at all in his performance—only sleight of hand, illusion and fake.

But let us consider now that for eons mankind has witnessed the handiwork of a Master engaged in fantastically wonderful accomplishments, and we hardly give it second notice! Science at length took a careful look into the acts of this Performer, and actually found in a great many instances just how He does it! But here is where the Master and the faker part company, for they are in different spheres altogether. When the men of science succeeded in finding out how these wonder works are performed, lo and behold! they found them all very real; that there is no illusion in a fluffy chick just hatched, no sleight of hand about the rain that falls from the sky to water vast expanses of thirsty earth, no trick in the tiny plant embryo buried deep in the heart of a seed, and so on ad infinitum. Moreover, these learned men consistently find the results so positive, so reliable, that all are predictable in advance! That they perform the same yesterday, today and forever! Here we all must concede that all things are wise and wonderful; that they surely bear evidence of having been designed, engineered, and purposefully materialized, and this with a perfection that borders on the incredible. Yes, amazing! In fact, men and women who delve deeply into the workings of the many facets of our creation have occasion to experience deep convictions, and ever afterwards believe more, rather than less, in the presence of an Intelligence far surpassing anything in our comprehension. Man with his finite wisdom can hardly be expected to grasp the infinite, but he can be still and listen! Robert Millikan, for whom the Millikan Rays are named, was one of many scientists, we are told, who became devoutly religious after astronomic findings opened his eyes to the wonders of the universe.

Were we asked personally to create even the simplest thing, and given the choice to do this intentionally or by accident, we would have to beg off with the honest excuse that such is beyond our capability. But honesty is a virtue, and making this acknowledgment has to be commendable in itself, for it indicates a wisdom that ours frankly is a subordinate capacity. Here we admit to some power greater than man, because the creation we cannot do does go right on under some positive continuity which we can only see and wonder about. And again we ask, Is it accidental? Or is it in accordance with an ordered plan?

As a child each of us did "creating" of sorts when we took our building blocks, built a tower, house, bridge, or some other thing. Each time we tore down one structure, took the same blocks and with them built another. Building blocks made all this possible—and rather convenient. The process really was simple because these blocks went together in many different ways and lent themselves to making almost anything we desired.

Building blocks? That's it! If we were to create our world and, in fact, the universe, building blocks would seem the most logical way to go. The block system would lend itself to a continuity that would know no end because they could be used over and over again in an infinite number of combinations, and from now until the end of time.

And *building blocks* are exactly what the Master Engineer employs in the design of everything in our creation! Science in probing into this secret of secrets made this discovery many years ago, and found the building blocks in question to be very wonderful indeed. They named these wonderful blocks *atoms*. Further, they found that these blocks come in a set, that there are over a hundred different kinds in the set. They also discovered that these blocks are very cleverly designed, each kind with its own characteristics, and that these characteristics permit arranging them in organized patterns. See the Periodic Table, Figure 1.

CERIUM 6.66 795 3,4 3468 58 Ce 140.12 2,8,20,18,8,2	PRASEODYMIUM 6.782 935 3,4 3127 59 Pr 140.907 2,8,21,18,8,2	NEODYMIUM 7.004 1024 3 3027 60 Nd 144.24 2,8,22,18,8,2	PROMETHIUM 1080 3 2730 61 Pm 147 2,8,23,18,8,2	SAMARIUM 7.536 1072 2,3 1900 62 Sm 150.35 2,8,24,18,8,2	EUROPIUM 5.259 826 2,3 1439 63 Eu 151.96 2,8,25,18,8,2	GADOLINIUM 7.895 1312 3 3000 64 Gd 157.25 2,9,25,18,8,2	TERBIUM 8.272 1356 3,4 2800 65 Tb 158.924 2,8,27,18,8,2	DYSPROSIUM 8.536 1407 3 2600 66 Dy 162.50 2,8,28,18,8,2	HOLMIUM 8.803 1461 3 2600 67 Ho 164.930 2,8,29,18,8,2	ERBIUM 9.051 1497 3 2900 68 Er 167.26 2,8,30,18,8,2	THULIUM 9.332 1545 3 1727 69 Tm 168.934 2,8,31,18,8,2	YTTERBIUM 6.977 824 2,3 1427 70 Yb 173.04 2,8,32,18,8,2	LUTETIUM 9.842 1652 3 3327 71 Lu 174.97 2,9,32,18,8,2

ATOMIC WEIGHTS BASED ON CARBON-12 (IUPAC, 1961)

KEY

PRODUCTS AVAILABLE

- PURE METAL OR ELEMENT
- ALLOYS AND/OR COMPOUNDS

	BERYLLIUM	
Density, G/CC† ▶	1.845 1284	◀ MELTING POINT, °C
VALENCES ▶	2 2507	◀ BOILING POINT, °C
ATOMIC NUMBER ▶	4	
SYMBOL ▶	Be	
	9.0122	◀ ATOMIC WEIGHT
	2,2	◀ ELECTRON SHELLS

†At room temperature for gases, G/Liter at NTP.

IA	IIA	IIIB	IVB	VB	VIB	VIIB	VIII	VIII	VIII	IB	IIB	IIIA	IVA	VA	VIA	VIIA	INERT GASES
HYDROGEN 0.0899 -259 1 -252.8 1 H 1.00797 1																	HELIUM 0.1785 -272.2 0 -268.9 2 He 4.0026 2
LITHIUM 0.534 179 1 1317 3 Li 6.939 1,2	BERYLLIUM 1.845 1284 2 2507 4 Be 9.0122 2,2											BORON 2.34 2300 3 2550 5 B 10.811 3,2	CARBON 1.88 3550 2,4 4200 6 C 12.01115 4,2	NITROGEN 1.25 -210 1,2, 3,4,5 -196 7 N 14.0067 5,2	OXYGEN 1.429 -218 2 -183 8 O 15.9994 6,2	FLUORINE 1.69 -223 1 -187 9 F 18.9984 7,2	NEON 0.900 -248.6 0 -246.1 10 Ne 20.183 8,2
SODIUM 0.97 97.9 1 883 11 Na 22.9898 1,8,2	MAGNESIUM 1.74 651 2 1103 12 Mg 24.312 2,8,2											ALUMINUM 2.7 660 3 2467 13 Al 26.9815 3,8,2	SILICON 2.33 1410 4 2480 14 Si 28.086 4,8,2	PHOSPHORUS 1.82 44 1,3,4,5 280 15 P 30.9738 5,8,2	SULFUR 2.07 113 2,4,6 444 16 S 32.064 6,8,2	CHLORINE 3.214 -101 1,3, 4,5,7 -34.6 17 Cl 35.453 7,8,2	ARGON 1.784 -189.3 0 -185.9 18 Ar 39.948 8,8,2
POTASSIUM 0.87 63.7 1 760 19 K 39.102 1,8,8,2	CALCIUM 1.54 851 2 1482 20 Ca 40.08 2,8,8,2	SCANDIUM 2.99 1539 3 2727 21 Sc 44.956 2,9,8,2	TITANIUM 4.54 1668 2,3,4 3260 22 Ti 47.90 2,10,8,2	VANADIUM 6.11 1890 2,3,4,5 3000 23 V 50.942 2,11,8,2	CHROMIUM 7.19 1875 2,3,6 2199 24 Cr 51.996 1,13,8,2	MANGANESE 7.43 1244 1,2,3, 4,6,7 2097 25 Mn 54.9380 2,13,8,2	IRON 7.87 1535 2,3 3000 26 Fe 55.847 2,14,8,2	COBALT 8.90 1493 2,3 3100 27 Co 58.9332 2,15,8,2	NICKEL 8.9 1452 2,3 2900 28 Ni 58.71 2,16,8,2	COPPER 8.94 1083 1,2 2595 29 Cu 63.54 1,18,8,2	ZINC 7.133 419.5 2 906 30 Zn 65.37 2,18,8,2	GALLIUM 5.907 29.75 2,3 2403 31 Ga 69.72 3,18,8,2	GERMANIUM 5.32 936 2,4 2700 32 Ge 72.59 4,18,8,2	ARSENIC 5.727 814 2,3,5 615 33 As 74.9216 5,18,8,2	SELENIUM 4.79 217 2,4,6 685 34 Se 78.96 6,18,8,2	BROMINE 3.12 -7.2 1,3,5,7 58.8 35 Br 79.909 7,18,8,2	KRYPTON 3.74 -157.3 2(4,6,8?) -153.4 36 Kr 83.80 8,18,8,2
RUBIDIUM 1.53 38.5 1 688 37 Rb 85.47 1,8,18,8,2	STRONTIUM 2.6 770 2 1380 38 Sr 87.62 2,8,18,8,2	YTTRIUM 4.472 1509 3 3200 39 Y 88.905 2,9,18,8,2	ZIRCONIUM 6.45 1852 2,3,4 3580 40 Zr 91.22 2,10,18,8,2	COLUMBIUM 8.57 2468 2,3, 4,5,6 4927 41 Cb 92.906 1,12,18,8,2	MOLYBDENUM 10.22 2610 2,3, 4,5,6 5560 42 Mo 95.94 1,13,18,8,2	TECHNETIUM 11.49 2140 4,5,6,7 43 Tc 99 1,14,18,8,2	RUTHENIUM 12.4 2250 3,4, 5,6,8 4900 44 Ru 101.07 1,15,18,8,2	RHODIUM 12.44 1960 3,6 4500 45 Rh 102.905 1,16,18,8,2	PALLADIUM 12.02 1552 2,3,4 3980 46 Pd 106.4 0,18,18,8,2	SILVER 10.49 960.5 1 2212 47 Ag 107.870 1,18,18,8,2	CADMIUM 8.65 321 2 767 48 Cd 112.40 2,18,18,8,2	INDIUM 7.31 156.6 1,3 2075 49 In 114.82 3,18,18,8,2	TIN 7.3 232 2,4 2270 50 Sn 118.69 4,18,18,8,2	ANTIMONY 6.68 630.5 3,4,5 1440 51 Sb 121.75 5,18,18,8,2	TELLURIUM 6.25 449.5 2,4,6 990 52 Te 127.60 6,18,18,8,2	IODINE 4.93 113.5 1,3,5,7 184.3 53 I 126.9044 7,18,18,8,2	XENON 5.89 -111.8 2,4,6,8 -108.06 54 Xe 131.30 8,18,18,8,2
CESIUM 1.873 28.5 1 705 55 Cs 132.905 1,8,18,18,8,2	BARIUM 3.5 710 2 1500 56 Ba 137.34 2,8,18,18,8,2	LANTHANUM 6.174 920 3 3469 57 La* 138.91 2,9,18,18,8,2	HAFNIUM 13.29 2230 2,3,4 5400 72 Hf 178.49 2,10,32,18,8,2	TANTALUM 16.6 2996 2,3,5,6 6100 73 Ta 180.948 2,11,32,18,8,2	TUNGSTEN 19.3 3410 2,4,5,6 5900 74 W 183.85 2,12,32,18,8,2	RHENIUM 21.02 3180 1,2,3, 4,5,6,7 5900 75 Re 186.2 2,13,32,18,8,2	OSMIUM 22.5 3000 2,3, 4,6,8 5500 76 Os 190.2 2,14,32,18,8,2	IRIDIUM 22.42 2410 1,2, 3,4,6 5300 77 Ir 192.2 2,15,32,18,8,2	PLATINUM 21.4 1769 2,3,4,6 4530 78 Pt 195.09 1,17,32,18,8,2	GOLD 19.32 1063 1,3 2966 79 Au 196.967 1,18,32,18,8,2	MERCURY 13.55 -38.87 1,2 357 80 Hg 200.59 2,18,32,18,8,2	THALLIUM 11.85 303 1,3 1457 81 Tl 204.37 3,18,32,18,8,2	LEAD 11.34 327.4 2,4 1737 82 Pb 207.19 4,18,32,18,8,2	BISMUTH 9.8 271.3 2,3,4 1627 83 Bi 208.980 5,18,32,18,8,2	POLONIUM 9.398 252 2,4,6 962 84 Po 210 6,18,32,18,8,2	ASTATINE 302 1,3 85 At 211 7,18,32,18,8,2	RADON 9.73 -71 2,4,6 -61.9 86 Rn 222 8,18,32,18,8,2
FRANCIUM 1 87 Fr 223 1,8, 18,32,18,8,2	RADIUM 5 960 2 1140 88 Ra 226.05 2,8, 18,32,18,8,2	ACTINIUM 1050 3 3027 89 Ac** 227 2,9, 18,32,18,8,2	THORIUM 11.66 1750 4 4200 90 Th 232.038 2,10, 18,32,18,8,2	PROTACTINIUM 15.37 1230 4,5 91 Pa 231.05 2,9, 20,32,18,8,2	URANIUM 19.07 1132 3,4,6 3813 92 U 238.03 2,9, 21,32,18,8,2	NEPTUNIUM 20.45 637 3,4,5,6 93 Np 237 2,9, 22,32,18,8,2	PLUTONIUM 19.84 639.5 3,4,5,6 3235 94 Pu 239.11 2,8, 24,32,18,8,2	AMERICIUM 11.87 <1100 3,4,5,6 2607 95 Am 241 2,8, 25,32,18,8,2	CURIUM 7 950 3,4 96 Cm 242 2,9, 25,32,18,8,2	BERKELIUM 3 97 Bk 243 2,9, 26,32,18,8,2	CALIFORNIUM 3 98 Cf 245 2,9, 27,32,18,8,2	EINSTEINIUM 3 99 Es 253 2,9, 28,32,18,8,2	FERMIUM 3 100 Fm 254 2,9, 29,32,18,8,2	MENDELEVIUM 3 101 Md 256 2,9, 30,32,18,8,2	NOBELIUM 102 No 254 2,9, 31,32,18,8,2	LAWRENCIUM 103 Lr 259 2,9, 32,32,18,8,2	

FIGURE 1. PERIODIC TABLE OF PROPERTIES OF THE ELEMENTS

So perfect did science find this matched set to be that when they came to a place in the pattern where a block was missing (had not yet been discovered) they could predict what it must be like, then with these clues searched for it and found it! One such block was the atom called Helium. Scientists found it missing and described it so well that subsequently astronomers discovered its presence in the sun, and then an ensuing search revealed it in our own atmosphere! The building block system was long a secret from the prying ways of man because the Creator in his infinite wisdom made the blocks so tiny that millions can be packed into the point of a needle. This diminutive quality gives unlimited flexibility in putting together many elements and making them infinitely varied.

Like the more sophisticated blocks of our childhood days—the ones that had keys, grooves and similar characteristics so that they could go together a certain way, or would lock together—the Master's blocks also have the features for going together in a selected manner and for locking together in the making of stable compounds. Each block has one or more bonds which science calls *valence*, but for this presentation we shall call arms or hands. An interesting characteristic about these building blocks is that they dislike being alone and empty-handed, and when other compatible blocks with free hands come near they readily "join hands" with them. Once they join hands these sociable little blocks are completely satisfied and tend to stay that way until some force or condition takes them apart for some other combination.

In view of the fact that many of us have learned to speak the language of science in our class work, our laboratories, and in our enlightened world, and since an approach to our creation in terms of theology as such is beyond our ready understanding, we shall proceed from here in terms of classroom language which we know, understand, and in a manner we can actually prove with scientific apparatus if we so desire.

By way of illustration, then, let us look at a few of these wonderful building blocks and their bonds. We find that some of the simpler kinds such as Hydrogen, Sodium, Potassium, and Chlorine atoms, to name but a few, are generally one-armed/one-handed building blocks. They may be represented as one-armed circles with their name symbols written inside. See Figure 2(a). Oxygen is commonly a two-armed block and it may be shown as in Figure 2(b), while Carbon is here a four-handed block, and may be shown to look like that in Figure 2(c).

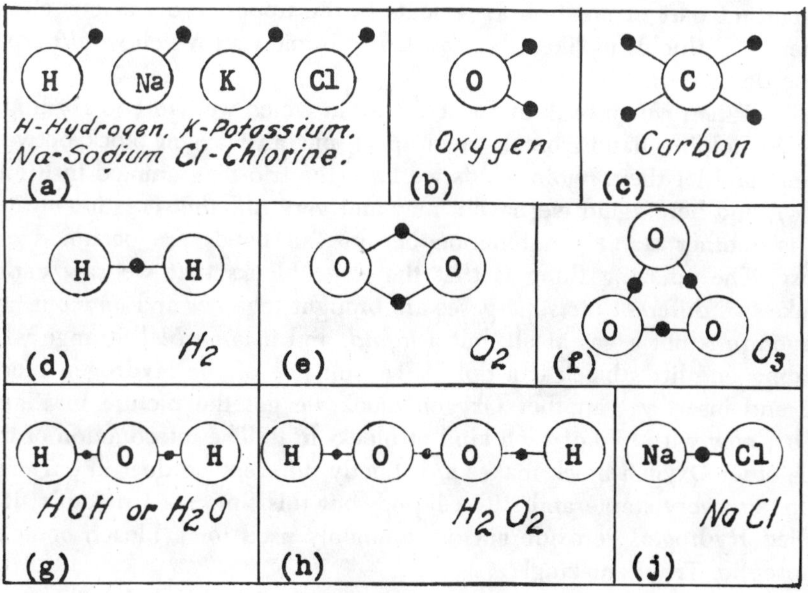

FIGURE 2

Remembering now that these blocks go together with handholds and that they are not happy until all hands are occupied, let us suppose the Master Engineer said: "Let there be hydrogen gas!" Here two Hydrogen blocks go together, and they hold hands as in Figure 2(d). In this we have a *stable* creation because all bonds are filled (there are no unused handholds) and the result is we have a gas which we know to be lighter than air—a gas which is used for filling ballons so they float upward in our comparatively heavy atmosphere. Similarly, suppose the Master said: "Let there be oxygen gas," whereupon two Oxygen blocks join both their hands and hang together in the manner illustrated in Figure 2(e). Thus we have the stable life-sustaining gas that is so necessary in our breathing. Furthermore, if we wish, we can break the handholds of the two Oxygen blocks and let a third Oxygen block come in and make a circle much as children do when playing Ring Around the Rosie, shown in Figure 2(f). With this additional one block we now have changed the whole picture in that we have a new and entirely different product which science has named Ozone—a gas produced by germicidal lamps to kill bacteria; also noticeable after a severe electrical storm when lightning causes formation of Ozone. Ozone, too, is a very important part of creation as it floats in the upper layers of our atmosphere and shields us like a blanket from cosmic rays which would otherwise destroy us.

When we go back to the structure in which we had two Hydrogen blocks holding hands, break them apart, put an Oxygen block between them, and let them rejoin hands we have the trio diagrammed in Figure 2(g), and here again we have a new and very different creation—water! It is another stable combination because all hands are occupied and busy. The amazing thing is that the *same* blocks that we saw earlier make two different *invisible* gases are brought together and now our new structure is not a gas at all, but a *liquid,* and it is *visible!* Strange what adding one little block can do! If we pull one of the Hydrogen blocks off and insert yet another Oxygen block we get the picture in Figure 2(h), now with two of each kind of blocks in it. The introduction of this one other Oxygen block makes a distinctly different product in our creation, also very stable and still a liquid, but this time not drinkable; it is called Hydrogen Peroxide and is commonly used for a bleach or as an antiseptic. Truly amazing!

Now to take one more example: The Sodium block (sodium is an unfriendly metal that cannot be handled with unprotected hands) and put it with a Chlorine block (chlorine is a poisonous gas), we get the creation in Figure 2(j), and here we have a surprising result, this time a white *solid* which bears no resemblance whatever to its parents! We call it Sodium Chloride, or common *table salt.* Heavens to Betsy! In their natural element, one a violent metal, the the other a deadly gas, yet together a strangely new creation, safe, tasty, and one so important on our dining table every day!

Thus these processes, so surprisingly simple with the building block scheme, go on and on. And everything great and small in our universe, including our own bodies, are put together similarly with various combinations of these wonderful building blocks. The fact that blocks which make up our bodies are not unlike those in the soil under our feet, in a real sense makes everything of a common order, and makes the story of the creation of man now take on more real meaning than ever before. At least we can now see the possibility that man might well have originated from the "dust of the ground," as the Book of Genesis puts it. Certainly, if we have reservations about man coming from dust, we only need consider the fact we know so well that his remains eventually return to the dust of the earth, and that should be convincing enough even for the most dubious.

Yes, science peeped over the Master's shoulder, investigated the details on his drawing board, and found out how He does it. But instead of exposing Him as a fraud always proved His works to be very real and truly wonderful! Science, too, discovered that matter and energy are one and the same basically; that the building blocks of one are inherent in the other. So now we know that matter can be brought about from energy, and energy from matter. And knowing that heat and light are forms of energy, the story of creating a sphere of solid, liquid and gaseous matter comes much closer to making sense in our minds. In this regard, the creating of mass from the early "vapors" which were "void and without form" in the Book of Genesis does not come out so far-fetched as some of the scoffers would have us believe. Much to the contrary, we are even moved with respect and admiration for these early recorders of "the beginning" who wrote so intelligently, and this at a time when the underlying knowledge of matter and energy was supposedly unknown! Truly, these men must have been divinely inspired!

An interesting and significant thing about the Master's building blocks is that each time the same blocks are arranged in the same way the *same* products are created. The positive and predictable repeatability thus gives us a new understanding of the Master's creation when we read that He surveyed the work of His hand and "saw that it was good." Very good, indeed! For eons now the basic creation has held steadfast—water stayed water, rocks stayed rocks, plants stayed plants, and animals, animals—and each "after its own kind"! All proved very stable not only at time of creation but have held true to the present hour—yesterday, today and forever! Had this arrangement not been good, everything would have become hopelessly intermixed a short time after creation, and the resulting hodgepodge would have turned out to be an utter failure and a senseless waste of time. Now before continuing let us pause and ponder the question: Could all this have possibly been the result of some freak accident?

To continue on the heels of the foregoing, we shall consider the cycle of a simple growing plant—any plant. First we have a seed for our consideration—really a wonderful little package—a complex structure put together with many kinds of the wonderful blocks we discussed earlier. It is in reality a package, all done up neatly with a special covering to enclose the precious things inside, sealed perhaps with a coat of wax on the outside to weatherproof it for a while and yet responsive enough to let everything happen that is supposed to happen in a prescribed time. Once planted the tiny embryo in this package stirs to life as the ground moisture breaks down the wax layer, penetrates the outer coating or jacket; then it begins to grow, and this says it must eat, for growing plants are like boys and girls—always hungry! But where does this infant seedling get its food? Simple! In this wonderful package someone had the forethought to *pack a lunch* for the baby plant. The highly concentrated starches, sugars and fats packed in the bundle dissolve in the moisture that seeps in and the products from this interaction nurture the embryo until it can feed itself through its own root and stem systems. Packed in this bundle (seed) are other wonderful things that speak volumes for some top-flight engineering designer. There is a "thermometer," "calendar," "timetable," and an "alarm clock." These help the embryo sense when conditions are right for it to come awake—and these are important lest the embryo begins its development when a few warm days come in midwinter, only to be destroyed by later blizzards long before spring has officially arrived. Mainly when all signals are "go" does the tiny life begin its cycle!

Now that the new life has begun, more wonderful things take place. The tiny plant extends its roots and directs them downward to remain in the ground where they do their work, and its stem system to penetrate the earth's crust to reach up to the light. See Figure 3. Here we pause for a question or two: How did this tiny life know to do these things in just the right way? What instinctive knowledge assured

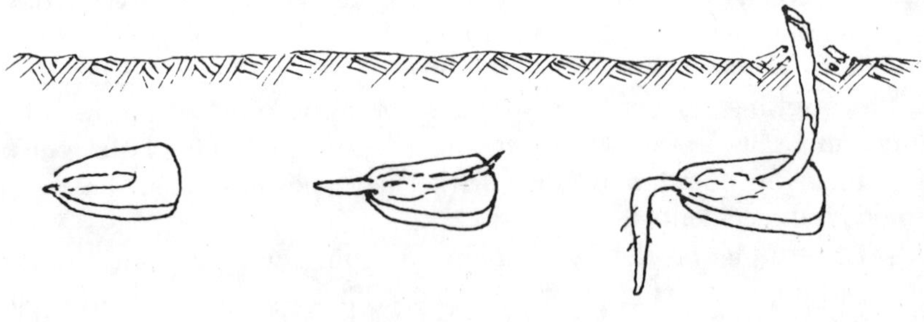

FIGURE 3

it that there are nutrients in the soil just outside the seed wrapper for its roots to absorb? How did it know where to find the light? Or even that it needs light? Perhaps another accident, but one that has been happening since the beginning of time—over and over again in the same way—yesterday, today and forever! If so, truly a remarkable accident!

Were this seed perchance to sprout in a dark place near a window, as for example in a cellar or an unlighted basement, would this plant waste away and finally die because of a lack of sunshine to help "cook" what food the roots were able to find and send forth? Not at all. It would bend and grow horizontally toward the light of that window, then once at or through the window it would straighten up and grow skyward. See Figure 4. Science again peeped here and discovered the parameters that make this plant do these "smart" things. These learned men found that the plant exudes a special substance from the tender tissues of its growing tip. This substance they named auxin. In further exploration they discovered that this substance has three amazing prop-

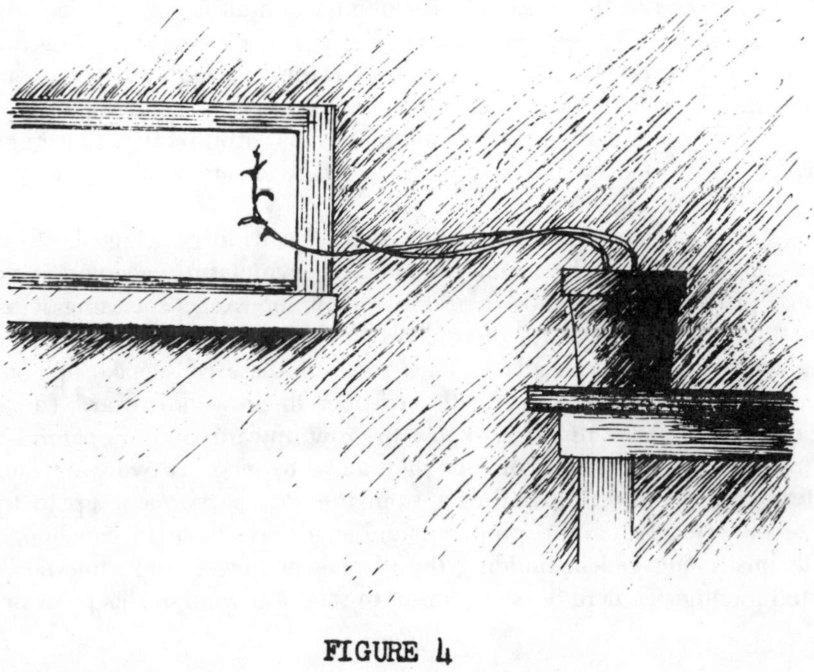

FIGURE 4

erties. First, it is destroyed or seriously impaired when light gets to it; secondly, it responds to gravity (has weight) so it tends to run down the stalk somewhat like water would under similar circumstances, and thirdly, it greatly stimulates growth of the cells it touches. From here on the scientists had easy sailing in explaining the behavior of the plant: The light from the window kills the auxin on the near side, but on the far (dark) side it remains active and keeps the cells stimulated so they grow comparatively longer and faster than on the side near the light. Long cells on the back side and short cells on the near side simply make the stem *bend* towards the light as it grows. Once the stem reaches open light the auxin on the more shaded surface underneath the horizontal growth tends to lengthen the lower cells more than those on the upper (lighted) surface, but more importantly, the pull of gravity concentrates more of the auxin below and so rapidly growing cells below and retarded growth of cells on the upper surface here cause the stem to bend and grow upward. Now safely in the light, the process of photosynthesis ("cooking" or preparation of plant food) goes on in a normal manner and the plant acquires a healthy green color (chlorophyll produced in the presence of sunlight) and all is well. So scientific men exposed the secret, and now we know! But did we discover a fake in all this? Never! All we discovered were the workings of an awesome phenomenon that literally makes one's spine tingle in amazement. Here we see a bit of supernatural "planning"—a thoughtful feature that might have been overlooked if you or I were left to create so simple(?) and so wonderful a thing as a plant.

The science of botany teaches that all cells in growing plants are basically structured the same—the nucleus, cytoplasm, vacuoles, inclusions, protoplasmic strands, and the membranous sac enclosing it all, and that they differentiate themselves in various ways to serve certain explicit functions in the plant. Thus some of these cells make up roots that are somehow gifted with the wisdom to grow downward (auxin again!); some make up stems, know to grow upward, and are careful to provide channels in the structure they make to serve as two-way traffic arteries for transporting nutrients from the root department up to the "kitchen" (leaves) to be prepared and made available to the hungry cells busily engaged in building the plant ever bigger, and some designated intelligence here does not forget to send a portion of this processed food back down to the underground root department to feed the hungry miners (cells) there engaged in extending the root system for the purpose of bringing forth more and more raw materials for the "cooks." Fortunately the cells in the many areas in the plant know what to do, and do it in exactly the right way—making roots, stems, leaves, bark, and whatever; and all in the right places and in proper respect to one another. What perfect organization! Otherwise, our plant certainly would develop into a nondescript mass of confused protoplasm!

Somewhere well along in the growing season another astounding development shapes up. As if by some decree of an unseen "board of directors" in a management system of the plant a new program is instituted. The new program, apparently born of a session in the long-range planning—and with high priority—allocates time, energy and other resources to this project which deals with a serious look into the future. The "directors" somehow understand that once frozen down by a coming winter (how did "they" know it was coming?) all of the tissues in the current plant will decay, and so making preparations for next year is very much in order. Accordingly, for this important business a special company of cells are delegated, as it were, to differentiate themselves into an unbelievable system of reproductive organs. Some cells make themselves into the calyx, some the ova, others the sepals, the petals, the stigma, the pistol, the pollen, but always in the preordained numbers, positions, arrangements, with consideration and regard for each of the others in the composite structure so vital for perpetuation of a treasured species in a hallowed kingdom of vegetation. Each group seems to know unerringly what it is to do and precisely where and how to do it. In the ovaries and pollen the cells, for example, form themselves with only *half* the chromosomes that the other cells elsewhere in the plant have. This was long a proprietary secret with these cells, with their purpose being that only the pollinated (fertilized) ovaries would grow into future plants and all others would wither away. Fertilization is the process where half the chromosomes are brought by the pollen cells from the stamen and are merged with the other half of the chromosomes in the ovary cells to make a full and correct chromosome count for the new life-to-be. Who would have thought of that! And since the creation was seen to be *good* it meant that pollen from a dandelion for example shall not mix with the ovary cells of a daisy, or soon we would have the hodgepodge mentioned earlier. Some clever Planner saw to it that this should not happen, and did it simply by allotting a different number of chromosomes to each of the many species of plants, and so ensured the perpetuation of the same strains, species, varieties year after year, eon after eon. Marvelous! Science discovered all these secrets also, but could find no sleight of hand, no deception, anywhere in the entire performance!

But what plans were made to ensure that the pollen cells are carried from the stamen to the ovary cells? Were this overlooked all would be a lost effort. But endowed with some all-pervading wisdom our imaginary "board of directors" must have thought of this, too, and contemplated all the possibilities—the wind, rain, insects tracking through the sensitive areas, and so on, and all were favorably considered. But how did "they" know that their Creator provided these other carriers in departments completely outside their own plant structure? Suffice it to say that there is some unexplained network of communication and "they" knew this all the time in a positive way and acted in full accord with this information. So certain cells differentiate themselves into a compound called nectar which is placed in quantities in the right places to accomplish the correct effect when the bees, flies, gnats, and other insects come tramping through the flower parts to gather up this delicious concoction. Sort of a trick on the insects it is, but really not a bad trick when we consider the nectar always proves to be ample reward for the visitors' trouble.

But the wonders of the "advance-planning department" go to even greater accomplishments. Present in this body is some expertise on the physics of light, and so orders are doubtless given to some cells to form in such a way that they absorb certain wave lengths (color elements) in the light spectrum, and reflect others. The parts reflected are conveyed to the eye of the beholder, who sees them as beautiful colors, this because the cells in the various plants are so constructed to reflect varying elements and portions of the wonderful components in our God-given light. Somehow the planning department had knowledge that light is made up of seven prismatic elements, and that they have leave to choose from these. These ingenious cells thus contribute their special efforts to help in the work of attracting the pollen-carrying insects. How, we may ask here, did these inner workings of this lowly plant know to deal so expertly and delicately with the elements in the sunlight that floods them day after day? And how did they know that out there somewhere would be foreign creatures with light-sensitive organs called eyes, enabling these creatures to *see* and be attracted to the blossoms? The beautiful way these "departments" work together defies any argument that all these functions are accidents, for were this true there would be a lot of wasted effort around us every day—many features offered with no takers, but every observing person knows that there are no such excesses. But there is more! Still other cells with their own assignments have the incomprehensible intelligence to differentiate themselves into substances which become air-borne as fragrances to entice these pollen carriers they also knew about, and they do a tremendous job in attracting the bees, gnats and flies—besides perfuming our world something wonderful to delight us! These cells must have had advance information on the function of passing breezes to carry these vapors, some foreknowledge that there will be organs of *smell* in their proximity, that many of the smellers would come and see what's in it for them, and thereby inadvertently intermix some of the pollen cells with the ovary cells in the process. Perhaps this also borders on a trick of sorts, but it accomplishes a most important function. And meanwhile the world is indescribably more delightful because of the heavenly fragrance!

Now we come to a "department" that caps them all, and here we are virtually moved to take off our hats in sheer respect and look on aghast! This "department," also subservient to the "long-range planning division," becomes aware that all the fertilized ova will shape themselves into seeds—the embryo and all the goodies included in the wonderful package we discussed at the beginning of this part of the presentation. These will eventually ripen and fall to the ground. And here is where a grave concern enters the picture, for there will be so many struggling plants clustered around the foot of the stem next spring that they would smother one another to death in the process of trying to grow. Now real genius is called upon to plan means for scattering these precious little packages (seeds) far and wide so each will have better opportunity for survival. So forthwith plans of many sorts are implemented. The "airborne division" with a mysterious knowledge of aerodynamics predicates that certain cells form themselves into wings, parachutes, nets, and the like, attach themselves as fixtures to the package and so they sail away into the wild blue yonder! Dandelions, milkweed, and the maple tree are some that use this method. Those with a penchant for hydrodynamics arrange for floating devices and merrily go drifting down the waterways in search of new places to stake out their claims. An example of the latter is the sycamore. Others versed in the characteristics and habits of creatures in the animal kingdom form themselves into the most ingenious hooks, barbs, and the like, and literally cover the outer surface of the embryo package so that the chance for catching on to the fur of passing animals is never compromised. These hooked parcels go great distances from the home plant to start life in the remotest areas imaginable. They further have the important but disturbing effect of pricking the animal when he sits down on the burr, whereupon he dislodges the pesky thing with his teeth and leaves it wherever he happens to be. Next year, lo! here sprouts a member of the old family in a fine new location with ample room to grow! Here we are moved until virtually our very flesh creeps! A bit of plant creation growing in apparent detachment by the wayside, yet aware in a very real sense of the presence of a passing dog, person, or thing! Else its carefully fashioned hooks would be a ridiculous waste of time and a useless lot of clutter! In this, can we be so indifferent as to chalk up another accident, or can we be generous enough to acknowledge here another interdependent function fitting indisputably into a great complex of spine-tingling wonders?

One would indeed have to be intentionally blind not to be awed by seeing a "simple" plant that is aware of, and interdependent with, so many essential elements of the same creation with it—soil, gravity, air, sunlight, water, cell growth, structure-building, co-operation among its own parts, planning for the future with reproductive organs, thoughtful packaging of its embryo, knowledge of helper birds, bees, insects, furry animals to carry its seeds to distant places, knowledge of the hunger of strange creatures passing by who eat of the "package" and spit out bitter seeds, knowledge of organs of sight and smell, "tricking" others for furthering its own survival, adjusting to changing seasons and acceptance of being buried (planted) by "smart" animals with food storage in mind, and so on and on. If this all can be an accident, we must admit that it is a very clever accident—one that "accidentally" keeps happening in the same way year after year, century after century, eon after eon.

In conclusion, it cannot be overemphasized that we are part of a nearly-incomprehensible jigsaw creation in which all things are wise and wonderful. It is doubtful, were men gifted with the power, and given his turn at the business of creating, that even the wisest among us would have had the faculty to foresee and include such clever features as: A simple tilt of the earth on its axis to give us four seasons; water's greatest density at approximately thirty-eight degrees Fahrenheit, lighter when nearing the freezing point, and lightest when expanded in ice so the latter floats and thereby safeguards marine life by preventing the pool's freezing solid; water evaporating, rising to condense in colder air strata where winds move along and scatter these clouds of condensate to help distribute the rain falling to earth (what a watering system!); bramble bushes to protect the lives of small wildlife from predators; natural processes of camouflage for creatures to evade detection, as the ermine's changing the color of his pelt from brown to white in wintertime; the flow of adrenalin to give near superhuman strength in time of a crisis; the drop in blood pressure to facilitate clotting of blood after a serious injury; hollow bone structure for strength and minimum weight, with utilization of even the space in the hollow for distinct other vital functions; the unique design of the human arm/hand structure which serves as fifty-some distinct tools and implements on command; in fact, so many, many awesome things, and all mutually sustaining one another, yet each actively pursuing its own functions! Even the remains of a fallen tree in the forest and the cover of last year's leaves are very much alive with an ongoing process of decomposition—a process which is an indisputable part of life itself. Here the many miraculous building blocks the Master had used. in former structures are now being taken apart, salvaged, and made ready for building new formations in tomorrow's creation!

In searching the farthest reaches of man's imagination, what other concept could be a possible improvement on this awe-inspiring plan we see in constant operation day after day? Yet, despite this we have those among us who somehow prefer to credit it all to happenstance! In this it may be well to observe that if man knows too little about the prodigious workings of the universe to accept it as an act of Divine creation, then he likewise knows too little about it to refute or reject it. And this in itself deserves long and careful consideration.

Indeed, when we behold the works of the Master Engineer and

Builder we are truly overwhelmed by the wonders of His superbly-planned and masterfully-conceived universe. These, we read, were all pronounced *good* at time of their making, have held unwaveringly constant and good through the ages. And in light of all this, whether we call them all accidents, or yield to a less prejudiced logic, whithersoever we are, even in the uttermost parts of the earth, we are nonetheless every place and always on Holy Ground!

CHRISTMAS IN THE HILLS

Christmas was but two days off, and already old man Winter had begun to make it a white one. The day had dawned with a disagreeable mist sifting from a sullen sky and borne upon a chilly southeast wind. Later in the afternoon a wild northwest wind gained predominance and changed the mist to an even more disagreeable mixture of rain and sleet. This king of winds whistled triumphantly through the leafless trees and over the rolling contour of the Missouri Ozarks, while the thickening blanket of sleet brought out the ridges and slopes more and more distinctly. Truly the hills were assuming an appearance very Christmaslike, for the wooded ranges everywhere, even though dimmed by the screen of falling sleet, were a somber contrast to the spotless meadows and pasture fields, and the icy panels of an occasional rail fence strung like tinsel across a meandering valley or zigzagged away over a sweeping ridge. Highways and byways as well as fields and forests seemed practically deserted of all living things, for the creatures in fur and feather were hidden away snugly in their dens, or had in the friendly lowland thickets found refuge from the rigors of the storm. Thus, with few exceptions, the outside world was surrendered, as it were, to the gods of winter and the magic of their handiwork.

"Giddap, horses!" snapped Herbert Billings sharply, not to say impatiently, from between the corners of his upturned coat collar, as he turned into the old River Hollow road which led past his farm some five miles distant from the highway. If indeed Herbert's voice betrayed any trace of impatience it may have been justified, for, because he was cold, wet and hungry, it was little wonder that the miles on his way homeward seemed like so many leagues. At any rate, he seemed unmindful of the fact that his wiry horses were quite as eager to get home as was he himself, for they maintained a spirited even gait that even the sharp whistle which broke forth at frequent intervals could not affect. With an instinct almost human the animals followed unerringly the undulating, winding trail through the interlacing foothills of Redbud Valley, and this even though their driver frequently held the lines between his knees while warming his benumbed fingers in his pockets. While the road followed a direction generally southward, Herbert was nevertheless obliged to shift in the seat of his wagon from time to time in order to keep his back turned to the biting northwester and the barrage of stinging sleet which it drove in wild, incessant volleys.

Herbert Billings was a hard-working young farmer who had already become resigned to a life of adversities which is so often the lot of the hill-country dweller. The fact that he was rather hard run was by no means a discredit to his fine character, for being poor was in no wise disgraceful in his section of the country, and certainly not when this condition prevailed in spite of thrift and industry, as was true in Billings's case. To make up in part for his financial deficiency, he resorted to cutting stove wood in his spare time and delivering it to the county seat, where he usually found a ready market.

On his way homeward from Blandon the old River Hollow trail invariably proved a welcome sight to Herbert; it indicated that he had passed the halfway mark, and was nearing his own community. Late in this December afternoon, however, due to the nasty siege of winter, it was a sight doubly welcome, for in spite of the fact that he had spent all of his thirty winters in the Ozarks, and had become accustomed to the uncertainty of her weather, he could recall no past experience quite so uncomfortable. The oncoming night served to add even more to the young farmer's eagerness to get home. Already the premature darkness was settling over the solemn hills, and the lamplight of the farm houses began to blossom dimly here and there like the faint starlight of heaven at the passing of evening's twilight.

"Hi, Herb!" shouted a familiar voice when Billings was passing the Rollins's farmstead. In the growing darkness he distinguished the tall, broad-shouldered figure of John Rollins. "Hi, John," Herbert responded huskily. "What's up?"

"I hate to stop you this a-way, Herb," began Rollins apologetically, "'cause I know you're just about froze stiff, but I've got a cow down on the pond and me and the boy cain't git 'er up 'thout some he'p. We 'lowed you'd be a-comin' along agin dark, an' we could git you to give us a lift."

Desirous though he was of getting home, the thought of refusing a slight favor to his nearest and most congenial neighbor did not for a moment enter Herbert's mind. And to be down on the ice a night like this was by no means a desirable place for any living creature to be. "You bet your life, John," said Herbert with his characteristic heartiness. "We'll see what we can do." He tied his horses to the paling fence which rounded the Rollins farm home, and having declined the elder farmer's very inviting offer to go into the house to warm a bit, went off with him to the lower end of the feedlot. With the combined strength of Herbert, the stalwart Rollins and his eighteen-year-old son, the unfortunate animal was soon on her feet, stabled and fed. Having assured young Billings that he was "much obliged" for his help, Rollins led the way to the house. "By the way, Herb," he ventured suddenly, "did you see Bill Harlen about givin' you a little more time on your note?" It was not inquisitive prying which prompted him to put this rather personal question, for Rollins had always liked Herbert Billings, and was almost as deeply concerned over the latter's financial difficulties as he was over his own.

"Yeah, I talked to him for quite a while," replied the younger farmer in a tone which was self-explanatory as to the result of their conference.

"Nothin' doin', eh?"

"No," rejoined Herbert dismally. "He says these hard times have hit him purty hard and he wants the money."

Rollins was a man who believed instinctively in the principle of live and let live; his mountain-bred sense of justice rose in resentment against Harlen. He shook a condemning fist. "Wants the money, bosh!" he said with something like a sneer. "Why that old skinflint has more dough now than he knows what to do with! Goin' to go ahead an' sell you out in January, is he?"

"That's how he's got it advertised," replied the young farmer disconsolately.

By this time Herbert had untied his team, and having once more declined Rollins's urgent invitation to warm and have a cup of hot coffee, he climbed into his wagon and continued homeward. Farther down the road the light winking through the kitchen window of his home already was greeting his eye. When he neared the trim white house with the friendly hearth glowing a warm welcome through the living room window, a feeling of depression settled upon his heart momentarily, and a cloud of gloom spread over his handsome face. It was indeed a distressing thought that this farm upon which he had begun his career, the farm which was the birthplace of his children, and the home that he had built several years before to shelter them, was his now in name only, and this for but a few weeks longer. His troubled thoughts drifted into the past for a few moments as he recalled the incidents that had brought about his unpleasant circumstances—first, the hospital bill resulting from his untimely illness, and the $500 debt he had incurred against his 120-acre farm to meet its payment; next, the bolt of lightning which had killed nearly half his modest dairy herd; the coming of the depression and the successive years of drought which found him unable to pay even the interest, far less retire the principal; then Harlen's positive refusal to extend his time; and finally, his inability to effect a loan elsewhere—all these trying misfortunes passed through Herbert's mind. Yes, Fate had surely dealt him a series of staggering blows, and every one of them an entirely unavoidable one! Now it seemed that within a very short time they would culminate in his economic ruin; meanwhile, the impending outcome threatened to blight the gladness of the coming Christmastide!

Billings's despondency vanished almost completely, however, when he turned his horses into their respective stalls and found that his wife had prepared feed for them. He lit the smudgy lantern he kept in the barn and made the rounds to his stock. Everything was in perfect order and the animals seemed wholly oblivious to the frigid weather outside. The sow and her half-grown litter were lying heaped one over another and grunting contentedly beneath their pummy-covered roof in one corner of the barnyard; the sheep in their shed were curled up with their heads tucked snugly into their woolly jackets; and in a leeward section of the barn old Roany's bell clanged and scraped against the manger as she sorted through her portion of timothy hay. Everywhere Herbert noted that the chores had been done, and done well. "What a gal is Beatrice!" thought he. "She deserves the better things of life if any women ever did!"

The sleet crunched softly beneath his boots as he made his way to the house. A tempting mingled odor of coffee, bacon and Christmas cakes that Beatrice had been making whetted his appetite as it wafted through the door little Bobby held open for him.

"Hello, Daddy!" he called out gleefully. The chubby eight-year-old held a mixing bowl in one hand, and around his mouth was ample evidence that at least one of the cakes had a chocolate icing. Little Virginia, two years younger, and with large brown eyes and dark hair like her mother's, stood close behind with a mixing spoon clutched tightly in her two small fists. Beatrice paused in her work of placing supper on the table to welcome her cold and wet husband, and to provide him with some dry clothing.

A definite air of contentment prevailed in the cheerful household and Herbert bitterly regretted that he could not bring good news about the mortgage. In due time, however, he told his wife of the futility of his appeal to Harlen, and of his failure to obtain a loan elsewhere. Disappointed though she was, Beatrice had hardly dared expect otherwise, and for the sake of her husband she deftly concealed her disappointment behind a cheerful smile, assuring him that everything would work out for the best in the end.

Inasmuch as Herbert had a tale of disappointment, he also had one more pleasant to relate. With a lighter heart he told of Mrs. Browning's offer to pay him double price for a load of heating wood if he delivered it before Christmas. It meant another cold trip to town on the morrow, but the opportunity to make this much-needed money was not to be taken lightly.

The morning dawned a sullen gray and cold. Droves of jagged, dismal clouds scudded hastily toward the southeast, though the rain-sleet mixture had ceased falling early in the night. However, the wind which had whistled the whole night through had formed a hard, glassy crust on the surface of the Yuletide blanket that had fallen the day before, and it rendered getting around not only tedious but hazardous. In fact, if Herbert had not found among his possessions, thrown back with other half-forgotten paraphernalia in his shop, a pair of sturdy ice creepers which he strapped securely to his boots, it is doubtful that he could have made the rounds of his morning chores in time to load his wood and make the delivery to Blandon.

The road to town wound through a section of rugged beauty characteristic of the Ozarks, and this was now greatly enhanced by the immaculate new cloak of winter. The white-clad fields lay like a ruffled sheet tucked around the wooded plots that skirted the sweeping ridges, and the dark limestone ledges brooded over the valleys that nestled below. Trees, large and small, wore on their windward side a shawl of lacy white, while their spreading crowns were draped with lustrous crystals that creaked and groaned as the breath of the northland rocked them to and fro. Pleasing and colorful was the contrast effected by an occasional ice-tinsled cedar clinging to a rugged slope, or by the delicate green of a lonely pine that lifted its head here and there among the dormant oaks. Herbert admired the wintry scene all about him. Fortunately he had not permitted his hardships to exclude from his life an appreciation of nature's simple beauties, and they somehow made it easier for him to carry on his rather unavailing labor. He loved the immutable mountains that enfolded him, the ruggedness of the great out-of-doors, and the friendly snow-capped farm houses which nestled here and yon among the sleeping hills, silently radiating an infinite cheer to a glorious ice-owned world.

"Hey, Billings!" It was "Uncle" Henry Williams who came half-walking, half-sliding to the gate, putting on his coat as he came. "Air ya gonna have a load on yer way home?"

"Well, no; not much, I reckon," replied Herbert. "Lon Fisher just asked me to bring him some flour, feed and dry goods for his store, but there'll be some room. Want to go along?"

"Naw, I don't need to go in particular," drawled the grizzly farmer, and pausing, he ejected an amber jet between his index and second fingers; "but if hit ain't askin' too much o' you, I wish you'd—dad gum this ice!—go to the station and fetch me a Victroly that our son-in-law is sendin' us for Christmas."

"All right, Uncle Henry," said Billings, who was accustomed to doing favors for his neighbors, and they, knowing this to be true, felt no hesitancy in asking such accommodations of him. "If hit didn't come yesterday, hit'll come in today," added Williams. "All charges air paid."

"All right," repeated Herbert as he drew up the lines, then added as an afterthought: "In case I have too big a load, I may have John Rollins fetch it out for you; he was a-fixin' to go to town as I come by. Better come along, Uncle Henry."

"Naw, Herb, I reckon I'd better stick around the house in weather sich as this. Old fellers like me shouldn't—wope! Well hang this darned ice!"

Blandon was a thriving country town of some two thousand inhabitants. It was located at the terminal of a prong of the Frisco railroad, and in addition, four major all-weather roads linked it with the outside world. In keeping with the high civic standard for which the town was noted, its principal street now was a continuous Christmas ornamentation. The windows of all the business places were profusely tinseled; around the elaborately decorated Christmas trees which adorned many of the show windows was a colorful array of toys and gifts of all kinds, and red-cheeked replicas of Santa Claus greeted the shoppers everywhere. Despite the icy roads a throng of happy folk were on the sidewalks, and automobiles with tire chains jingling were coming and going continually. Everybody seemed to be intoxicated with the Christmas spirit; young folk were especially exhilarated over the hoilday ice, and skates and sleds were a common sight.

Among the bustling crowd of carefree shoppers Herbert pushed his way, intent on buying a few simple but useful gifts for his loved ones. He was well aware that the five-dollar bill which he had received for the wood would not go a long way in buying presents, especially when there was a list of groceries to be taken care of first. However, he resolved to get some oranges, bananas, a pair of warm stockings for each of the children, and perhaps a few inexpensive toys. There would also be enough to buy several yards of gingham and a box of handkerchiefs for Beatrice. Not a lavish lot of gifts, he admitted to himself, but it was all he could afford this year.

As the young farmer passed the Howell Furniture Store the clock in the window struck the half hour after two. He had already made the round to the wholesale house and the Farmers' Exchange on behalf of the country merchant, and his meager Christmas shopping was finished. He even had had another fruitless talk with the tight-fisted Harlen. As he glanced at the clock he paused to admire the beautiful gray kitchen range and the glossy linoleum spread beneath it. How Beatrice would enjoy Christmas if she could have the range for which her heart had yearned so long; and the lineoleum would take one of the drudgeries out of her housework! But he had no time to spend in dreaming—the clock had told him that half the short winter afternoon was already gone, and he had yet to drive to the station for Williams's freight, so he hurried to his wagon.

Much to his disappointment, Billings was informed upon arriving at the depot that no freight was there for Williams, and it meant that he had to wait for the train, which was scheduled to arrive one hour late. To aggravate matters, the young farmer had to stand out in the cold to watch his horses, which had twice broken loose when they shied from passing sticks a group of boys were sending down the hilly street which led to the depot. Blissfully unmindful of the fact that their sport was discommoding anyone, the boys delighted in watching the pieces of wood dart down the hill, shoot over a steep bank and glide across the railroad tracks.

After a time the boys tired of playing with the sticks and began to coast with their sleds. They did not follow the course of the sticks, however, for it was a steeper grade than they cared to descend; instead they turned and coasted down a side street. How it thrilled their childish hearts to round the sweeping curve! Merry shouts and laughter filled the air, and gay woolen scarfs were flying in colorful array as they darted, one after the other, down the street. Herbert watched them with a good deal of interest, for he was reminiscent of his own childhood and the fun each snow and ice used to bring.

Presently the faint musical note of the Frisco far to the north told him that his waiting was nearly ended. He heard it again and again, each time it came more distinctly, and soon the black smoke could be seen curling up from the pulsing locomotive as it rounded the long curve at the foot of the grade, and the rhythmic clanging of the bell told its passengers that they were at their journey's end.

Suddenly a blood-curdling scream for help, followed by a din of wild shouts and frantic cries farther up the street arrested Herbert's attention, and what he beheld sent a succession of icy chills up his spine. One of the lads had so intently watched the oncoming train that he had passed up the curve, and his sled out of control was darting down the hill toward the close approaching juggernaut. Herbert and the others who appeared almost instantly upon the scene saw the boy make desperate efforts to swerve, but panicky with terror, he turned so sharply that he upset his sled, and was now sliding helplessly down the smooth, glassy grade where he and his companions had sent the sticks a little while before.

Everyone who witnessed the scene at once sensed the gruesome tragedy that was impending; yet all stood as though frozen in their tracks, for they realized the folly of trying to stop the hapless, screaming youngster. If there had existed even the faintest hope of rescue, it faded completely when the sled—which had righted itself in the meantime, and darted down the hill with the velocity of a rifle bullet—was crushed to fragments beneath the wheels of the slowing train, thus foreboding a similar fate for its owner.

As Herbert collected his wits he became conscious of an urging sensation creeping over his body. His finer qualities would not permit him to stand by and look on when a human life was at stake. Instinctively he sprang forth with desperate strides, and with one supreme effort he made a flying hurdle and caught the scarf of the boy as he passed. This heroic attempt brought a chorus of cheers from the onlookers; but the cheers died on their lips when they saw the young farmer thrown off his feet by the speed at which the boy was moving by this time, and an even deeper shadow hung over the scene now that two lives instead of one hung in the balance. A panic of deathlike terror held them spellbound; women fainted; men stood speechless and looked on with ghastly faces. Surely the lives of both were doomed, and in another half minute all would be over! Even the passengers on the train had flung up the windows by this time and were looking on wide-eyed and mute, awaiting helplessly the awful tragedy which seemed so inevitable.

Herbert, slipping head first, was trying with desperate main to alter this position so that he might gain a foothold on the ice with his creepers. He was fully aware that not more than some sixty feet farther down was the steep bank, and if he could not right himself before he reached its brink, the greater slope would accelerate their speed and fling both beneath the wheels of the train.

A shout went up when Herbert somersaulted and dug his creepers into the ice. It halted him for but a moment, and he was slipping again. After what seemed an eternity, Herbert succeeded, with another frantic effort, to bring his feet foremost once more, and now his creepers were plowing hopelessly in the ice. For a moment his heart stood still, then, Hurrah! His foot had caught a firm hold at last—and not a second too soon—for when he tugged at the scarf the boy swung in a semicircle right on the brow of the precipitous bank.

The thunderous peal of shouts and cheers which burst forth from the spectators rent the air in wild acclamation of the farmer hero. Herbert, however, sat motionless with the boy for several moments. His face, as well as the boy's, was of a whiteness which rivaled that of the sleet ice; his lips were colorless, and his jaws protruded grimly; large drops of perspiration stood out on his forehead, and his heart bounded wildly. As he slowly collected his senses he became aware of the extremely dangerous chance he had taken with his own life. Two seconds more, and Beatrice would have looked in vain for her husband's return this Christmas Eve! He would have been but a faint memory during the lives of his children, and what hardships would have been their lot in their early years! Fortunately, though, Providence would not have it that way, and the young farmer's heart swelled with deepest gratitude. He then turned to the frightened, weeping boy, and in a faltering tone gave him a bit of stern, fatherly advice as he led him safely to the street.

Herbert Billings may well have imagined himself in a new and strange world, for never in all his life had he experienced being the center of such attention. For a time it seemed that he would be torn to pieces, so hysterical were the bystanders in expressing their admiration for the courageous farmer, and each wanted to be first in the scramble to reach him. His arms were shaken until he thought they would surely be dislocated, and his shoulders became the target for a score of hearty back-slappers.

Notwithstanding Herbert's modest protests, the mad demonstration showed no sign of letting up. As a matter of fact, it did not subside until several minutes later when a short, portly gentleman of slightly past middle age came elbowing his way hurriedly through the crowd. From his general appearance he was a man of means; his clean-shaven, spectacled face was shadowed by a light gray Stetson, and a smart woolen topcoat hung open from his shoulders. About him was an air different somehow from that of the others, and the nervous, important manner indicated unmistakably that his presence was prompted by more than a mere desire to shake the hero's hand. When he succeeded finally in thrusting his way into the center of the crowd, Herbert was surprised to recognize facing him Richard Bowers, president of the Farmers' and Traders' Bank, and even more surprised to learn, after the man finally found words, that he was the father of the boy he had just rescued. In a halting, broken tone the banker told Herbert of having witnessed the breath-taking rescue from a window of the incoming train, and apparently oblivious of the others around them, he went on pouring out his heart in gratitude to the young farmer whose presence in town that day, he insisted, was a kindly act of Providence.

An hour later Herbert left the little country town behind, and was once again on his road homeward. The wind had subsided, and the great crimson sun was sinking from a cloudless sky. It flung long shadows across the snowy billows, and bathed the high points in the rarest gold. Herbert saw the light fade slowly from the western sky, and dreamily he watched the bright stars take their places in the darkening heavens. The hills were wrapped in a restful silence, broken only by the muffled rumbling of the wagon, the faint barking of a farmer's dog, and the occasional hoot of an owl on a distant ridge. Truly this Christmas Eve Herbert's heart was filled with the same sacred peace that enveloped the slumbering Ozark Hills!

"I'll bet you're nearly frozen," said Beatrice as she swung open the kitchen door, "it's—why, Herbie, who's been imposing on you this time?" A puzzled look radiated from her face as her husband piled one package after another on the kitchen table. "Nobody," responded Herbert in a matter-of-fact manner as he laid off another bundle; "this is our stuff!"

"Herbert," Beatrice eyed the packages and her voice indicated an intense seriousness, "it's nice of you to do all this for us, but you know we have more debts now than we can ever pay!"

Herbert could withhold the happy tidings no longer, and in one joyful stream he poured out the whole story. He told in detail how he had saved Richard Bowers's son from a terrible death; how the banker had expressed his gratitude not only in words, but also by insisting that he take a reward.

"But t-two thousand dollars," gasped Beatrice, "that's all the money in the world!"

"Well," shrugged young Billings, "there was nothing I could do; when he saw that I wouldn't take anything, he simply pushed the check into my pocket, and said he'd have given all he has rather than have had anything happen to his boy." Thus for several minutes the young farmer and his wife discussed their good fortune. "And I went to Harlen and not only paid him the interest, but also every cent of the principal—here, you can put these papers away," he concluded. Beatrice was conscious of a lump in her throat, and with the corner of her apron she brushed away the tears that welled up in her eyes. "Oh, Herbert," she sobbed, "I'm so happy!"

"Hey, Daddy! There's somebody a-comin' up our road!" Bobby shouted excitedly as he peered through the parted curtains at the living room window.

"Oh, yes!" Herbert jumped to his feet. "I guess that's John Rollins with the new range and the linoleum and things," and he sprang with boyish agility out into the starlit night.

A very generous array of toys, candies, as well as articles of clothing and other necessities were placed around the most dexterously ornamented Christmas tree in Red Bud Valley that night. The joy of little Bobby and Virginia knew no bounds as they played by the glowing hearth with the new and strange toys that Santa had sent them.

After a time when the children had finally gone to bed, Herbert and Beatrice sat and talked for a long while over the wonderful events the day had brought forth, and as they knelt side by side to murmur a Christmas Eve prayer, their hearts were filled with the joy and peace that "passeth all understanding." How wonderful the Santa Claus of all Santa Clauses had been to them and theirs, and how beautiful the method chosen to bestow the gifts!